Dark Pools

The Dry Fly and the Nymph

DARK POOLS

THE DRY FLY AND THE NYMPH

Charles Jardine

The Crowood Press

First published in 1991 by
The Crowood Press Ltd
Ramsbury, Marlborough
Wiltshire SN8 2HR

British Library Cataloguing in Publication Data

Jardine, Charles
    Dark pools: the dry fly and the nymph.
    1. Angling. Trout
    I. Title
    799.1755

ISBN 1 85223 396 6

Acknowledgements

Artwork by Charles Jardine

Dedication

This book is dedicated to:

The past: my father for his precious gift to me – fly fishing;
The present: my wife Carole for her generous help and forbearance;
The future: my children Annabelle and Alexander, that we may leave them streams worth inheriting so that they, in turn, may do the same.

Disclaimer

Throughout this book the pronouns 'he', 'him' and 'his' have been used inclusively and are meant to apply to both males and females.

Typeset by Context, Greenlea House, Green Street, Coopers Hill, Glos GL3 4RT.
Printed and bound by Times Publishing Group, Singapore

Contents

Acknowledgements

Although a book is attributed to a single person or sometimes a partnership, this belies the many people without whom a project could never be undertaken, those who are the foundation stones for the venture. This book is no exception.

Firstly I would like to thank unreservedly Bob Church and David Goodfellow, who were variously instrumental in guiding the project and Chris Dawn for allowing the use of ideas that were originally conjured up for *Trout Fisherman*.

Eternal thanks go to those kind people who have increased my knowledge of river fishing, the experts who were generous enough to share their information with me. These are Jim Hadderell, the doyen of Test instructors, Nick Mitchell, Ron Holloway, Peter Gathercole, Roman Moser, John Goddard, John Hatherell, Tim Greenfield who got me fly tying, and many more unsung heroes.

I owe my good friend Dermot Wilson more than I could repay, as it was he who set me on the 'primrose path' to trying to understand chalk streams.

I must mention here the contributors: Dr Jeremy Lucas, whose elegance with words is matched only by his prowess with a rod, and Dr Barrie Rickards, a renowned pike fisherman, a Doctor of Geology at Cambridge and a great companion.

My wife Carole, veteran of a myriad encounters with the word processor, without whose support this book would not have happened, deserves my special thanks, as does my mother, who smiled at my epic tantrums, bearing them as stoically as in days gone by; and my children for, sometimes, being quiet – while daddy is working!

May I finally express my gratitude to the chaps without whom the whole thing would be superfluous – the trout of the stream, who get it right far more often than I do.

Foreword

Whenever Charles Jardine comes to stay with me – which is not often enough – he brings a bottle of whisky. Tradition dictates that we sit down and consume it, swapping fishing stories, genning-up on the latest in tackle and techniques and generally putting the game-fishing world to rights.

These occasions are times I look forward to greatly, since Charles is not only a fisherman par excellence and a wonderful wildlife artist, he is also a true friend. Three of his paintings gaze down from my sitting-room wall as I write this. Supremely evocative, they serve to help me through the tedium of the long closed season.

As an angler, Charles is a rare creature. He comes from a line of great fishermen and is anxious to preserve the traditions of our sport. But he is not a stuffy 'traditionalist' who turns a blind eye to the huge advances in tackle and techniques that have taken place and that are still taking place. Charles delights in trying out new techniques and bits of tackle – many of them gleaned from his numerous fishing trips abroad – to see if they will work in this country. Sometimes they do, sometimes they don't; but you can be sure that whatever Charles has to say about them is based on practical trial and not theory – upon which many people seem to base their opinions today.

Charles Jardine is a great fisherman and a supreme fly-tier. None of his opinions can be lightly cast aside since they are all based on practical experience. Any book that bears his name, therefore, should be read and re-read, for within its covers will be a wealth of sound advice that will help every one of us to be better fishermen.

Sandy Leventon
Editor
Trout and Salmon

Preface

Most of my thirty-seven years of life have been spent playing about with fly rods, thirty-one of them on chalk streams. I have witnessed great change over this period, in climate, attitudes, tackle, fly choice and in the water itself. During the far off 1950s, I imagine that none of us thought that fishing would ever be frowned upon by some members of the community; in those days, angling was wholeheartedly accepted. There were no diversions either, no carping, trout fishing, salmon fishing, pike fishing, roach fishing, etc., just plain *fishing*. Now we are pigeonholed into being a specimen hunter, a stillwater specialist and so on. The effect of these self-inflicted divisions bears out that saying 'United we stand, divided we fall'. Hopefully, this book will not fuel that division but will appeal as much to rain-fed river or stillwater anglers, as to the chalk stream fisher. It is, in essence, about a way of life, and I hope it will be fun; for fishing, after all, is only fishing and not, as some would have us believe, a matter of life and death.

`I felt that fly casting should be dealt with in detail as it is absolutely vital to chalk stream tactics. There are so many times when we can benefit from increased line speeds and various long-range presentations. All of us know how difficult this subject is to write about. Being a casting instructor myself, I am aware of the importance of practical exercise.

Of course, flies and their imitation will be a prime consideration in this book. Often we are blinded by science – yes, of course it is smart to be able to reel off *Ecdyonurus venosus* or some such, but this is still merely the late or false March Brown and, to the trout, a large brown object which is good to eat. An over-simplication perhaps, but not, I fear, far from the truth.

Each year sees the 'death' of another chalk stream. The preservation of rivers has never been so important, and not merely for fishing purposes, although that is our personal crusade. To lose them is to desecrate the countryside.

So there you have it – an odd book, in many ways, possibly old-fashioned in concept, but entertaining I hope.

The late Charlie Brooks, the great American fly fisher, wrote the following in his introduction to *The Trout and The Stream*: 'you will find the personal pronoun 'I' used in almost every case. If man has something to say, let him say it and, for God's sake, let him have the courage to say, "I said it, no one else; I believe in it and I am responsible for it" . . . That does not mean you should believe everything I say – I'm now and then wrong, but if so in this book, it is not for lack of trying to find the right answers.' I have enormous empathy with that statement. A book is personal, it has to be so, and this is my offering to you and my thoughts.

Charles W.B. Jardine
Dunkirk, Kent, 1990

PART I

1

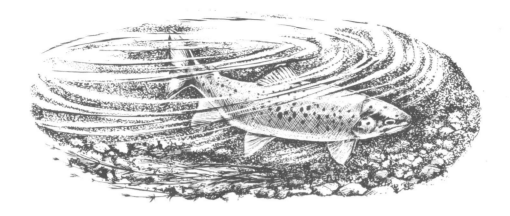

Then and Now: The Influence of History

To fish a river, any river, is not merely to extract its contents, rather it is a haven where mind and senses can soar. This is reflected in the Fly Fishers' Club motto: 'There is more to fishing than catching fish'. Any fly fisher who lacks the ability to take pleasure equally in sitting and drinking in the atmosphere of the chalk stream should, I would suggest, seek his pleasure elsewhere.

The pioneers of the past have added a further dimension to fishing and have helped to make the rivers what they are; without their colour, the landscape would be partially grey. Most of these fly fishers' histories are well known and documented and, rather than trudging through their birthplace and recounting their doubtlessly important school-days and so forth, I offer instead an entirely personal view of them. Some mentioned will be known to you, some revered as the founders of an international sport, others merely unsung heroes who have added pearls of wisdom.

I found it impossible to start with anyone other than Frederick Michael Halford (1844–1914), his mere mention being synonymous with dry fly fishing (and I use the term advisedly). I am sure I would have enjoyed meeting him. Halford's influence did not really affect me until my time on the Test and Itchen. Before this period, although known to me by name and legend, I had little sympathy for his ideas and ideals, finding them – in my boyish ignorance – to be old hat.

Halford actually started life sea and coarse fishing. I believe this is significant because most people that I have met who have made the quantum jump between disciplines – that is from natural bait fishing to artificial – bring to the sport an insight, understanding and tactical mastery that often evades pure fly fishers. Halford most certainly did, bringing to the art of fly fishing a rationale that has endured.

However, it was not a solo effort; Francis Francis (1822–1886) and George

Frederick Halford.

Selwyn Maryatt (died 1896), who was considered by Sir Edward Grey of Fallonden to be the finest fly fisherman at that time in England, also played their part. To the best of my knowledge, these three gentlemen fashioned the whole concept of upstream dry fly fishing, which is a remarkable feat if one considers that its theory and practice have remained unchanged for generations.

They lived in a different time, with different values and lifestyle. Both Maryatt and Halford were independently wealthy, allowing them full scope for experimentation and theorizing. This is usually impossible now. However, we can learn from their knowledge, and I urge you to do so. Halford's books remain educational even in this age of enlightenment and the strong influence of Maryatt. In fact, authorities suggest the Maryatt should have credit for at least half of Halford's debut book *Floating Flies and How To Dress Them*, published in 1886. Sadly Maryatt never penned his own work. If he had, I believe it would have been a book of astonishing insight and been veritably timeless.

Maryatt was not as dogmatic as Halford, as is evident by his fly boxes, which are secreted in that shrine to fly fishing, the London Fly Fishers' Club. Among his little Maryatts (pale watery imitations), which are still effective today, spent drakes and quills, nestle wet flies, which Conrad Voss Bark considers may well have proven do be the reason why Maryatt sought anonymity from the book's authorship. Yet, for all the argument and discourse over who was the thinker, I find myself drawn to Halford, not because of his purism, but for his abiding thirst for knowledge. Everyone needs a catalyst and, undoubtedly, Maryatt provided this, but Halford's patterns testify to his ingenuity, powers of observation and angling skill. The detached cork-bodied Mayflies, similar to styles we think are so advanced today, the Rough Olives, Blue Duns, Red Spinners, Ginger Quills and many others. I urge anyone to study these dressings, as they will give a rare insight into floatability, deftness of tying and understanding of materials in an age without fly floatant and when many fishing practices that would cause apoplectic shock these days were being employed, for example, dapping with natural flies and the use of live minnows and the garden hackle (worms) up and down the Test Valley. I vividly remember when first gazing across the tiers of that fly-pattern chest in London that I could not help reflecting, 'Don't we re-invent the wheel a great deal?'

The nerve-centre of this dry-fly doctrine was primarily the Houghton Club on the Test. Established in 1822 by a mere twelve founder members at the Grosvenor Hotel in Stockbridge, it is always closely associated with a dynasty, the Lunn family, who have been the keepers of the water since 1887 and created what has become a paragon of chalk stream fly fishing, unsurpassed anywhere in the world. The manicured banks, carefully nurtured and sculpted weed-beds and dappled brown pristine trout bear testament to the devotion and gentle care lavished upon this stretch of water in Hampshire. This art of river keeping and management, which William Lunn appears to have started, is now sadly regressing, for pecuniary reasons.

For anyone wishing to know how best to create an environment for trout, I would recommend John Walker Hill's masterful book *River Keeper – The Life of William James Lunn*. It is all there: fly boards, the introduction of the augmentation of species (grannom, mayfly, caperer), fish culture, and all other aspects of stream upkeep. And Lunn's Particular, Lunn's Yellow Boy and Caperer are bankside names, but there are thirty-seven other fly patterns, to my knowledge, covering every major species and stage of development found on chalk streams, and even a

William Lunn.

G.E.M. Skues.

few nymphs. All fashioned in a manner that only a patient and deeply observant naturalist could achieve.

Mick Lunn continues this tradition and a more helpful and deeply knowledgeable man you would be hard-pressed to find. The nurseries, stock and stew ponds still exist in their original location and produce brown trout of a calibre unsurpassed. A legacy of three generations of devoted care and expertise.

Moving on from one Hampshire valley to another, we come to the Itchen, and George Edward McKenzie Skues (1858–1949). This man bestrode the fly fishing world like a colossus. His insight and perception still have a great effect on how we view the sport today. I feel that Skues has to some degree been unfairly cast, almost stereotyped, as the personification of the nymph fisher, often overlooking the valid statements he made in dry fly terms.

I was introduced to Skues' writings at a comparatively early age, my father having illustrated the posthumous publication, *Itchen Memories* (Barrie & Jenkins). Skues was an extraordinarily gifted writer, he could convey a picture, fly pattern or theory with a simplicity, expediency and wit that befitted his profession as a solicitor. His dry fly fishing and dressing aside, it is for nymph fishing and flying in the face of convention that he is best remembered.

Most authorities subscribe to the view that Skues' evolution of the nymph on chalk streams was more by accident than design, the floating fly having drowned, enmeshed in the surface film, and been taken by a trout, who was in the process of feeding on another stage of insect development altogether. I wonder just how true this is. Cross-pollination of ideas between anglers from different regions must have occurred, although less freely than today. I feel certain Skues knew about T.E. Pritt and W.C. Stewart, both fishers of the tempestuous northern streams, who used sparsely dressed spider patterns, which are nymphal imitations if ever there were. Perhaps this triggered Skues' imagination off, because if you analyse a Skues imitation nymph, there is a very definite suggestion of North Country spider, combined with the field knowledge and recognition points he uncovered during his many autopsies with a marrow spoon, an item of equipment, stolen from the kitchens, that has endured.

Skues' well-recounted debate with Halford over the usage of the nymph still causes acrimony. This is sad, because I do not believe that Skues was unsporting or trying to threaten the establishment, rather he was attempting to offer the chalk stream world an alternative to be used at such times as was necessary. Having used Skues' styled nymphs, I have come to the realization that he was perhaps doing nothing more unethical than using a damp dry fly or, as we now call it, an emerger. Not truly wet at all.

I have a great affection for another contemporary of the Skues/Halfordian era: Dr E.A. Barton. He published four books: *Chalkstreams and Water Meadows*, *Running Waters*, *A Doctor Remembers* and – to my mind one of the most evocative pictorial offerings ever dedicated to these rivers – *An Album of Chalkstreams*, where each photograph is a fusion of atmosphere and expertise. He was a fishing companion of Skues, as were H.S. Hall (the originator of eyed-in hooks in their familiar state), Francis Francis, George La Branche and 'Lamorna' Birch, the wonderful artist of the Cornish school. Dr Barton, with his gift for photography and poetry, must have nestled in well. What a period it must have been; artists, literary giants and eminent men, all brothers under one spell: chalk streams.

Dr Barton's sepia-toned photographs still reflect what exists today, little on the surface has changed. Many pictures are instantly recognizable. However, one wonders what he, or indeed the others, would have made of carbon fibre and 'dog nobblers'. A chastening thought, although tempered by the knowledge that Skues was reputed to have fashioned the odd fly from rubber bands – and we think we are modern!

Frank Sawyer (1907–1980) was a man whom I knew – not well – but sufficiently to realize that he was blessed with quite extraordinary ability, and was the personification of the countryman, caring deeply about all natural creatures. It was

Frank Sawyer.

he who gave me my first professional casting lesson when I was nine years old, and already a veteran of a three-season campaign! His gentle knowledge made a lasting impression on me as a youngster. Later we met again on the banks of the Test where he came to fish as a guest of Dermot Wilson, who was employing me at the time in a similar capacity to Sawyer, as a guardian of the river.

A few years ago, Merlin Unwin of the Unwin Hyman publishing house asked if I would illustrate a reworking, albeit posthumous, of *The Keeper and the Stream*. I was overjoyed at the prospect, and hastily made arrangements to visit Sawyer's river, the Upper Avon. I received invaluable help from Sidney Vines, a well-known angling author and Sawyer's biographer, who escorted me to various stretches of river that are relevant to the book. It was autumn drifting into winter, a sad and disconsolate time, the reeds were bent in damp brown misery, the grassy water-meadows pock-marked with frost damage and the work of industrious moles. But there was the river as jaunty as ever, sweeping around corners, tumbling over shallows and flowing sedately over deeps, carrying sienna and yellow leaves along like a great raft race. Sidney mourned Sawyer's passing; the river, a testament to his keepering skills, was slipping back into the clutches of nature.

I made various sketches and imagined casting a fly, even hooking one or two of the grayling rising to large dark olives through a gap in the procession of discarded leaves. I sat where Frank Sawyer died and drank in, as he must often have done, the beauty and grandeur of that Wiltshire valley.

Frank Sawyer's rightful role as nymph fisher extraordinaire is undisputed; I believe he, and not Skues, was the father of this style. This is dangerous ground, I know, but certainly Sawyer conquered the difficulties of deep-lying fish in current by ballasting his patterns. I can find no record of this previously. His patterns are still the mainstay of a nymph angler's fly box; often we conjure a slightly different pattern, but it always seems to end up looking rather similar to Mr Sawyer's original.

His patterns, the Pheasant Tail, Grey Goose, Killer Bug, Bow Tie, Buzzer and Swedish nymph, bear the hallmark of simple genius. They are sparse, utilitarian and deadly, and are the only patterns I still buy (from Mrs Sawyer, Frank's widow), as I cannot seem to get their simple forms to look how they should. For all his genius, Sawyer was merely a hard-working river keeper, and yet he was accepted into the then élite of the fly fisher's Fario Club and honoured with the MBE. Thankfully he left a rich legacy behind, not merely his fly patterns, but his two books, *Nymphs and the Trout* and *Keeper of the Stream*.

Major Oliver Kite, or 'Ollie' as he became known, was perhaps the extrovert to Sawyer's introvert. I believe anglers are divided into the Sawyer or the Kite camp. He came to fly fishing late in life and from 1958–68 lived virtually opposite Frank Sawyer's cottage in Nether Avon. Kite learned a great deal from Sawyer, enabling him to refine further the techniques of nymph fishing, to develop the variation, the induced take. Kite conveyed both fly fishing and country matters expertly and enthusiastically during his five-year television slot, *Kite's Country*. More recently seen on video, it brought to many homes an infectious enthusiasm, seldom matched in the media. He was a showman and perhaps it was this that separated the two fly fishermen.

There is a bitter-sweet story, which I hope is apocryphal, concerning this division. Kite had mentioned to Sawyer that as soon as he possessed a white Jaguar he would feel he had 'arrived'. Obviously the television programmes assisted, for sitting outside Kite's house finally was a gleaming white Daimler. Apparently, Sawyer never spoke to Kite ever again, which must have been intolerable in a circumspect, tiny Wiltshire community.

I confess to being a Sawyer man, as I believe his mind to have been more perceptive in angling terms, but I do acknowledge Kite's undoubted abilities; his Imperial still remains one of the most successful dry flies of all time. He should also be remembered for the enjoyment he brought to an armchair-bound audience and the insight he gave into affairs of the river bank, delivered in his delightful Wiltshire burr. His book, *Nymph Fishing in Practice*, is full of sound information as befits a man of army rationale, especially in the cataloguing and division of nymph types. My good friend, Jim Hadderell, who knew him, always recounts with a twinkle Kite's favourite breakfast: curry and a pint of beer. There are few characters like that left these days.

During the years spent on the Test and Itchen, many legendary fly fishing figures fished at the kind invitation of Dermot Wilson. Some were from America, and brought with them a tactical dexterity, profound knowledge and often a lethal execution that left me in awe. Mainly it was my job to guide them (I always felt this to be something of a practical joke on Dermot's part, wondering just who would guide who!). I learnt fast and listened a great deal. It was time well spent, for who could not help improve under the inspiration of such as John Goddard, Brian Clarke, Conrad Voss Bark, Ernie Schweibert, Ted Simeroe, Dan Zahner, Perk and Leigh Perkins, Dick Walker – the list is endless. To all of them I offer my thanks for tolerating a fledgling fly fisher, with humour.

Two particular people – one English, the other American – shine like beacons in my memory, not because of their angling ability, although considerable, but for their zest and joy of the river bank. The American, Ed Zern, I met only once. He is perhaps one of the best known field-sports writers in the US, if not worldwide, and he was everything a 'frontiersman' should be, not overly tall but barrel-chested, with a red bandanna knotted around his neck, over which spilled an ebullient bushy beard beneath a pair of twinkling eyes, which pondered the next mischievous adventure.

Tackling up by the notorious twin fishing huts (their liquid assets would shame a pub), I realized the prime motivation that day would be fun, and so it turned out. I thought Ed might derive a certain amount of interest from being introduced to the top pool, a hatch pool laden with muscle-bound rainbows and browns, all quarrelling with the considerable current. Here normal chalk stream tactics of delicacy and precision were made null and void by the white water confusion and resulting mêlée. Leaded nymphs were the only viable proposition and I have to come clean and admit some attained the size, proportions and weight that Ed would definitely be familiar with on the brawling Western freestone streams. Ed greeted this alternative chalk stream method with alacrity, and, of course, knowledgeable expertise. We did catch fish, but it was the day's humour that stays in my mind. Ed was later to write, in *Field and Stream* that 'Dermot's guide Charlie took me to the top pool where he insisted I used flies the size of English house sparrows' – an exaggeration, although not much.

The Englishman is Dermot Wilson to whom I owe more than I could ever repay. It was with his assistance that I chose the pastoral world as my vocation. We hatched ideas together and still do, and created 'Mr Vole', a cartoon character

Alex Jardine.

Mr Vole.

who adorned two tackle catalogues and inspired us both. I later came to realize that there is something I call 'vole vengeance'. This story concerns one D.W. and one R.E., the then editor of *Trout and Salmon* magazine. I, busy with another client, was despatched to the Itchen, Dermot with his usual abandon exhorted R.E. to try the Test. Somehow R.E. cast sufficiently accurately to hook perfectly a water-vole in the ear. I presume a tussle erupted, quite probably of reel-singing dimensions. Dermot, ever handy with a net, landed the protesting mammal with great aplomb. Practising what he preached (having instigated an occasional catch and release policy) he took the necessary action and attempted to detach the fly from the creature's ear. The vole, being already considerably upset by anglers, decided on punitive action and sank a pair of well-directed incisors through Dermot's index finger.

That evening our paths crossed and Dermot, having wound down his car window, looking wild-eyed at me, shook what appeared to be a minute Egyptian mummy stuck in his hand, and hissed through clenched teeth, 'Look what's happened – it's that damned vole; it tried to eat me! Look, my finger will probably have to come off'. I protested that I was merely the artist and not the instigator of some terrible water bank curse.

Dermot Wilson's book, *Fishing the Dry Fly*, must surely be regarded as a classic. Its pages are filled with common sense, for Dermot, rather than adding to the mystique of fly fishing, has stripped away many of its superficial shrouds and offered a thirsty fly fishing world logic, direction and simplicity, swathed in humour and rare insight.

Two people have primarily fashioned my thinking, Dermot is one, the other

Dermot Wilson.

was my father. Alex Jardine may not go down in the annals of fly fishing folklore, but he gave me an understanding of *why* we fish. Through him I learnt woodcraft, natural history and the myriad complexities which form the whole we call fly fishing and that is perhaps the greatest gift of all.

Of course, the river predominates, but where would our heritage and sport be without the characters who fashion our opinions, and chalk streams seem to have been blessed with more than their fair share. To all of them, this student salutes you and the history you helped to create.

2

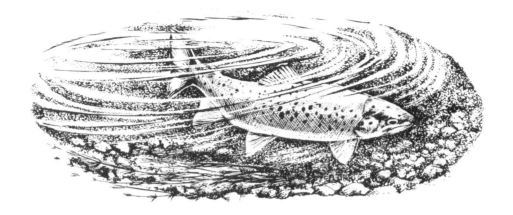

Source and Mouth and In Between

THE GEOLOGY OF CHALK STREAMS
by Barrie Rickards

You might be forgiven for thinking that a chalk stream is a water flowing milky white! However, for most of its life it is exactly the opposite, and is filled with the clearest water imaginable. A chalk stream is simply one which drains from land underlain by chalk rock. As such, chalk streams occur in Yorkshire, where they run down from the Yorkshire Wolds; the Lincolnshire Wolds; Cambridgeshire, as tributaries of the Great Ouse; Norfolk and Suffolk; and north of the Thames from Baldock to Marlborough; but most celebrated are those south of the Thames in the counties of Dorset and Hampshire.

Chalk streams are spring fed and the water is held in the chalk aquifer, not, as many people imagine, as underground streams, but in cracks and joints and between the tiny grains which go to make up chalk rock. These are almost 100 per cent composed of microscopic fossil plants (algae), called coccoliths. Coccoliths are skeletal spheres and plates of the mineral calcite, in very pure form. The crucial fact from the anglers' point of view is that the mineral is relatively soluble in water, resulting in the lime-rich, or hard water that typifies chalk streams.

Yellow flag iris.

Other rocks are lime-rich, such as the limestone of Derbyshire, western Yorkshire and parts of the Midlands and Wales, but these rocks are harder and slightly less soluble and do not result in the richness of the chalk streams. Even within the realms of chalk stream counties, those in the south are richer than those in the north, because the chalk is softer and goes into solution more easily from better aquifers.

Once the calcite has gone into solution it gives a numerical measure of alka-

Yellow king cup.

linity/acidity to the water in question. Neutral is 7; anything over that is alkaline. Chalk streams are alkaline and they have a pH reading in excess of 7, often 7.8 or over 8.0. Highly alkaline streams like this encourage a rich invertebrate fauna, enable a great diversity of plant life, and this leads to a rich and healthy water, which can sustain superb fish stocks, and excellent growth rates.

WILDLIFE

River banks are, in many ways, a microcosm of natural life, a veritable 'motor-way' of natural events. Therefore, fly fishers ought to be as quiet and unobtrusive as possible. I have come across people whose sole ambition is to catch trout and who are impervious to all about them, shrugging off natural beauty, as though it were worn-out clothing. They have not grasped the reason why we do it. I believe it was Izaak Walton who penned, 'Angling is a contemplative sport', along with another pearl, 'A study to be quiet'.

Working on and living with rivers on a daily basis has afforded me a rare opportunity for nature-watching. A whole phantasmagoria of insects, birds, plants and animals has made my life a privileged one. It is because of this that many intriguing and often humorous instances have been encountered.

I do regret my almost total ignorance of flora. I could be swathed in a sea of orchids or toadflax and report purple loose strife in a field notebook. A case of non-blissful ignorance, I am afraid. The one thing I do know is how much I look forward to the arrival of king cups and yellow flag iris each season. Their riotous yellow splashes set amidst the deep verdant green always inspires. However, I find

The kingfisher is an increasingly familiar sight on our rivers.

it difficult to become euphoric about sedge and alder, both of which have tended to divest me of my fly-tying efforts at an alarming rate! Despite sedge's almost total anonymity during the easier casting hours of daylight, their presence at the water's edge at last light seems awesome, invariably during the evening rise, and their appetite for spinner patterns is colossal. Seldom is there any other course open to the angler than to put down the trout which has been stalked for the previous twenty or so minutes and risen magnificently, in order to retrieve the fly pattern which hangs seductively over the water from a single sedge stalk. Alder trees are even worse. Fly fishers should make wide detours around these avaricious gatherers of fur, feather, tinsel and hook.

The need for survival is uppermost in nature. The inescapable truth is that for one creature to prosper, another must be sacrificed. Nature is cruel and yet we *Homo sapiens* do have a habit of sentimentalizing the wild world. The mayfly is a prime example of the harshness of nature: what a miserable existence this creature must have. Initially, it is incarcerated in silt tubes for up to two years. Then it breaks free from its prison only to have trout descend upon it, along with other avaricious fish. If it survives this, it then hatches and once more comes to the culinary attention of fish. Once its wings are dry and flight can be achieved, the mayfly ascends into a maelstrom of aerial attack from wagtails, swallows, martins and a host of other birds, that relish this delicacy erupting from the silver stream.

However, it is man who commits mindless, senseless cruelty. One instance of this remains with me with the clarity of the piscine water in which it occurred. It was high summer and I was on a fishing trip. I emerged from the head-high foliage

that encircled the spring pool, a horseshoe lake that fuelled the Little Stour, home to numerous springs which percolated in the pool. So clear was the water that even at depths of 10ft and over, stones and water weeds looked touchable and tantalizingly close. Great trout swam here, indigenous rainbows (at that time this was one of only six places in England where they successfully bred) finned the crystal depths, each spot and sinewy movement in sharp focus and absolute clarity. It seemed a magical place, graced with tranquillity and an air of joviality.

The day was bathed in sunshine, two large willows casting flickering, dappled shadows across the wide-leafed plants in a green kaleidoscope of light and shade. Suddenly my foot touched on something beneath the bankside reeds, something hidden, secret and camouflaged. I bent down and picked up the beginnings of a tethered strand of thick nylon which resembled sea fishing-line. Inquisitively I tugged it, meeting resistance somewhere toward the middle of the pool. I knew of the poacher and his ways; having a stream full of trout provided quick learning ground for my father and me. I knew of long lines with their baited, gorging hooks. The small resistance gave; hand over hand I pulled the length through the water, the thick spring nylon falling over my feet. It was not, as I expected, a stream of hooks – just one. A small black bundle furrowed through the surface and dangled beneath me. As I cupped my hands around its sodden little form, I

Potential hazards. It is not a bad idea to have a glance behind you before making a cast.

23

saw it was a moorhen chick, no more than a few days old. It had died disgustingly, tethered, gorged, lonely, and lingeringly painfully. I wanted to scream my outrage, and a small boy's sunny day turned suddenly black. To this day, I have never returned to fish there.

I suppose that of all the creatures I enjoy watching, the kingfisher is my favourite bird, with its shrill little haunting cry, followed by that blur of indigo, sapphire, cobalt and reddish orange, as it wings its way speedily across the water; and otters are my favourite animals. As a keeper, I could never begrudge these creatures an odd meal, even if it was destined for a client's catch. Yet, in all my years on chalk stream banks I have never actually seen one, although I have seen plenty when sea trout fishing. I have heard their eerie night call, freezing one momentarily to the marrow, and seen their holt and their playground, but never seen the animals themselves, except maybe the odd wisp of a tail.

Barn owls I have recorded, and during the day too. Often when unlocking the 'den of iniquity' – our booze-laden fishing hut on the Test – I would see their ghostly white forms noiselessly sweeping across a field by the carrier. I am told, that this, sadly, is now a rare occurrence. Indeed, I have spotted very few in recent years.

Not so their smaller relative, the little owl. This sprightly character does not obviously see itself cast in the role of 'court jester', but who can take seriously an owl which alights on fence posts or tree stumps, and bobs continuously up and down with blinking and dilating eyes, with all this being done with an air of a Dickensian clerk?

Bats, too, can seem idiotic, particularly when their radar malfunctions. I have experienced two occasions, many years ago, when during the gloaming, with the

Mallard that have been alarmed.

24

A sparrow hawk swooping down on a martin. Sparrow hawks are more common now than years ago, and can be seen frequently along riverbanks, especially those covered by woodland.

trout lazily sipping away through the evening rise, I realized that, rather than creating a fairly interesting back cast, the vertical line and leader, to my bitter consternation, was flying in haphazard circles about my head. To a small fly fisher alone in the water-weeds, with swathes of marsh mists hanging eerily over the landscape, silvery in the darkness, it is the stuff of nightmares. I am happy to recall that, in both instances, the bats were caught and released. Selectively fishing for bats is not to be recommended.

This brings me in mind of an incident, which occurred only two seasons ago on the tiny Allen River on the Hampshire/Wiltshire border. It is a stream of cloistered, almost jungle-like proportions, serpent-like it winds its way beneath boughs and branches, as though only secretly admitting to having a trout season. In many ways, it is a true trout stream, demanding cautious and deft approaches and extremely precise and gentle casting. Foraging my way, like an old badger, up the stream one afternoon, a small fluttering movement to my right caused me to glance, but nothing more. I dismissed the movement as simply a dead leaf on a branch, but then something – possibly the way it moved – made me look closer, until I realized that the dark shape in the gloom, whatever it was, was alive. I waded the stream and managed to reach with my rod tip the branch that held the object, looping the fly line and rod tip around an outstretched twig which looked substantial enough to act as a lever. I gingerly eased the alder branch and the small fluttering form towards me. As it came within reach, I realized what it was. At some point, I can only assume (and pray) it was the previous evening, a fly fisher had made an inaccurate cast, lofted his leader up into the alder branch and, obviously disgruntled, pulled for a break, thus leaving a length of nylon in a small ball-like shape on the branch, which freakishly allowed the fly to dangle on about 6 inches of loose tippet. A bat, detecting this fluttering artificial, had mistakenly assumed it to be the real McCoy and taken a swipe at it. The pheasant tail dry fly was still firmly embedded in the bat.

Very carefully I cut away the mêlée of monofilament, which incarcerated the

The elusive otter.

Roe deer in 'velvet'.

pipistrelle bat, and dislodged the dry fly. Mercifully the bat was fine; he was discomforted and disorientated but nonetheless able to fly away looking relatively chipper. Wherever I go the memory of that wretched fly goes with me and serves as a poignant reminder of how a split second's anger and haste can needlessly run the risk of destroying – quite hideously – an innocent creature.

Those of our number who knowingly leave nylon on hooks and other objects that are potentially lethal to wildlife on river banks, such as cans and bottles which trap mice and voles, in my opinion, have no business fishing – they should seek their 'pleasures' elsewhere.

Often, over the years, and especially when keeping a low profile during the evening rise, it has astonished me how acceptable I have become to wild creatures, even the more nervous variety. One particular evening on the River Test during early September stands out, when the blue-winged olives were busily hatching and making life momentarily tiresome. The trout (as is their wont) were rising with gusto at anything that was non-artificial. Hard concentration was the order

of the evening. In their almost hypnotic state, it is easy for them to ignore the angler.

Roe buck drinking.

Intent on rising trout sipping in duns, a mere whisper in the reeds opposite caught my attention. Almost unconsciously, I gazed in the direction of the movement, a drinking roe buck paid me no heed and I drifted back to the task in hand and he to the business of quenching his thirst. We must have remained like that for a further quarter of an hour. I watched him unhurriedly depart when a clumsy cast had put pay to my intended quarry. The buck, I like to think, seemed to take me as a part of the riverbank life, rather than a visitor or, worse still, a trespasser.

All the creatures of the river bank are important to the fly fisher's year. They are the notes and tunes of the orchestra and we the audience. The spring-like melodies of the blackbird; the lazy soft cooings of the woodpigeons drifting over the meadows; and the water-vole's arguments of chattering, dips, hops, scuttles and plops under the water are truly marvellous to observe. I cannot help but wonder what the river world would be like if they were not in evidence.

3

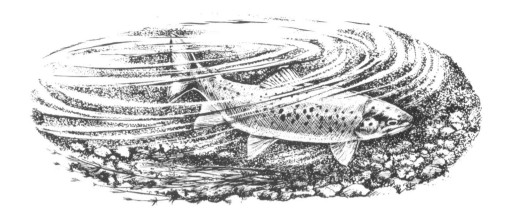

To Have and Have Not

'If only' are two of the saddest words in our vocabulary; *if only* we had acted sooner, *if only* we had heeded the obvious changes, *if only* we had bothered. I am afraid this is a rather doom-laden chapter. The irrevocable signs are there: our rivers, it appears, are merely convenient commodities in a transient throw-away society that cares little for the future. The river near to my home testifies to this. Last season I waded around discarded bicycles, prams, black plastic bin-liners, car tyres and other paraphernalia. An American who fished with me, on hearing tales of ecological destruction, wryly summed it up, 'You can create a stillwater, but hell, once you've lost a river, you've lost it forever'.

Dr Jeremy Lucas is a dear friend and a fly fisher of extraordinary ability but, more importantly, he is an ardent conservationist and passionate champion for the natural cause. He is better qualified than I to discuss the dilemma facing anglers and the general public. My only regret is that this chapter was necessary at all; these are his words.

CHALK STREAM CONSERVATION
by Jeremy Lucas B.Sc., Ph.D.

Chalk streams die in various ways. In Britain today the conservation projects and good river management schemes in operation are swamped under a devastating avalanche of destruction. It stems from ignorance – from an individual level to political – and carelessness. It manifests itself either subtly, in a river's ecosystem being infinitesimally altered, invisible to all but the most studious and experienced observers, or obviously in the sad spectacle of a river in the shadows of existence.

TO HAVE AND HAVE NOT

All readers of this book will have an interest in chalk streams and will probably know of the major threats to these fragile systems. What I want to do is support Charles Jardine in his view of the calcium-rich, running waters being, collectively, an environment which is wonderfully diverse and beautiful. The chalk streams' virtues lie beyond even the appreciation of the dedicated fisherman, although it is he, perhaps, who will most closely observe and understand its nature.

Memories are so short and they so poorly transcend generations. We need to recall the perfect state of a limestone- and chalk-enriched river of yesterday and compare that watercourse with what exists today.

We often hear mention of a chalk or limestone area. Elementally there is no difference between the two. The essential difference is geological. Limestone is effectively inorganically formed calcium carbonate, while chalk is the deposit laid down from organisms which have utilized the element calcium and from their subsequent death and decay processes over considerable tracts of time, especially from molluscs and crustacea. Calcium carbonate is the major component of their shells.

A river is an individual entity, no two being exactly alike. Limestone and chalk characteristics are often mixed. The truest chalk stream types are almost entirely in southern England. The Yorkshire and Derbyshire rivers have a significant limestone component while rivers like the lovely Eden in Cumbria are entirely limestone sourced, rather than chalk. Even in remote north-western Britain, where there are only isolated outcrops of limestone, we find streams and lochs with surprising calcium content, even on and close to the acid moorland.

The chalk is an enormous, porous sponge through which the water soaks, from which the springs and rivers drain. A limestone river derives from rock possessing a high amount of limestone. This rock is far less porous than chalk and therefore the rivers of this type tend to be more subject to inconsistent flow, largely dependent on rainfall in the short term. The chalk stream is naturally only affected by rainfall in the long term, since the chalk of its source continues to unleash its load over a period of many months.

We need to understand the composition and source of the rivers in order to appreciate fully the threats and the measures we can take to protect them. Calcium carbonate itself, either from chalk or limestone, is virtually insoluble. It is the carbon dioxide dissolved in rain, forming very weak carbonic acid, which dissolves the carbonate to form calcium hydrogen carbonate, an alkaline substance, which is more soluble. Living organisms such as molluscs and crustacea in lakes and rivers can utilize this dissolved compound by precipitating out, via biological processes, the calcium as calcium carbonate. Many aquatic plants also need the alkaline nature of these streams.

Limestone and chalk can thus be seen to be very important minerals in these days of high acidity in rainfall. The burning of fossil fuels drastically increases carbon dioxide input to the atmosphere. The resultant heavily acid rain is counteracted where it falls on calcium-bearing rock. Where there is little or no calcium present the acid reacts with other elements, such as deadly aluminium, which then leaks into the ecosystem with disastrous effects.

Chalk or limestone rivers are not usually susceptible to acidification or serious pH changes. Only those that are maintained alkaline artificially, by agricultural liming in the catchment area, or those with marginal limestone at their sources – some of the Cumbrian and northern England rivers and streams – are affected.

The joie de vivre *of the leaping brown trout.*

ABSTRACTION

The greatest dangers to chalk streams are pollution and abstraction. The rivers are terribly vulnerable to both, and the areas which we most utilize for water abstraction processes are those possessing the chalk sponges. Artesian boreholes can be easily sunk into the soft chalk to force the water out into the waiting conurbations and industries that demand it.

The lifeline for the appalling spread of housing in southern England is not, as many would suggest, the motorway links to London, but the vast water table of these lowlands. Ironically, it is the presence of chalk and water that make beautiful, lush southern England so special, which has also actually caused the man-made pressures which destroy it.

On a much more rapid and dramatic scale we witnessed the death by abstraction of the little chalk steams of Hertfordshire, the Bean, Mimram and Rib, within only a few years. Through the 1960s, the late Richard Walker was one of the few champions for these once-delightful rivers. Again, the massive growth of housing and industrial development in the county meant that it could only be sustained by escalating the exploitation of local water. Where these rivers, just a few years ago, contained stable and typical chalk-stream ecologies, including wild trout in abundance, today they flow feebly, with virtually none of their diverse organic past. Where they contain trout it is entirely due to episodic stocking, particularly with rainbow trout – artificiality in the extreme.

Despite the detrimental effects of abstraction seen in Hertfordshire, the same pressure is being applied to central southern England (although here the chalk source is far larger and terminal abstraction will take longer) and even in the last chalk stream domain of the south-east, the Great Stour in Kent. Sourced in some of the most beautiful scenery in southern England, the North Downs, the Great Stour curves down towards the delightful Weald, through Ashford and then turns back through the Downs to Canterbury, across the flat plain of East Kent, where it is met by the Little Stour, also chalk-sourced, before reaching the sea at Pegwell Bay.

One cannot envisage a scene more English and lovely than the Great Stour flowing through the parkland at Olantigh and Godmersham, where Jane Austen wove her literary magic, or the tumbling, swirling intimacy of the divided stream at Chilham Mill. Even parts of the Test or Dever, so obviously chalk and lush, could never reach so deeply into my own affections as the Great Stour. Here are echoes of my childhood and memories of living on the Downs, and even where I fished so much when I was first married. It hurts a great deal to see what happened in Hertfordshire now taking place in Kent.

Abstraction, this time for the increase in population in Canterbury, Ashford and much of the rest of the central county, has already completely destroyed the Little Stour to the extent that, in a dry summer flow, it is reduced to nothing and the entire river bed is sometimes exposed. It is incredible to think that Charles Jardine's father, Alex, once caught a 5lb wild trout from this stream. Now even the Great Stour is reduced to the level where much of its ecosystem has been altered and, over most of the river, it is doubtful that trout, sea trout and salmon now breed naturally.

Abstraction has several effects on a river's ecology. In the first instance, it reduces the average volume of the ecosystem, a much overlooked factor which directly controls both the diversity and abundance of species. It also reduces flow, which some organisms cannot tolerate. Several plants, even *Ranunculus*, and countless invertebrates, need a high average river flow. When this is reduced, oxygen concentrations fall and the partial pressure of carbon dioxide increases. Silting is a major by-product of reduced flow which also has a profound effect on plant and animal species.

SILTING

Consider a typical length of chalk stream affected by reduced flow as a result of abstraction. The fast-water plants dwindle and disappear, being replaced by plants adapted for slow-moving water. On carriers of the Great Stour, for example, even lilies, doyens of stillwater, have formed dense beds. Worse, certain algae take hold and can discolour the water (this, along with fish farm effluent, severely discolours the Test), further affecting higher plant and animal species and also further reducing concentrations of oxygen.

Silting is a great enemy of the chalk stream environment. As silt settles on the leaves of aquatic plants, they become unable to photosynthesize and to conduct respiratory processes adequately. Moreover, many of those invertebrate species, so typical of the chalk environment, cannot tolerate silting. Many ephemerids, for example, live on lightly silted or silt-free gravel, or stable silt beds. When such areas are episodically heavily silted, or suffer continuous low levels of silting, these vulnerable insects cannot survive. Also, with the loss of the fast-water plants, many insect and crustacea species that depend on them also disappear.

In appearance these affected streams tend to carry more colour with fewer gravel beds, and visible silting – furring – of plants and gravel. Observation reveals fewer species of insect, particularly ephemerids, although an increase in slow-

Man's legacy – the River Stour during the summer of 1960.

water species such as various chironomids. Minnows and dace are the coarse fish most affected by reduced flows and lack of highly oxygenated shallows. The shoals tend to drop downstream or become highly localized in favoured areas. A reduced suitable environment for these fish results in heavy predation by animals such as pike, mink and heron. Eventually, minnows and dace will be the first fish to be exterminated from seriously affected rivers.

Conversely, some vertebrate species will benefit, at least in the short term. Bream, for example, have moved from the lower reaches of the Great Stour upstream as far as Ashford (they were entirely absent above Canterbury before the days of heavy abstraction), while there are even good populations of tench (the archetypal species of stillwater) in certain stretches.

A major problem of silting also manifests itself on the breeding redds of salmon, sea trout and trout. The salmonids simply cannot breed on mud or even moderately silted gravel; their eggs and alevin would not survive even if they managed to spawn successfully.

With the reduction of water volume and available breeding and feeding opportunities, both the numbers and average sizes of fish present fall. On the Test, throughout stretches which once boasted common catches of 2lb-plus grayling and roach, and dace of 1lb and more, these specimens are now much less common, although the grayling, at least, remains abundant. On the Great Stour, famous for very large roach and a high average weight of trout, the big roach is almost absent upstream of Canterbury and the trout are only maintained by stocking.

Abstraction and silting together produce intolerable damage to the chalk stream

33

environment. To some extent they have affected even relatively big chalk streams such as the Avon (an atypical chalk stream), the Itchen and the Test. Added to other problems, notably the various types of pollution, the largest rivers in the land have not escaped from the various detrimental incursions of human populations and activity.

POLLUTION

Pollution is at its worst in the abstracted stream. The pollutants are more concentrated and take longer to run through the system. There are many harmful substances which we deposit, either accidentally or on purpose, into our rivers, even the chalk streams. Industrial pollution is more prevalent on larger lowland drainage rivers than on chalk streams. Certainly, heavy industry is entirely confined to big rivers. Small industry, including food processing, perfume manufacture, cosmetics, confectionery, light engineering and paper milling, is located on the banks of even the upper chalk streams, using the water but returning it, ideally, at a high standard, although rarely at its pristine quality before use (at best it will have been affected by heating, which itself can be detrimental to natural processes).

The industrial units are always aesthetically ruinous to the chalk stream and water-meadow environment and physically rob the landscape of very rich areas. Most of them, however, are located in or close to towns through which the rivers flow. At worst, these industrial concerns release harmful substances into the water. The amount of any substance that they are allowed to release is set down by law and it is the responsibility of the National Rivers Authority (NRA) and the Regional Water PLC's, formerly the Water Authorities, to monitor, advise and, where necessary, take action to safeguard the water environment.

In practical terms it is a case of too few having to do too much. There are not enough officers of the NRA to check on the outflows from so many industries, together with other polluting sources, their powers are not strong enough and the money is simply not available to administer a system which can adequately protect our rivers.

I will never forget attending a talk given by an officer of the NRA who had special responsibility for pollution control in one of the regions. On sustained questioning it became increasingly clear that he was unaware even of the existence of problems in some of the most important streams and rivers in the region. He obviously knew, and worked to protect, water systems near where he lived, but had given far less attention to rivers farther afield.

Apart from industry – and actually more importantly for chalk streams – the most serious addition of pollutants to the aquatic environment comes from agriculture. The case against nitrate and phosphate fertilizers has been well documented, but the problem has not been solved completely. The years of very high run-off from heavily fertilized fields are probably over except for a few isolated cases. The sheer cost of these materials has reduced the levels of nitrogen and phosphorous fertilizers which are placed on the land. Also, the introduction of 'slow release' fertilizers (actually slow dissolution pellets) reduces episodic flushing of high concentrations of these substances into rivers.

A subtle problem of excess unnatural fertilizer leaching into our waters is that of trace element chemistry. Only comparatively recently has the importance of trace elements in biochemical systems been fully appreciated. 'Trace' implies that the elements are present only in very low concentrations. Plants and animals have adapted to make use of these elements. The problem is that some metals can be rendered unavailable by precipitation by phosphate. The metal is chemically locked away to the extent that the ecosystem which depends on it experiences deficiency.

The more urgent and obvious effects of fertilizer pollution are eutrophication and an increase in the standard measurement of pollution, the biological oxygen demand, BOD.

Eutrophication is the unrelenting multiplication of algae, feeding on dissolved nitrate and phosphate, especially at high partial pressures of carbon dioxide. At first, as these organisms photosynthesize, they release oxygen, most of it passing into the air. However, as the waters turn green, the algal organisms become superabundant and then die. It is in their death that they become lethal, for decay brings about the release of carbon dioxide and the depletion of oxygen. Fish and, indeed, any aerobic (oxygen requiring) creature suffer. In a eutrophied river or lake all fish, even low-oxygen demanding species such as tench, can be killed.

The BOD is an empirical standard for measuring pollution. As oxygen is needed by the micro-organisms, which remove certain pollutants by utilizing it in their own life cycles, we can measure the rate of depletion of oxygen in a sample over a set period of time (most usually five days) in order to obtain a comparative scale and measure of pollution. The more fertilizer and other pollutants, especially farm waste and slurry, which leach into the system, the higher will be the BOD, thus reducing the oxygen that is available to species such as fish. Some fish are much more susceptible to low-oxygen concentrations than others. Dace, minnows and all the salmonids are top of the list for British fish.

Pesticides might well cause longer-term damage to the ecosystem, especially in water habitats, than fertilizers. We simply do not know the medium- to long-term effects of so many pesticides, particularly the very active halogenated organic compounds. Memories of DDT, Aldrin, Parathion and Dieldrin have lasted, but still there is widespread use of some of these and other potentially very hazardous chemicals.

Not only do the target pests at which the chemicals are aimed become involved, but it is virtually impossible to prevent these very complicated organic compounds from affecting non-target organisms and, worse, being concentrated by the food chain until they affect higher animals, even ourselves.

While micro-organisms can deal with fertilizer pollutants, even if this results in short-term damage to the water environment by oxygen depletion, these same bacteria cannot utilize and break down organic pesticides. Persistence of these is a major threat, particularly as they are now beginning to be found as contaminants, albeit at low concentration, deep in water-bearing strata from which boreholes abstract drinking-water supplies and chalk streams are born.

Effluent resulting from human waste is pumped into rivers, although this tends to be low down on their water courses, or even directly into the sea itself. Though human waste is not a particular, identifiable problem for chalk streams, waste from farms certainly is, especially that from large stock such as cattle and pigs. Besides the high levels of nitrogen and phosphorus, a pot-pourri of substances runs into the streams in this raw effluent. Even growth hormones and other medicines and compounds with which farm stock is treated are present, with unknown long-term effects.

The insidious proliferation of trout farms over the last decade now causes much concern. The tonnage of waste products, actually raw effluent from the trout themselves, together with waste food that escapes from big farms, is, in the opinion of some experts, the severest threat after abstraction. There are hundreds of large trout farms in Britain, most of them situated on the banks of chalk streams, simply because such rivers always provide the optimum flow and near-constant temperature so suitable for trout growth.

We demand the produce of trout farms both for a growing table market and a boom in fly fishing. We cannot have these without some environmental impact. There are ways to reduce the damage other than by transferring the problem to non-chalk or limestone areas, even freshwater lochs or sea inlets. Treatment plants for the outflow from fish farms is the only suitable answer, but these are presently very expensive and must substantially increase the cost of our trout, for both table and sporting markets.

CHALK STREAM MANAGEMENT

Good chalk stream management is, like the streams themselves, dying. We have cited reduced flow as being detrimental to the animals and plants. However, even with abstraction, it is possible to maintain flow in the shrunken river. Good bank maintenance is the key, even considerably narrowing the river so as to increase

Victim of a careless world – a dead trout.

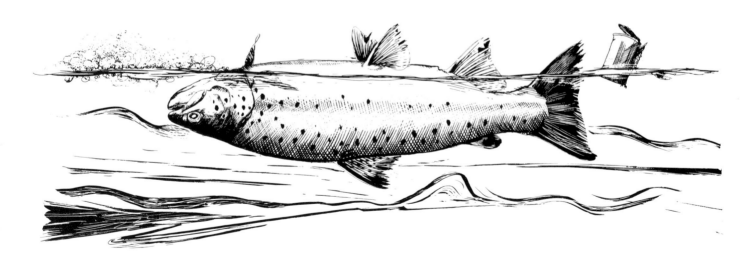

flow. Banks can be staked for rapid short-term results, or planted with trees such as willow and alder for a long-term policy. Groynes and supported gravel bars can be constructed for the same purpose.

Weed-beds can be cut in strips, either along the direction of flow or even in bands to produce a series of pools and rapids. Diagonal cutting is also practised to produce desired flow patterns. Less careful weed control is often seen nowadays. Sometimes it is quite ruthless and thoughtless, indiscriminately machine-cut along entire stretches of river, not only exterminating so much vertebrate and invertebrate life, which depends on the water plants, but causing weed choking and decay pollution downstream.

The days are well and truly over on all but a cherished few of our smaller chalk streams when management meant little more than controlling grayling and coarse fish populations. Today these are indiscriminately controlled, in size and number, by pollutants and abstraction. Also, we should be looking far beyond our penchant for stocking with more and heavier trout to maintain the sporting potential of a chalk stream fishery. The River Test today has earned the sad accolade that it is the biggest stock pond in the world. Tainted waters now flow along this, the world's most famous chalk stream, and we wonder how few wild trout still live there. It cannot be many.

Chalk streams need simultaneously to be managed from the source downstream and from the estuary upstream, each section, each influence, to be dealt with with due regard for the whole, although cherishing the source more than anything. Without a clean, abundant source, we cannot have a healthy river.

Yet the aquatic environment is wonderfully resilient. Time and nature are, indeed, great repairers of even ferocious damage. If more reservoirs can be built to supply our drinking-water needs and our chalk streams are allowed to flow unabstracted; if fish farms can be adequately controlled; if detrimental run-off from agricultural land may be tamed; if good management shores up the banks and stocks intelligently, with not too many vagrant rainbows so alien to our rivers; if politicians can see the value to our community, our health, our pride, of our lovely rivers; if only . . . Then we will again have some of our most precious heritage.

4

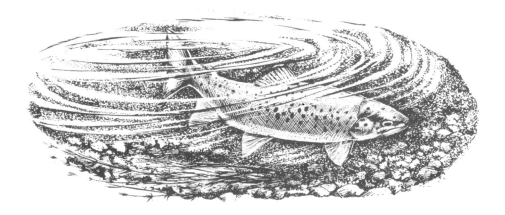

Master of Its Element

There can be few of us who, when crossing a bridge over a river, can possibly refuse the magnetic draw to peer over the edge and gaze into the tranquil depths below. This particular occupation pacifies the minds of most of us, enveloping us like a Merlin spell. This sparkling world is another dimension, tangible yet, at the same time, mystical and apart. In my childhood, like most small boys, I found the lure of water to be the very essence of adventure. This feeling has not diminished, I am still transfixed by the easy glide of rippling currents, the lazy contortions of water-weeds and the darts and silvery flicks of stickleback and minnow.

To understand fly fishing is to understand the very character of the water in which trout live, to interpret nature's signs and subtleties and convert them into angling notions. This is essential; more important than fly choice or tackle. I would urge everyone to spend a part of their time *without* a fly rod, just walking the banks and familiarizing themselves with the underwater mysteries. The most useful information that anyone has ever offered me were the profound words of my father, 'Charles, if you want to catch fish, then you have to think like one'. That was thirty years ago. The fact that a trout's brain is the approximate size of a pea might indicate also his opinion as to my academic potential. As with most things, he was right both in the former and the latter.

The best anglers seem to possess an ability to transcend the hard tangible reality of terra firma and submerge themselves mentally into this water dimension. They are the people one meets from time to time who fish an area shunned by all and, for no accountable reason, proceed to catch an abundance of large fish. They are the anglers who can tell by a sixth sense when a trout has taken a nymph, although nothing is seen, heard or felt. In short, they are guided by instinct and insight.

A trout in this game plan is a quarry to be studied. It has the upper hand; generation after generation have secured a lineage which is almost perfectly adapted to the surroundings. (I am, of course, talking of brown trout, the indigenous species of Britain, and not the rainbow.) You only have to observe the next

38

brown trout you catch, whether it be from a beck, a boulder-strewn northern river or a sedate chalk stream, to see that nature has contrived one of her more subtle camouflages. Certainly it may have silver flanks or even a buttercup yellow belly, but look at the top, as a predator might, and immediately you will notice how the sinewy motion of weeds are echoed in the olive hues of the back, and how the intermittent spots on perhaps a darker brown back fade into a pebbledash bottom. If we take one particular variation, 'the Kennett Greenback', which is sadly in decline, we see that its natural colour scheme uses a palette which echoes perfectly the weed-laden layers of that Berkshire stream.

Fortunately for anglers, the trout tends to give itself away in a number of ways; the difficulty is in knowing what to look for. All the best tackle in the world will not achieve as much as your own eyes, cunning and stealth.

THE TROUT'S MOVEMENTS

I have been privileged to take many people to the bankside on what was often their first or formative trip. It constantly surprised me just how difficult people find looking into the water or 'trout spotting' to be. Indeed, even veteran reservoir anglers seem to be similarly stupefied. It is essential to learn the trout's lifestyle; how he reacts to certain conditions and periods of the day; what kind of water is suitable for feeding, resting, sleeping and, of course, observing quarry when hunting. In short, what we need to emulate is any practised hunter. A predator, to be effective, must first evaluate the prey, in its many guises. As Jim Hadderell once said to me, 'Time spent in reconnaissance is seldom wasted'.

The next step is to understand how the fish move. It may sound contrite of me to say it has fins, but very few fly fishers I meet seem to realize just how crucial these appendages are to reasoned fly fishing tactics. They are, without question, a vital aid in evaluating how the fish is feeding and, occasionally, the food form that will be chosen. Sometimes, by knowing how the fish is lying from watching fin movement, one can detect underwater current speeds faster than those occurring on the surface. Occasionally it will afford you the ability to skip the odd fish because it is sound asleep. A resting fish tends to hug the bottom with fins projecting slightly downward, and, more often than not, lies just behind or in front of a weed-bed or obstruction, which allows for areas of slack water or countering bank washes against the main push of current. The trout may actually give off a palpably comatose air.

However, the same slothful fish might, on another occasion, although in the same position, be slightly fanning the pectoral (which are by the gill covers) and the pelvic fins (situated under the body, midships) and idly waving his tail (caudal) and dorsal fin. This is a sign that the fish is alert, although it may not seem so by its position. This trout knows it will not have to work hard for food because of the slack water it occupies. Any passing nymphal titbit will, before being sucked up and moved on by the main stream current, hover and remain stationary for a period, so that the trout, at best, only needs open its mouth and at worst, move its head slightly in order to enjoy its meal.

Therefore, rather than simply noting that a trout is in a particular place, the fly fisher has learnt a great deal more: that the speed of the water is slack where the trout lies; that he eats nymphs and shrimps; and that there is a need for both

*Various aspects of the
trout.*

accuracy and exact depth control with the artificial because the fish will maintain its station. If the fish adopts the comatose air, the angler would be well advised to seek pastures new.

If, when we look at the same deep-lying trout, we notice a hurried air about the pectoral, the pelvic fin is making fairly fast fanning motions, and the dorsal and anal fins marginally erect and waving, then immediately the nymph fisher's pulse should quicken. This fish, irrespective of the surface current, is actively feeding on subaqueous forms in a fast current near to the bottom, offering a steady, although undulating quantity of food forms. Very often this particular trout will betray its feeding presence further by flicking its head from side to side or darting forwards, or indeed drifting backwards to intercept a passing creature. However, if a fish's pelvic, pectoral, dorsal and anal fins are held almost static to its sides, with only its tail moving from side to side, it is not feeding. It can sometimes be persuaded, but often this will prove a fruitless exercise. These are just some of the permutations; they are as infinite as the water that trout inhabit, each current dictating policy.

THE TROUT'S HEARING

The basic component parts of the trout.

What is essential is not to overlook the auditory abilities of fish, and trout in particular. The lateral line is, I hope, a well-known sensory area to you. My father

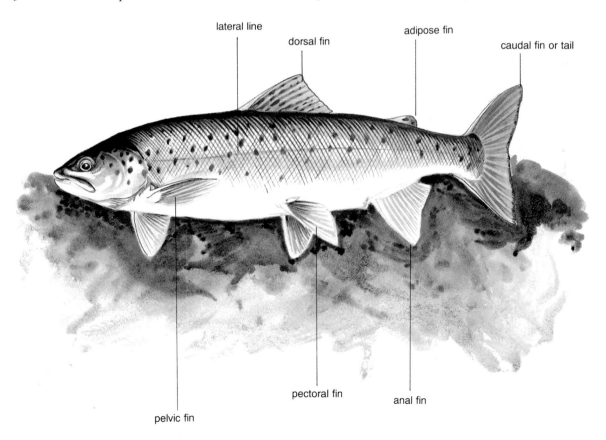

lateral line

dorsal fin

adipose fin

caudal fin or tail

pectoral fin

anal fin

pelvic fin

was the first to press home this important faculty of the trout. Our fishing escapades were always conducted in sepulchral silence; heavy footfalls, loud noises and, heaven forbid, a dropped item of tackle, were all greeted with stormy red-flushed fury. It is surprising how quickly even a six-year-old learns! Any sonorous and trill antics, sooner or later, reach the trout via the lateral line, i.e. vibrations. Any shock wave of reasonable proportions can be picked up approximately thirty feet away, in other words half a fly line's length, which is even more alarming. After that the trout's ears take over – yes, ears. Of course these are not fleshy appendages strapped to the gill covers, instead they are situated actually in the head and pick up high-frequency sound, whereas the lateral line responds to the low. These two factors control feeding and evasive action during times of danger, sifting the various waves into instinctive areas of approval or approbation.

This is, of course, important to the bank angler and should guide his conduct, especially when placing his feet is concerned. However, perhaps more importantly, it affects wading. I have simply lost count of the amount of times I have witnessed 'the enraged bull elephant syndrome' or the fly fisher emulating a sailboarder in his eagerness to cover water and trout. These anglers, although creating a very artistic spume of spray and a remarkable show of balance combined with movement, have done nothing at all to disguise the fact they are there and posing a threat to the trout population.

Wading should be noiseless, gentle and controlled, echoing an otter slipping through the river system. A crunched rock or dislodged bank of stones, or even an overly pushed wave will alert the prize. Bearing in mind that two sets of sensory organs, honed over hundreds of years, are deducing and reacting on information received just half a fly line's length away; trout are practised survivors.

THE TROUT'S VISION

Of all the sensory organs that bind fish and fishermen together, the eyes – except in the case of carp fishing and other similar species where taste comes into the proceedings – are the most important in terms of fly fishing.

Precisely what a trout can see, which colours are important and what form

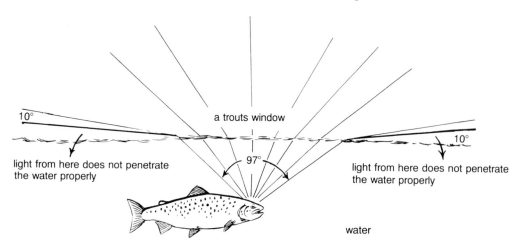

10°   a trouts window   10°

light from here does not penetrate the water properly   97°   light from here does not penetrate the water properly

water   *The eyes of the trout.*

images take is still largely supposition, although deductions can be based on the sound, scientific knowledge that we have of the precise make-up of the eye. The retina resembles our own in terms of being comprised of rods and cones; the cones allow for colour vision and the rods allow the eye to react to various light levels. Thereafter the lens is for focussing and the area of vision.

I realized when still a boy that, in order to catch trout, I must keep low, quiet and out of sight; I certainly did not need a table of the trouts' area of vision to tell me this. However, not to explain the function of the eyes and how this has direct bearing on fly fishing would be unforgivable, so I shall endeavour to do so. Please forgive my unscientific approach.

One of the primary considerations is the water and the trout's position. Obviously, in coloured water, in rivers carrying a great deal of sediment and debris, and where there are algal blooms in lakes, vision is obscured. In these circumstances I suspect the trout is guided far more by vibration than we believe, the lateral line and inner ears taking over from the eyes. Therefore, disturbance flies, such as Muddler Minnows or Elk Hair Caddis, would seem a good choice, at least offering the trout a target.

Another aspect which must affect a trout's vision is whether the surface is broken (rough) or calm. We know that a vague impressionistic fly comprised of buoyant materials like deer hair, such as Humpies/Goofus Bugs or Wullfe's, are taken with alacrity. This is not necessarily because the trout knows that they are buoyant, but because their size and body mass cast a larger shadow or area of light dimples. However, when a fly is positioned in the film or just beneath, very careful attention must be paid to a pattern's authenticity in masquerading as an insect because of the trouts' switch from obscured to total vision, owing to the fly being in its own element instead of being distorted through surface movement.

In calm water, the trout has problems for different reasons. It will have an image of floating flies, but only just, since meniscus (the surface film) is thick on such water, which obscures the vision of the object. Therefore, the trout still only has a vague impression of shape and outline which is, more often than not, only interpreted as light spots or pin-pricks on the surface. Of course, the emerger, or nymph, which is actually just beneath the surface or further down, can be seen equally as well as it is only the surface film that creates deception, barriers and refraction.

This might suggest that nymph patterns should be totally accurate in every way but that floating flies can be any old thing – not so. Other elements affect the trouts' eyesight and its reactions to food. Trout, blessed with a brain the size of a pea, embody logic and sense beyond their capacity. The chalk stream trout, in particular, seems to see no good reason for chasing about after nymphs when the river will present him with a constant supply of succulent goodies borne along on its current. The fact that these food items do not come in a straight line is accommodated for by the position of the trout's eyes: to its front (the nose area) it has binocular vision, which can compute accurately depth of field; to the sides it has monocular vision. Combined with binocular, and subtracting the blind spot toward the tail area, gives the trout an overall vision encompassing approximately 300 degrees.

Theoretically, this would suggest that the only way in which a trout will not see the angler is if it is approached from immediately behind. Mercifully, this is not always the case, primarily because of refraction, i.e. light bending around corners.

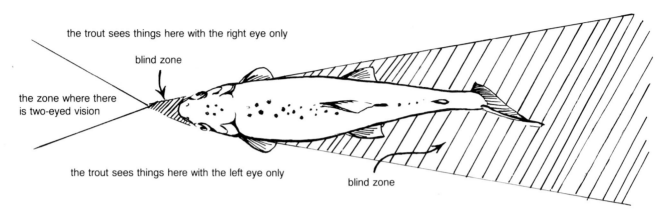

the trout sees things here with the right eye only

the zone where there is two-eyed vision

blind zone

the trout sees things here with the left eye only

blind zone

The trout's blind spots.

The degree of this is dictated by the trout's position in the stream to a large extent; the deeper the fish, the greater its cone of vision. Trout see in three dimensions, like ourselves, but objects viewed from far away have a blurred image. The nearer a trout is to the surface, the sharper the focus on surface-borne items, but the area of vision is narrowed. Therefore, a deep-lying fish has the advantage of a greater field of vision, but one that becomes hazy at its maximum focusing distance, whereas a shallow-lying trout can sometimes see very finely and clearly in front and immediately to its sides, but is largely oblivious to everything outside of this area. This may account for the general impressionistic fly working when trout are lying deep and the more accurate patterns being required when trout station

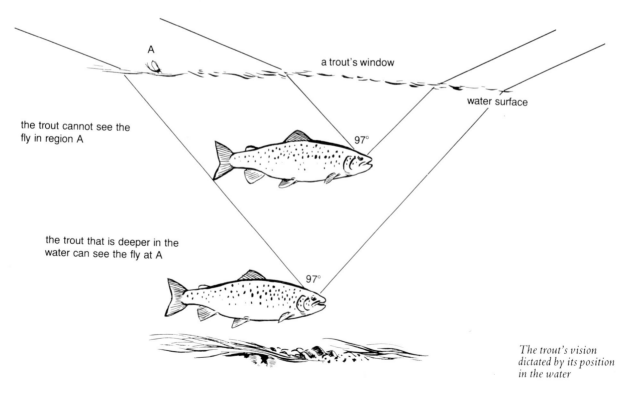

A

a trout's window

water surface

the trout cannot see the fly in region A

97°

the trout that is deeper in the water can see the fly at A

97°

The trout's vision dictated by its position in the water

44

to the trout, the fisherman
would appear to be here

The trout's vision.

water surface

the path of light rays between
the trout and fisherman

to the fisherman, the trout
appears to be here

themselves near to the surface. What remains unexplained is why a 'parody' of a nymph works at all, as a fly in this element, given that both monocular and binocular vision are working, must get very close scrutiny indeed.

Colour and Light Intensity

Many people consider colour unimportant, believing that only shades of black and white (incorporating grey) are relevant. However, trout *can* determine colour; the rods in the retina see to that. Another consideration is light intensity or rather the lack of it, which affords extremely good night-time vision; whereas during periods of extremely harsh direct sunlight/ultraviolet rays, such as midday in high summer, it is less tolerant. Yet neither of these instances are reliant on colour. To explain this if you hold a fly up to a light source – the sky or a light bulb – you will see the fly as a tone and a shape, rather than detailed and in perfect colour, an outline in other words. Now, into this equation we add water which further confuses the question of colour, perhaps not in dry flies, but certainly in nymphs and pupae because colour becomes less clear at various depths. A trouts' eyes assess oranges and reds (the warmer end of the spectrum) better than blues and greens. The cold colours, olives and blues, are more easily seen at depth. That most insect larvae are in olive hues, or at least cool-toned, may account for the effectiveness of drab, impressionistic nymphs.

Of one thing I am certain: reflected surface light has enormous bearing, especially during the evenings. Both insects and their imprints on the surface echo the colour of the sky which, I believe, triggers the trout into feeding. Patterns, especially spent spinners, that echo sunset colours of red, orange, amber, etc. somewhere in their make-up, outfish other types. This may also account for why Mallard and Clarets and claret-based flies are so successful towards darkness. After dark, I would suggest trout are triggered by silhouette rather than colour; the rod's influence overriding that of the cone's.

Basically, I believe the fly fisher should see the eye of the trout as a camera loaded with colour film with bias towards red, and incorporating a macro-zoom lens which can revolve through an angle of 180 degrees either side of its head. Given this analogy it is a wonder we catch trout at all.

THE TROUT'S HABITAT

Trout do not live just anywhere in river systems. They fashion a very particular lifestyle, often based around two distinct areas: a place for feeding and a place for rest. Depressions in the bottom, large stones, weed-beds and a host of other encumbrances will alter and deflect current significantly, which in turn alters trout behaviour. As with the example of the resting trout, described previously, sometimes all is not what it may appear to be. The only answer is to look hard, then act.

Before looking at specifics, let us first analyse things in the broader sense.

To understand your river is to understand the trout's domain. Broadly these areas can be categorized. Here, I will unabashedly use the Gary Borger system. It is practical and excellent, mirroring this American fly fisher to a 'T'.

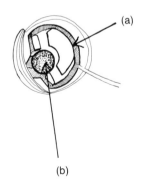

Trout's eye. (a) The retina, home of the rods and canes which allow for both monochromatic vision (at night/low light) and colour during daylight/or light of sufficient strength. (b) The lens used for focusing, be it 4cm or 4yd and offering 180 degrees vision.

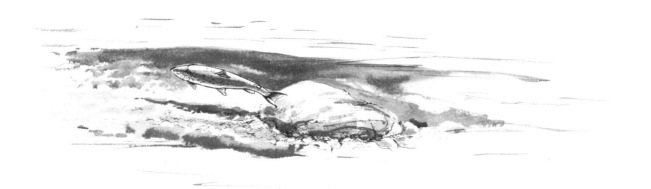

A trout 'on station' in front of (or behind) an obstacle, in this case a rock. This gives it an opportunity to rest and feed, though the nearness to the current makes it difficult to fish.

Sheltering Lies

Although very much a feature of the more rumbustious northern freestone rivers, areas of retreat are an integral part of chalk streams too. Here, I might be wrong but, I believe they relate to larger than average trout, i.e. leviathans. The occasions I have heavy-footfalled a veritable 'submarine' from undercuts in the banks and then watched an olive brown shadow sink solemnly into the darker recesses of tree root confusion, are legion – and testify to my clumsiness.

These fish rarely concern us, especially if our exploits centre expressly on the gentlemanly hours of about 10 a.m. till dusk. They are, I believe, creatures of the night and, under cover of darkness, these veritable monsters go about the business of feeding, probably in the very areas vacated by anglers only hours before. By and large, although sheltering lies are important, they should be viewed as a pointer rather than places of enormous consideration.

Feeding Lies

Feeding lies are essential, both in terms of angling and fish culture. Specifically in a chalk stream context, feeding lies could also be termed shallows, i.e., stretches of water with an average depth of between 1–3ft, generally made up of reaches of gravel stones and interspersed with long fluttering tendrils of *Ranunculus*. This area, although encompassing scintillating fly fishing possibilities, can also be viewed as a necessary area for small fish, especially trout and grayling, who harvest the abundant aquatic life and frolic in the oxygen-infused water.

Very often it is such areas that gave them life. Shallows also equate to redds, the breeding areas. Therefore, sometimes I will deliberately not fish these areas, especially during the earlier months of the season. This is tempered from June onward with the realization that there are times, particularly during dawn and twilight, when these shallows can contain disproportionately larger quarry.

One instance echoes this theory. Stretching below the fishing hut at Kimbridge on the Test, a long reach of shallows sparkles, often heavily weeded and abundant in fly life. It is often profuse with rise forms, escapee rainbows mingling with youthful browns to enliven the most jaded fly palette. As you may imagine, it is not a place of demanding tactical nuance. However, it is extremely effective for deducing a new fly pattern's effectiveness or trying out new ideas. The fish are indeed accommodating.

On this occasion, the sun had slipped out of the July sky, bathing the landscape in apricot afterglow interspersed with indigo tree shapes. The bats were a-wing, and a hatch of small spurwing were still trickling off, their diminutive forms no more than dark impressions on the spangled surface. It was 11 p.m., the light was fading and I wanted to know how I could discern rises in near darkness. Was it possible to react to audible sound? Could I discern rise forms by looking for a reflective edge on the ripple? In short, how can a take be detected at night other than tactilely? Given to spasms of madness, I persevered with a size 20 Adams which, although ably acquitting itself during daylight hours for the spurwings, gave little (or rather no) chance during dusk at sight fishing in fly terms. This suited my prognosis perfectly.

I pitched the fly towards a run of fast water, undercutting the far bank from my mid-stream vantage point. As I surmised, I could not see the fly at all, but I did note that I could see the shimmer of the leader butt and the fly line as it dented the surface film, creating a halo effect of bright light along its length. I was reasoning that, given the situation, I could look for a take in nymph style, by keeping line and leader as taut as possible between rod tip and fly, and reacting on any draw or uncharacteristic movement of either as an indication, when, just beyond the visible point, the darkness seemed to rock, and the faintest ripple was suffused with barely discernible pin-pricks of light. A rise, I thought, and lifted the rod. Imagining that it must be a youthful rainbow up after bedtime, my resulting action was, to put it mildly, unceremonious. In rather cavalier fashion, the grudging force pinioned to the fly was urged out of the weed-beds, hustled from channels, battled out of this and that with a considerable force that belied the given leader strength of 2.4lb. It looked larger than normal. Wanting to release it in as quick a time as possible, I applied even more pressure. I estimated a bigger fish than expected – 1½lb compared with 12oz – I slipped my hand down toward the battling shape at my wadered knee and realized that my hand would not span its girth. Quickly I pressed my net into service. The shape bulged in the bottom like a diamanté splattered 'U'. I decided to weigh it and keep it. On reaching the bank, I despatched the fish and ferreted about for scales. My little torch revealed that this was to be one of three brownies of over 5lb that I caught from the Test during my four-year association; it weighed 5lb 2oz. I went a little weak at the knees. This episode supported my original theory about sheltering lies and also pacified any qualms I had that low-diameter nylon may not be up to the job and, of course, demonstrated that fly fishing in semi-darkness can be, shall we say, an enervating experience.

Prime Lies

Borger's description says it all. These are a combination of the two previous areas moulded into one, offering both shelter from predators and a readily obtainable food supply. Whereas on many other types of water, such places may only account for a small percentage of water area, chalk streams offer a veritable profusion. There will, of course, be favoured places, often so much in demand that if a trout vacates, another will almost instantly set up residence in the lie.

The basic criteria of a prime lie are a current which allows a comfortable stance, a constant procession of food or the close proximity of organisms, and a degree of cover. Undercut banks that include a deepish depression, perhaps flanked by

Different chalk stream areas and their significant features.

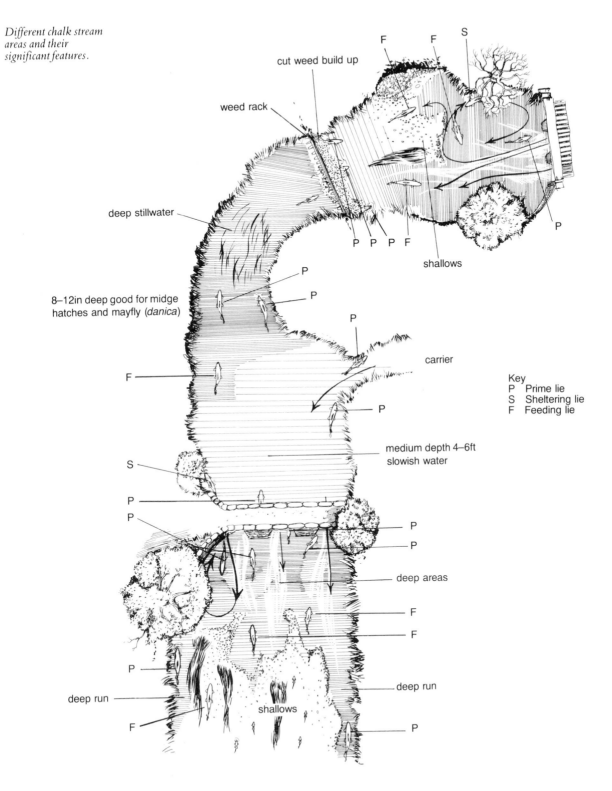

cut weed build up

weed rack

deep stillwater

8–12in deep good for midge hatches and mayfly (*danica*)

shallows

carrier

Key
P   Prime lie
S   Sheltering lie
F   Feeding lie

medium depth 4–6ft slowish water

deep areas

deep run

deep run

shallows

49

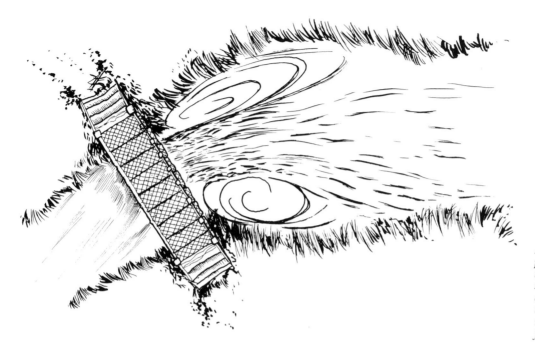

A plan view of a hatch pool, weir or anywhere that produces slackwater back current: trout will tend to move to such areas, rather than the main flow.

weeds, are good examples, as those fringes of gravel bounded by weed-beds of one sort or another might be by overhung trees. Indeed, anywhere where food and cover combine must be deemed suitable residences for trout. The depth of these trout-rich domains can vary, anything from 3–10ft appears to be equally favoured.

This brings me to a leading question: 'When does a trout not face upstream and into a current?' The answer is, 'when the river is reversed in flow due to an obstruction'. Such places must be construed prime lies. Eddies and backwashes around fallen trees, bank outcrops or branches, can all bring about this state of affairs, as can weirs or hatch pools with their quite marked back currents and undertows. Sometimes, if you look hard enough into the water at such places, you will notice trout, often big ones, assuming the impossible; facing downstream whilst the current also races the same way. This is because the effects of backwash and eddies can be transported quite inordinate distances.

This, of course, drastically affects fishing strategies. How on earth does one make contact with this trout if terminal tackle and fly line are being whisked coastward?

I would urge you to learn upstream mending casts, i.e. throwing a slack fly line upstream above the fish whilst the leader and fly – often quite heavily leaded (where permitted) in order to reach the desired feeding depth – are allowed to travel unimpeded with the current's undertow. This is tricky to master, but deadly if executed correctly. There is seldom any need for extreme delicacy; of all the chalk stream situations, these areas will often have the most agitated surface, and ripples and contortions hide a multitude of sins.

Throughout the valleys of the chalk stream country, a penance must be endured by hard-working folk both in and out of season: weed cutting. Although taxing

50

to every muscle and sinew in the human body, it is essential to fishery management, if rivers are to flow efficiently and effectively. Weed growth has a nasty habit of accelerating during periods of prolonged light and summer warmth and keeping it at bay is a constant problem. With most rivers specific days are allocated for this to be carried out. Traditionally, these are barren periods for the fly fisher. Great rafts of scythed weeds drift aimlessly with the current like severed islands and the water is, at best, debris-ridden and, at worst, gloomy and muddied. Fly fishing, if then practised, can be very hit and miss. Trout are less inclined to feed and rise due to the intrusion of foreign bodies in their defined homes, and become near torpid, owing to the sinking silt deposits coursing through their gill rakes. Should the fly fisher be given a rising fish, he almost always overlooks the unseen floating menace that, at the ultimate moment, catches the imitation, whisking it impotently downstream. Such are the dubious charms of fishing during the weed cut. The aftermath is entirely different.

Rivers these days are not what they used to be. Weed racks – bridge-like constructions containing grills of wooden perpendicular slats – were once a common feature, but disrepair and modern contrivances (wire strands and so forth) have largely caused their decline. However, where they do exist, they continue to ensnare the floating masses of weed and, more importantly in fly fishing terms, provide trout with a happy hunting ground. Bridge pillars, tree branches or bushes at water-level operate in much the same way as do any outwardly projecting snags. Especially efficient at weed retention are the slacker areas of the main river flow, such as a culvert or the side of a carrier.

Anywhere that arrests a mass of weed for a period of time demands our very closest attention. Trout obviously feel comfortable with the ceiling-like seclusion above them, but this is not the whole story. Along the perimeter of the build-ups of weed, the surface film (meniscus) is at its thickest and most tenacious, ensnaring any fly that happens to come along. In fact, so 'thick' can this water surface be that dust can be seen in its make-up, and it can actually look like an oil-slick.

Again, observation is the key; both visual and auditory senses should be directed at this area. Trout do not give themselves away in such situations. It is a world of

Trout 'taking up' a feeding position just in front of a weedraft or similar projection – often all the angler will see is a tiny rising form or dimple on the outer edge of the weed.

subtlety, very often all that can be heard is a delicate hissing noise and, on closer inspection, some gentle half rings can be seen ebbing outwards from the weeds' edge – this is a feeding trout. I have witnessed, on the Itchen, up to five trout working such areas, where a neb (a trout's nose) was my only clue. It is not a place for full-hackled imitations, rather it is the domain of emergers, floating nymphs and hackleless flies. As always, think along the lines of the natural world: natural flies would be pinioned and unable to move, in fact drowned in many instances. The need for accuracy of pattern at such times and places is paramount.

THE TROUT'S FEEDING HABITS

Having discussed places where trout might reside, the next step is to look at their feeding patterns. The fact that most fish (the civilized ones that is) face upstream, remain relatively 'on station' (holding in one area) and, given a reasonable hatch of insects, rise and betray their presence, would seem to suggest that chalk stream fishing is easy, particularly as the water is usually clear enough for us to observe. Sometimes it is easy, but a great deal of the time it is not.

Nymphs

Generally speaking, the reaction of the trout to this subsurface form varies little from species to species, but it can vary quite markedly in slow to faster water movement. By noting the speed of current, the angler can glean some idea as to which species will be present in numbers. It is unlikely that *Caenis* or chironomids will be habitating roaring torrents or agitated shallows; these are the domains of that agile darter, the *Baetis* nymph, and the blue-winged olive.

In fast water, nymph feeding is done more by sleight of hand (or should I say fin?). It is so fast, barely perceptible and oh, so subtle. The only clue an angler may have is a nod of the head, a tilt up or down, a feint to left to right, a quickening of the tail movements or quick fanning of the pectoral. Sometimes the body will swing but this is rare. At any of these signs, if you happen to be physically fishing – lift! (I used to say 'strike!' but once, whilst teaching a young boy, I enthusiastically urged him to strike and then watched transfixed as a ½lb brownie defied gravity and landed in a disgruntled heap on a thorn-bush behind us).

There is one sure way of detecting a nymphing fish or, indeed, a take in fast water, whether the trout is near to the bottom, at mid-depth or close to the surface. Nature has played a nefarious trick and given the trout a white inner mouth. Given that the water is clear enough and you are not immediately downstream of the fish, this stark signal is visible from almost any angle. Even in quite ruffled water, with a mere whisp of trout outline to go on, this blink of white as a mouth opens to take in a morsel can sometimes be clearly visible. On tumbling shallows with a markedly broken surface, where a trout might only be a shadowy shape or a shade darker or lighter than the weeds, or in intensely tree-shrouded or harsh light, an underwater flash, similar to quickly turning a silver coin against light, can indicate the trout's presence.

If there is any movement from a trout feeding at whatever depth in fast-water situations, you should strike first and reason afterwards; it is so instant and fleeting. More than once, some sixth sense has guided me to a trout that otherwise

B.P. Buzzer,
[Subsurface]

would have gone undetected and missed. Concentration in all nymphing situations is paramount, as is speed of reaction.

In fast water there is a constant procession of edible bits and pieces passing the lie, a veritable conveyor belt of food. Because of the pace, the trout has little option but to take the view, 'If it looks edible, eat it – if it's unpalatable, spit it out'. Slow-moving currents allow more time for caution and appraisal; the trout can select. The angler, in turn, *must* give full vent to careful observation and fly choice, for trout do lock in on particular species. How they go about this feeding tends to vary. Some areas, especially prime lies that have cover such as tree branches, an immersed obstruction or a weed bank, will contain fish which are behaving similarly to those in fast water, as a constant source of food is being borne to them and often collects in slack water before being whisked downstream. They have little need to seek out a diet. However, in mid-stream, with perhaps weed-beds and often silt banks to deflect current and create lies, their lifestyle can be varied.

The type of area I refer to is specific – lazy water speeds which slither, snake-like over sometimes quite deep channels, a place of candlerush and idly gyrating long tendrils of weed – and are often homes to the bigger fish in the river system. Their character can be defined: slothful, almost forbidding and languid. Trout here often appear to be hanging in suspended animation, almost ghost-like in appearance. Their reaction to fly life reflects this semi-torpid world; they casually drift to either side in order to accept a passing, hapless being enmeshed in the oily current. Trout in this situation occasionally move comparatively long distances to intercept an insect. Sometimes this is a movement forwards, occasionally a drift backwards from the holding area or lie. On balance, the trout in slow currents is a much easier 'animal' to follow, as its decided body movements, combined with its cavernous open white mouth provides tell-tale signs of its presence.

If a slow stretch is long and reasonably deep (6–10ft) and a number of trout are present, you may find that the fish will behave as if feeding on a stillwater, i.e. zigzagging up the stretch until an invisible barrier is met, then returning by repeating the procedure. This patrol-route feeding in a haphazard fashion should send you scurrying for a midge pupa pattern, as there is clearly chironomid harvesting going on. This took me three years to work out.

Speed, or rather the lack of it, will often dictate which organism will be present because silt appears to be endemic to such areas and thus chironomids, mayfly (*Danica*), nymphs, *Caenis* and blue-winged olive and the agile darter (*Baetis*) will be present, and a great many other aquatic creatures will have been flushed down by the faster current above. Therefore, there is a vast aquarium brimming with edible variations. The trout are fully aware of this and can be, by virtue of this fact, very fussy. There is no short cut here, the amount of times a trout has ambled up to my fly, begun to open its mouth then drifted noiselessly away with a disconsolate air, are innumerable. You simply learn by trial and error.

When trout are busily feeding on nymph with no adult activity, there are no clues. My only policy then is one of small and sparse, using 18 or 20 nymph sizes, even 24 will not cause alarm. This presents a problem: how does one get a nymph of that size down to 10ft? But as I have said, this is not the easiest area to fish. Mercifully, trout in the slower stretch are seldom lurking at the bottom. It is far more likely they will be from mid-depth to just subsurface. Shrimping is another story.

(a)

(b)

(Overleaf) Rainbow Trout.

(c)

(d)

A nymphing trout seen in various light conditions. (a) In bright light, the trout gives only a shadowy image, which needs careful observation. (b) The trout in standard midday light. (c) When the water throws up harsh reflections, only a portion of the trout may be visible. Strike at any signs of fish movement. (d) The same trout seen in bright light with a rippled surface. If the shadow moves – strike!

55

The Moment of Decision
(A few more inches)
British Water Rainbow

Shrimping

Agreeably, shrimp, hoglouse, snail and indeed their stillwater comrade, *Corixa*, can occur almost anywhere in the river system, their resilience in varying habits being astonishing. The shrimp (*Gammarus* sp. and *Crangonyx* sp.) deserves special mention. I have never conducted a complete survey on river trout autopsies, but I believe snail and shrimp would feature inordinately highly. In fact, if I was allowed only one subsurface 'fly', I would plump for a shrimp pattern in various guises and sizes. They are important almost anywhere on a chalk stream from hatch pools to shallows, from weed-strewn depths to dark holes.

Cutting weed on the Itchen was one of the more dubious high spots in my keeping/guiding years. However, it did give me time for observation. Plenty of tea-breaks were a prerequisite and allowed for tranquil surveillance of water without a rod. On many occasions I witnessed the phenomenon (for that is what it is) of shrimping trout. Generally, this was in areas with banks of starwort. The trout would literally dive headlong into a weed-bed, then drift backwards tearing weed like a terrier with a rat, then move back a little further and commence feeding.

I have seen similar enactments on the Test, again at comparatively shallow depths, and one occasion, at Longparish, I witnessed a group of trout working the shallows, their tails waving above the surface, resembling carp or tench. These fish must have been almost vertical in their feeding and harrying of shrimp. In essence, what appears to happen, is that the trout rip away weed to dislodge the shrimp, swim away, then dine at leisure on the homeless, disorientated and easily targeted crustacea. The trout, when feeding in this frenzied fashion, have a happy knack of being almost oblivious to all about them. With a modicum of care, a well-placed facsimile, tends to work like a charm. A further plus factor is that the resulting mêlée tends to produce plumes of silt, further indicating feeding areas, casting areas and aquatic form.

Emergers

Now to emergers: the half-in, half-out world. Until recently, this area has had little coverage; hatching insects seem to be the preserve of stillwater. Perhaps it was known but not mentioned in polite conservation. Skues, without question, fished emergers. Subsequently, John Goddard among others has refined it to an art form. I shall be dealing with emergers in actual fly fishing circumstances later. The deduction of rise forms to this stage can be devilishly difficult as there are so many permutations. These range from a 'smutting sip' or 'kiss' in the surface film to a subsurface boil or lump, and just about everything in between.

In my opinion, an emerger is any fly at the point of hatching, even the ascending nymph prior to emergence fits this category. Mostly this revolves around upwing dayflies – Ephemeroptera – but not exclusively, as caddis pupae and midge chironomids nestle into this category too. More precisely, it is any fly 'twixt larvae and adulthood'. It is an area which has given me perhaps the most consistent fishing of all. It is open to conjecture whether it is dry (damp) or nymph fishing. I will let the theorists and dogmatists work that one out.

An emerger, by my definition, is also a creature with wings, all be they embryonic. It is also in a state of 'undress', about to discard its juvenile larval coat

A trout agitating the shrimp and then feeding on them at leisure.

The trout's tail wriggling about above the surface in shallow water suggesting shrimp feeding.

in exchange for the pristine opulence of adulthood. This fact is important. Creatures, when entering this instar (state of change) are at their most helpless and prone to predation. Trout, practised hunters that they are, waste no time in making the most of what must appear an easy protein-rich offering. This change from one element to another renders all but the most agile and expedient insect in momentary peril as it strives to discard its nymphal case whilst at the same time struggling through a veritably impenetrable surface film, which often transfixes them. It takes supreme effort and precious time. Therefore, here we have a creature all but static, imprisoned in the surface, drifting helplessly downstream.

The one vital element in the world of hatching flies is the surface. However, different river speeds are important too, as they were for the nymph although for different reasons. Fast water tends to hurry the feeding procedure. It is here that the subsurface boils and defined lumps occur in the water. Rise forms tend to be more under than in the film. One reason for this is that the swifter water movement causes inert insects to sweep, tumble and cavort in the undertow currents, enmeshed but none the less moving. Also the surface is generally broken, which disperses the adhesive quality of the film, facilitating a hasty emergence from one dimension to another. Therefore, the trout's decision must also be hasty and sure, and possibly conducted slightly below the surface.

Medium-to-slow currents require a different philosophy altogether. The trout has ample chance to select and disregard at will, and does so. It is here that the permutations of rise forms are given full range.

Many are the times I have argued with myself that they cannot possibly be feeding on anything other than spinner (imago), only to find (by fortunate accident or the occasional dim-witted trout) that I am hopelessly wrong in my deduction – 'emergers, not spinners!' is my usual twilight utterance. Blue-winged olives (*E. ignita*) are the normal *bête noire* in this charade and, generally, they

A simple rise form depicted in its different stages of progression. (a) The trout sees the fly, as it is in his field of vision. (b) It rises to meet the food form. (c) It accepts the insect. (d) It turns down the bounty in its jaws.

The nose and tail or head and tail rise. This is often done with a gliding movement.

emerge in the evening at the same time as a fall of spinner of perhaps the *Baetis* tribe, spurwings and so forth. Be on your guard to the switch, for I am often foxed by the spinner- like rise. That is one permutation: the nebbing, lilting motion rise.

Another is the sip. This resembles a tiny black hole in the surface that just opens and closes in an instant. The rings emanating are merely rocking contusions of the surface harmony.

There is also what I term the 'nodding dog syndrome', as it resembles those captivating creatures once found in the rear windscreens of cars. The trout, although not making any discernible movement on the surface, merely hovers just below it, flicking its head from side to side and up and down in monotonous regularity.

However, there is a classic: the 'nose and tail syndrome'. As soon as I see that languid neb see-saw up and down, followed by a dark back and tail, my pulse races. This is an emerger feeder if ever there was one. There are other variations but to mention them all would leave no room for duns and spinners.

This world of infinite variation tends to guide me to fishing an emerger if any doubt exists. Indeed, so effective do I feel this stage to be that, even in the height of a rise obviously to duns, a studiously fished emerger will still reap untold spoils.

Mention must also be made of stillborns and crippled flies, for they also fit neatly into this category of 'film' fishing. Wherever a major hatch occurs, be they pale watery or mayfly, a proportion will succumb to the rigours of emergence. They die or become entrapped half in and half out of their pupal skin. Some might have unformed wings, others are missing an appendage or two. These unfortunate creatures provide easy prey for the voracious trout. It is a complex instance and so often misleading and hidden. A 'hidden hatch' would be a good term. The trout, given the opportunity to take an inert insect instead of a cavorting one, would be pretty silly to pass it by.

The feeding pattern can be equally confusing, paralleling either spent imagos (spinner) or emergers. I spent four of the most frustrating hours fishing I have ever experienced on the Frying Pan river in Colorado. Pattern after pattern I threw at those confounded trout, receiving not so much as a half-hearted glance for my trouble. Then I noticed some crippled fly at my wadered feet. I literally tore off a wing of a spent pattern, and succeeded in inveigling three trout. Each one contained stillborn and semi-hatched duns.

Having itemized most rising instances, there would appear little more to add, but trout rising to duns (sub-imago upwing flies) can add further spice.

Duns

Years ago, theorists maintained that when trout were feeding on blue-winged olive duns, they betrayed the fact by a kidney-shaped whorl. I believe this to be more the creation of the river surface than a feeding pattern. I wish one could ascertain types of fly by the resultant rise, but I have found it not to be possible. Rather similar is the maxim that grayling always leave a bubble when they rise to a surface fly. Certainly they do, but any fish poking its nose through the surface and taking a fly will leave the same signature, whether chub, dace or trout.

The dun rise, as much as any other facet, is open to speculation. For instance, the rise in fast water will be moderately hurried, as the river is sweeping the natural fly away, and this is further compounded by a relatively easy take-off due to minimal surface tension. If flies get airborne a good deal quicker, trout correspond by feeding faster.

Medium-to-slow currents may contrive all the aforementioned instances of rise forms. However, one particular dun rise is best termed nebbing, whereby a trout maintains its position but constantly tilts its nose up through the surface, generally accompanied by a slight 'clopping' sound, which is surface fly for certain.

male

female

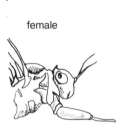

Differences between male and female upwinged species.

A typical dun rise, indicated by a kidney-shaped whorl.

The sip or kiss. This is frequently seen when trout are feeding on spinner, or during heavy hatches or falls of flies.

The next significant area appertains to spinner, as well as emerger on occasion, and is dictated by the actual position of the trout, together with the reaction to the fly, be they imposters or naturals. The late Vince Marinaro, the supremo of Pennsylvanian unforgiving spring creeks, categorized them into the simple, compound and complex rise. Up to now we have only looked at the simple rise: trout sees fly, trout takes fly. A compound rise tends to occur in 'even' and slow currents. They do not usually happen when there is a disguising ripple or on fast water. A trout may adopt a cautious or suspicious attitude because of the depth it is holding. It lifts itself up in the current, follows the fly downstream for a while then, only when satisfied, takes it, thereafter resuming its original lie.

The complex rise is a variation on the other two but containing a much longer drift of inspection of the fly. In some extreme instances, this can continue for a matter of feet, which is a long way in river terms. The trout eventually takes the fly with its head pointing downstream! The complex rise is comparatively rare and often goes hand in glove with previously caught and returned fish, lost fish or areas where constant food chains allow for dalliance. They do add spice.

There is another type which I term 'foldback' rise. It is generally found with trout, that hold station in a resting lie but have a feeding zone just outside. Classic instances are weed rafts of some width, undercut banks, or bushes where branches

view from underneath

side view

Male claspers.

The half rise or foldback. The angler may only see half the rings as a bright leading edge in low-light conditions. Nevertheless, the fly has been accepted.

might be trailing in the water. Here trout invariably fix their sights on a pre-or-dained area. When a fly reaches it, the fish move forward, take at that spot, then drift back under cover again. This is very difficult to assess, because the rise is not where the trout is, if you see what I mean, and if, like me, you try and cast as tight and accurately as possible to the area of activity, then the feeding area will be missed altogether. This rise requires a fly to be pitched a good 3–4ft above the last rise form if success is to be achieved.

Imagos

Now to the imago or spent spinners. Here, the same rise forms tend to occur as with the emerger, although the chances are, with more trout engaging in the same activity, a good fall of spinner is likely to produce a fairly definitive rising pattern. The unknown quantity is whether it will happen or not.

So many times I have awaited the spinner fall 'carnival' – my anticipation fuelled by the rise and fall antics of the male spinner columns across the water-meadows as they earnestly attempt to attract a mate – only to find, as the sun sinks in the western sky, that not a trout anywhere is tempted by the insect's demise. I cannot find a rational explanation as to why this is so. Barometric pressure, the rescuer of many a theory, may be the cause. Then again, it may purely be the recalcitrance of the trout. Yet, for all that, when a good spinner fall occurs, and the trout do play their part, it is a jubilant time full of rises and opportunities.

Rather than rise forms, an impression can be given of rings of rising fish, fusing with others, producing a dilemma over which to cast to next. These fish *are* selective. Sometimes they are so intent on their task that they become both oblivious and impervious to all but the most ham-fisted of efforts. Leaders drifting over them, splashy touchdowns of flies or even the odd (gently) wayward fly line, do not appear to disturb unduly this feeding frenzy.

Generally speaking (although this is a dangerous thing to say in fishing), trout feeding in such a manner will hover just beneath the surface, constantly tilting their heads or nose/neb (hence *nebbing*) through the film, seldom moving an inch from their chosen lie, as they know that the fly coming overhead is either dead or dying, ensnared in the surface film and so unlikely to move away from its path. Nature's economy and expedience leaves the angler with little option other than to be accurate.

Although patterns are important, correct presentation is paramount, to be 1in wide of the target is tantamount to being miles out. Occasionally, and especially during late July, August and early September – the time of blue-winged olives when seemingly spent spinners are the chosen fly – an abrupt change can be wrought, which can be foxing in the extreme. This phenomenon generally coincides with approaching darkness, when the trout, for no obvious reason, and without altering position or rise form, will forsake spinner for duns, sometimes blue-winged olive, often small spurwings. Not to note and react to this change is to invite a frugal time, as trout will simply not entertain the idea of a spent wing pattern, craving rather an upright wing dun pattern or fully hackled fly. The only certain way of deducing this is to scour the surface. Generally, whether you are wading or bank fishing, tangible evidence will emerge in the shape of some dun or other and, if no reaction is forthcoming to the spinner dressing, a speedy change of tactics must be made.

Centroptilum wing (spurwing)

The difference between a typical Baetid *wing (pale watery, large dark olive, etc.) and a centroptilum (spurwing), though these are classified as* Baetis *as well.*

Baetidae wing

64

Skues appeared not to care for spinner falls, especially blue-winged olive, but I rather like them. They are taxing, precise and mentally stimulating, which is everything trout fishing should be.

Caddis Flies

Sunk spinner.

So far, I have dealt only with upwinged species of fly and the trouts' reaction to them; now I shall widen our entomological horizons. I have long held a belief that caddis flies (sedges) play a far less significant role on chalk streams than experts would have us believe. Certainly, I feel they are very much secondary to midge, upwinged species (Ephemeroptera), and crustacea (shrimp etc.). With the onset of night, even in pitch darkness, great water upheavals can occur, often beneath trees or beside overgrown banks. Sedge are deemed to be the culprits, but I wonder. Moths are similarly shaped and might incite this response. It is difficult to say.

More and more I see the sedge rather in a daytime role – especially the afternoons as most species hatch out between 2 p.m. and 5 p.m. – and as attractors rather than deceivers, especially in the 'dry' sense. A prospective cast, made with an Elk Hair Caddis or a similar generalized imitation, cast under tree canopies or likely-looking areas, can very often encourage the odd somnolent trout to rise. It is a wild card worth playing. Rise forms can be energetic and splashy, similar to a mayfly (*danica*), and quite alarming if you are day-dreaming.

The USA is well populated with caddis species, which tend to be more important, in the angling sense, than in our own waters. Most American authorities subscribe to the opinion that many of these upheaval rises can be attributed to the ascending pupae venturing to the surface to hatch, the trout giving chase and being propelled through the river surface in their alacrity to seize the insect. One must construe from this that the water can at times be rough and food scarce. Chalk stream trout are lazy, possibly overfed, and seldom display this petulant attitude unless the food form is sufficiently large enough to warrant it. Therefore, I think it can be safely said, that if an upheaval or splashy rise is heard or seen, it will be for either a mayfly (*E. danica/vulgata*), a caperer or a large cinnamon sedge and, after dark perhaps a ghost swift moth or water ermine moth, augmenting nightfall adult caddis activity.

The slash rise. This is often seen when larger species are being eaten, such as mayfly (danica) and caddis adults.

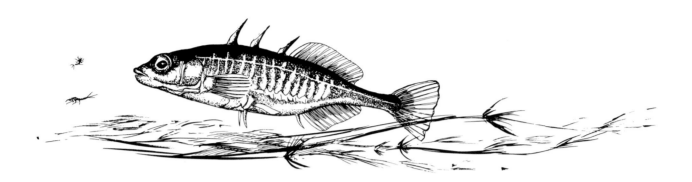

MASTER OF ITS ELEMENT

Stickleback.

Having mentioned the pupae in an American context, I feel it is only fair to align it to our own waters where it is largely overlooked. Often I have felt that given the complete lack of ephemerids hatching or in evidence, there are opportunities, especially during the afternoons, of using caddis pupae imitations. Last season was a consummation of such notions, when trout feeding aspects paralleled that of emergers or hatching nymphs. These, it turned out were caddis pupae, though taken in exactly the same way as emergent upwing duns, stealthily and subtly, with not a speck of white water in sight; merely underwater lumps, swirls, whorls or 'flashes of flank' from trout turning on prey.

Penultimately, there is the daytime kiss and sip reminiscent of spinner rises. Generally by the side of reed mace, sedges (the plant) or indeed, any bankside water-plants, one hears, rather than sees, the barely audible intake of water. Looking in this direction may reveal some gentle contortions in the current and, if very lucky, an apparent black hole in the water surface. If this happens during the hotter months, you have encountered the challenging 'smutting' trout. 'Smuts' is a loose term generally referring to reed smuts, blackfly, black curse or, as I call them, specks, because of their size! I have encountered them mostly on the Test, seldom on the Itchen and only occasionally elsewhere, where water flows slowly over silt and is fairly deep.

Curiously, these minuscule flies hold an attraction for large trout. Quite why this should be so, I cannot fathom. What is required is ultra-fine nylon, as low as 12oz b.s. and never heavier than 2lb b.s., and flies between 26 and 28. Whether you succeed or not is in the lap of the gods when fishing to the daytime sipping trout; some you will catch, others you will not – but what excitement!

The hidden rise. In rough and broken water, a feeding trout may only darken or flatten the ripples to betray its rise form.

Fry Feeding

I could not leave this chapter without at least mentioning one other feeding instance, in the full realization that it will meet with great disapproval from the traditionalist and the purist. Fry feeding is an established high spot in the stillwater fishers' calendar, to suggest that it does not occur on rivers would be folly.

Why is imitating a small fish, which is obviously the sought food form, any less proper than using a mayfly? Nymph fishing is imitating shrimp, hoglouse and other non-flying creatures. Even midge are not true flies. The Halfordian tradition, although laudable in many ways, is restrictive. We should be pushing away barriers, rather than being comfortable in our self-inflicted incarcerations.

Many is the time – across shallows of the Test especially but also other rivers – that I have witnessed feeding 'V' wakes, as trout rampage through shoals of minnows and stickleback like starving wolves. These are fry feeders, make no mistake. I have also witnessed great shadow forms in pools drift casually in the slipstream current, then turn mightily into an unsuspecting clutch of small fish in a slack area. These trout would seldom rise to a fly.

Autopsies have revealed not only minnows and sticklebacks but also parr, small roach, bullhead and often crayfish; all are viable to the trout, but not the angler. Perhaps one day we will attain enlightenment and be granted equality with the American fly fisher. In fact, our American cousins go further, imitating newts, frogs, mice, even leeches. This open attitude is very much in my mind when I gaze forlornly into a pool where an epic brown trout is striking terror and mayhem into the scurrying fledgeling fish, its electrifying shark-like dorsal cutting a wedge across the silver-dappled night-cloaked shallows.

In summary of rise forms and their various feeding patterns, I would only reiterate that it is a world of infinite change, variation and possibility. There is seldom a classic case; all warrant our careful attention and vigilance if the feeding patterns are to be unravelled and interpreted in our artificial restriction. By all means, be guided by principles and theory, but trust your own eyes and observation more. Nothing is cast iron.

5

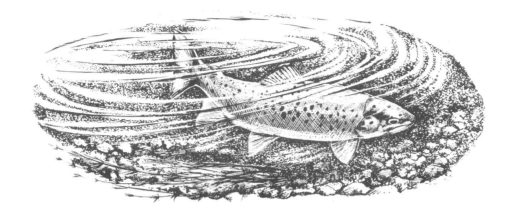

The Natural Larder and Its Imitations

There was a time when I thought I had found my Holy Grail (Halford would have been pleased as it was his ethos): exact imitation and carefully constructed realism I felt held the ultimate key to my goal. That was *then*.

I slavishly read, reread and read again John Goddard's *Trout Fly Recognition*, and memorized to the best of my ability the lineage and oblique names, until *Baetis fuscatus*, *Baetis rhodani*, *Ephemerella ignita*, *Baetis scambus*, and *Centropilum luteolum* tripped from the tongue. However, then I got to realizing that my adversary – the trout – is not a scholarly, analytical creature, rather it has a brain the size of a pea. Its assimilation of knowledge is neither great nor profound but simply instinctive. It could not baffle with Latin and was not trying to be clever – just trying to survive. I realized at that point, not for the first time, that Jardine had got it wrong. No matter how adept you are at spotting *Baetis rhodani* at 500 paces, if you cannot interpret that into simple fly fishing terms and dovetail the information into strategies, then it is of no use to you as a fly fisher. Therefore, the past five years has seen a drastic change in my philosophy.

In painting, in order to create abstract art, it is necessary first to know what it is you are abstracting. A bottle must be drawn and painted precisely like a bottle, before one ventures forth to break the rules and parody or change it to something else. Similarly, with fly fishing you have to know the permutations before you test, deduce and minimalize. It is a good idea to know, for example, the salient points of a blue-winged olive and to be able to create it in lifelike terms, before you strip the original dressing away, leaving an interpretation containing the obvious recognition features. Look at it as an abstract artist with a fly rod. Fly fishing, as in any other pursuit, involves a learning process.

Often anglers invent a fly which is successful in say the first season or during the formative period, without knowing why. When it fails – what do they do

The fisherman's fly order, the basic shape of the adult insect with larval stage.
(a) Upwing dun.
(b) Midge. (c) Caddis.
(d) Stonefly.

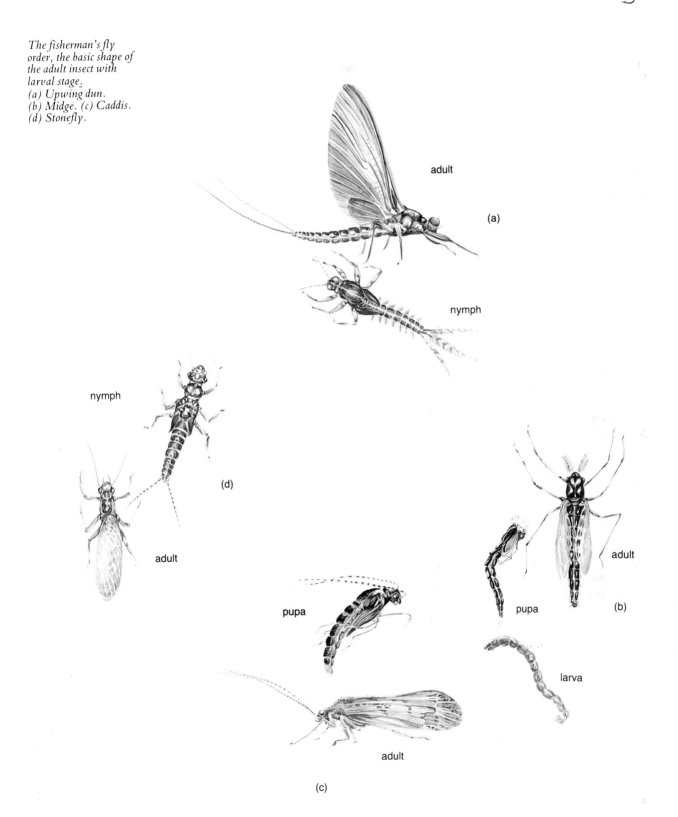

adult

(a)

nymph

nymph

(d)

adult

pupa

adult

pupa

(b)

larva

(c)

then? They have perhaps only scant knowledge of insect life and trout behaviour and do not have the ability to re-create the fly into what will be once more a winning formula. The fly is discarded and forgotten and thus perhaps a panacea, given a few modifications, is lost forever.

It is not necessary to be fully conversant with every insect and its habits. Halford gave us the extreme of this, creating artificials to cover even male and female differences in insects. However, Sawyer created a handful of patterns of just a general nature, with deadly effect. Although I am not within a day's march of these great men, my own philosophy lies somewhere in the middle. Once I was infatuated with realism, now I favour calculated suggestion. Trigger points are a fundamental to my fly patterns, with the odd unexplained one thrown in for good measure.

Observation is once more the key. Days spent by a riverside are worth volumes of books. It is a game of practicalities, not theories. Often I have forsaken the physical act of fishing, in order to simply watch insects hatch, mate, die, cavort and be consumed by trout. Oddly, chalk streams offer less variation and species than may at first be imagined: I would say possibly less than on equivalent freestone/rain-fed rivers. What one does find is weight of numbers, certain species dominating at certain times of the season. Here chalk streams can vary dramatically. The Yellow May dun is a classic case. The Itchen around mid-May would regularly offer sparse hatches of this beautiful and instantly recognizable fly, clad in primrose yellow. During four years of almost constant vigil on that stretch, I never once saw one taken by a trout. Yet, in neighbouring Dorset, on the river Allan, I have on good authority, from Phil White (now head keeper for the Haddon estate in Derbyshire), that this fly is taken with alacrity. Quite why this should be so, I cannot say. Maybe there are a few more to make it viable for the trout or, at least, recognizable as a food item. Therefore, the angler would be ill advised to carry multitudes of patterns to imitate this fly on the Itchen, but foolish not to on the Allan; it can be *that* localized.

The situation can even dramatically alter within a mile or so of water. The Kentish Stour, upstream of my home stretch sees a good and steadily improving mayfly hatch, whereas my stretch receives only the odd straggler. This, not unnaturally, leads to confusion: someone will remark on the Stour's good mayfly hatch and the newcomer to our beat will turn up positively bristling with mayfly artificials and stoically await the arrival of this non-event.

If one studies the upwinged dayflies (Ephemeroptera) and places the different species side by side, one would be hard put to differentiate between them. Some of their bodies err to yellowy light tones, some to a darker brown olive shade and wings may vary from gun-metal grey to smokey blue hues, but vast similarities exist, as they do at the imago/spinner stage. Indeed, were it not for size – and even this can be marginal – the only way of separating species, especially some *Baetis*, is a different-shaped hind wing (the smaller secondary wing close to the thorax) or different coloured occuli (eyes), legs or tails. Do the trout note these subtle differences? I suspect not. So what is the use of recognizing the various types? Probably not very much in real fishing terms. However, to remain ignorant of the differences is to divorce fly fishing from aestheticism and deny rationale and thought processes.

Trout, I am convinced, are motivated by trigger factors, familiar features that suggest food. For instance, at an ordained time, little nymphs leave their cloistered

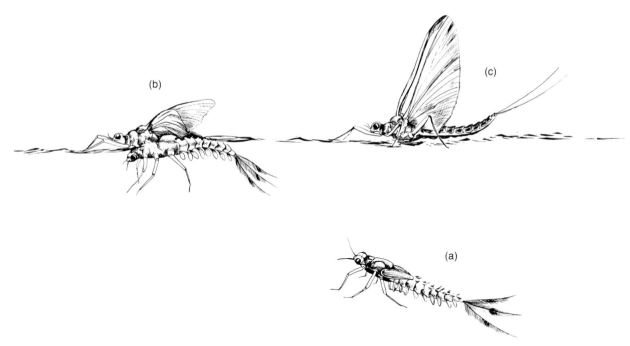

The stages of development of the upwing (Ephemeroptera).
(a) Nymph ascending.
(b) Nymph emerging.
(c) Dun at rest, drying wings.

surroundings of weed-beds to hatch into another world. Their journey is a perilous one and yet must be undertaken. I do not fully understand what instinct tells these little creatures that now is the time for adulthood; light intensity, barometric pressure, possibly even lunar phases may exert an influence.

Trout will be aware of this mass migration and see it as an opportunity for easy feeding. They also might recognize it as a 'masque for an overture to come', realizing that the little nymphs metamorphose into winged adults and that the barrier of surface film is a killing zone as well. This is easily substantiated by watching trout over the course of the day change feeding depths and positions within the confines of their lies. For the fly fisher, at least, trigger factors exist: the slim aquatic nymph ascending; the mêlée of wings and shedding nymphal skin at the surface; the dun (sub imago) with lofted wings awaiting arrival ascent; ultimately the returning female spinner (imago) spent and in death throes, inert on the surface.

Knowing of, and indeed anticipating, these situations is a great advantage and one afforded by some knowledge of the species. Thereafter, further recognition factors can be incorporated into dressings: the sparsity of a nymph in movement is imitated in Sawyer's Pheasant Tail; the dishevelment of hatching by emergers incorporating wing buds and soft hackles; the dun by a buzz of hackle/legs either set high or low depending on aspect, and lofty wings to echo the natural; and finally the spinner by a pattern prostrate in the film giving the likeness of out-stretched diaphanous wings.

(Overleaf) The nymph fisher's zone. A trout holding a particular lie and the area where a trout is likely to be most active in its acceptance of an artificial.

SELECTIVE FEEDING

If there is an abundance of one food organism, a trout would have to be jolly foolish not to make the most of nature's bounty. However, there is this strange

phenomenon of selective feeding, where a sparse hatch of something or other is preferred to another that may be more numerous. A classic example of this being the 'mayfly madness' period.

This preoccupation occurs between three and four days after the trout has become acclimatized to the insects' size (this being considerably larger than the majority of chalk stream offerings!). Thereafter, the trout tend to throw themselves headlong into a feeding orgy like children in a sweet factory. Obviously, it is a time when mayfly patterns are *de rigeur*. However, a point is generally reached when the trout, almost in unison, cry 'Enough is enough' and then swing into a selective feeding mode. This can take as many turns as a river course.

It may be that trout, even though still enjoying their substantial diet of mayfly, slip into a *modus operandi* of feeding, the trout taking every second, third or fourth fly which ventures into its watery horizons. This is selective feeding and most definitely requires the fly fisher to make very certain that the artificial fly conforms to this sequence or pattern.

Another selective situation, often referred to as a 'masked' hatch, where one insect is shielding the influence of another, can appear towards the end of the mayfly hatching period. Trout, having sated themselves on a constant and prodigious diet, will suddenly develop a taste for a completely different diet. Often this is a humble diptera of the *Bibio* tribe, the black gnat. This land-based (terrestrial) creature, despite its small size, can turn the head of many a blasé trout, but is often overlooked by the fly fisher during this period. *Bibio johannis* – a fitting title – is small (5mm–7mm) and thus tends to encourage a small dimple rise form, almost as though an emerger has been taken. Therefore, usually a tiny (size 18–20) Blackfly will unlock the door to a trout that are supposedly feeding on mayfly. Another example of this selectivity is the iron-blue dun. Trout, even given a heavy hatch of medium or small dark, or other olives such as spurwings, will select this little, dark grey ephemerid, and ingest it with relish, even if they are far less numerous.

One possible explanation for this whole escapade is that the iron-blue is easier to spot. This fly is a lover of dark, chilly overcast days in early and late summer and its dark shape can possibly be seen more clearly amidst the lighter ones, as even on dark days, the sky is appreciably lighter in tone than one imagines.

Just because the selective trout appears to show signs of superior cunning among aquatic souls, do not become infatuated and pay homage; it is merely operating on piscine autopilot in response to a given situation. Certainly, it may prove a trifle difficult to tempt, but it is the same trout which rose with such gay abandon to a Beacon Beige a week or so before, which looked nothing like the fly you were trying to imitate. Such is the perversity of chalk stream fly fishing. The clues for anglers when dealing with selectivity, preoccupation or straightforward random feeding are interwoven in the stream. Deduction and observation will always point the way forward in respect of pattern choice and actual tactics, but I digress. Let me first take you underwater to the world of nymphs and pupae.

THE TROUT'S FOOD

Nymphs

Quite why a fly pattern from the Sawyer collection of nymphs should be so

Correct presentation of foodstuff is vital. Here, the angler is keeping a low profile whilst fishing a river that is at shallow summer levels.

effective will always remain a complete mystery to me. I have tried to present nymphing trout with more realistic examples, more accurate colour tones and generally more lifelike movements and my efforts have lead me to the conclusion that trout do not give a fig for underwater, although they react differently to what is floating on top of it. (However, there are some notable exceptions, which I shall look at in due course.)

Agile Darters

The nymphs that gain trouts' most persistent attention (or predation), are the clan *Baetis* or agile darters, although other nymph types are popular at certain times in the season. For example – *E. danica* the mayfly nymph and a silt-bottom burrower for one or two years – will incite positive euphoria in trout when it swims to the surface, and during adulthood. The humble and diminutive *Caenis* – a silt crawler for almost all of its juvenile twelve months – will, when swimming through the layers to hatch, also find itself the centre of trout attentions, as will the moss creeper, the blue-winged olive nymph (*E. ignita*). The sheer constancy of the agile darter make it the chalk stream fly/nymph fishers' primary consideration. The natural's inclination to flit about from weed-bed to weed-bed, its quantity, its many tonal variations, sylphlike shape and liking for chalk stream habitats, all make this unfortunate creature an ever-ready target – a trout convenience food, if you like. The single, most difficult task is in ascertaining just which nymph turns into which adult as they all look very similar except in size, which is not a criterion, and in tonal variations. However, to be perfectly honest, it does not matter.

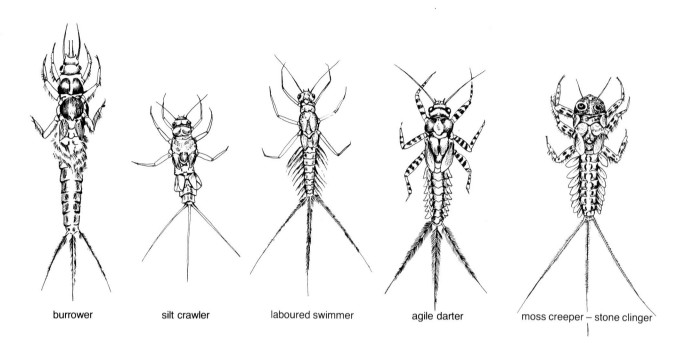

| burrower | silt crawler | laboured swimmer | agile darter | moss creeper – stone clinger |

Upwinged nymph types (Ephemeroptera).

You may well ask just why, if this group of nymphs are various shades of olive, should a pheasant tail, which is reddish brown, work? I simply cannot say. I once designed a nymph called the G.E. (general Ephemeroptera), which is olive, has the mandatory three tails (or a bunch of five or so wood-duck fibres) and legs of partridge-dyed olive. It works, but certainly no better than either the Sawyer Pheasant Tail or Grey Goose. However, I do baulk at the 'bare hook' nymphs designed by Oliver Kite, as there seems something deeply sacrilegious about using such utilitarianism, a travesty of a natural creature in the role of a nymph.

A suggestion may be that underwater, especially in and around weed-beds where nymphs (agile darters) live and are hunted, it is not clear or tranquil, even if appearing so from above. It can be a heaving cauldron of stream-born debris, tiny plants, bits of twigs and sections of leaves, all intertwined with undulating currents. Trout do not have the luxury of deliberation in such a topsy-turvy world, and so feed opportunistically. This would explain a great deal. For it is the slower, deeper areas of chalk streams, which require the greatest degree of realism in fly patterns and a considerable amount of analysis and querying of old principles and notions.

Midges

Certain river areas and their indigenous inhabitants have been dramatically changed in the last years, most especially the aquatic forms of insects with lower flows and shrinking levels, although there are notable exceptions, such as the Upper Itchen where life remains as it has done for hundreds of years. Heading the list of insects found in areas displaying a silt bottom and reasonably, or substantially, slow-flow rates and currents, often typified with deep sections and channels, are chironomidae, the non-biting mosquito-shaped midges belonging to the

Mare's tail and midge pupa.

family *Diptera* (flat-winged flies). Often the fact of their existence and usefulness is overlooked or reviled by traditionalists, which is a pity. Certainly they do not have the pretty birthright of Ephemeroptera or the revered lineage of the caddis, yet the term 'trash flies', which I have often heard levelled at these inoffensive creatures, is utterly undeserved.

Most anglers' idea of midge on chalk stream is of a tiny speck in a watery world full of other tiny specks. Absolute confidence and nerves of steel are required when using tiny flies. What is overlooked is that there are also larger species, which I have known to be taken with equal gusto. Indeed, I have seen trout move as much as 6ft from their feeding lie to intercept a midge pupa, which is a phenomenal distance in terms of normal feeding activity.

Of the three forms of midge/chironomidae stages of development, the pupa is far and away the most important and, thankfully, like the Ephemeroptera nymph, only requires some size variation and different colour combinations, given that there exist in the British Isles something in the region of 300 or more different species. In fact, you can get by with a Golden Olive pattern in size 12–16, a black one ribbed with fluorescent red in 12–16, an all-black one in 14–20, a Dark Olive in 14–20, an Apple Green in 18–20 and a red one in 16–20. Further pruning could be done, at the sacrifice of some sport, to possibly the Golden Olive, Apple Green and the all-black one. I have most frequently come across – either in water areas or through autopsies – the small (tiny) apple green, a brownish-black variety (although carrying a heavy reminder of its bright red larval state in the rear abdomen), and golden olive, which tends to be larger.

Size tends to be more important than colour, with shape or silhouette being the overriding trigger. It is, in fact, midge pupae's shape and their use of it to aid movement which separate them so thoroughly from the other creatures found in the river system. The attenuated abdomen and bulbous thorax conspire to render this insect exceedingly agile and lithesome, but poor in propulsion and swimming, especially in currents. I believe it is these factors which fashion the pupa's critical fishing area.

As in stillwater, one would confidently assume this to be the surface film, the viscosity presenting the little emerging midge with an almost impenetrable barrier and the trout with an easily acquired meal. However, I have found the area most useful in fly fishing terms to be mid-water, a fact supported by frequent autopsies where so many partially formed pupae still displaying the marked redness or greenness of the larval state, can be found. This does offer a vital clue as to the saga of their life up to the trout's culinary desires.

They spend their larval life as a blood worm (other colours include green and tan) amidst the comparatively passive currents at the bottom of deep, silted river areas

larva

pupa

The stages of development of the Chironimid.

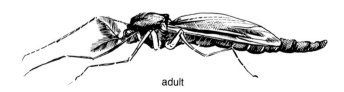

adult

that often support the verdant favourites Mare's tail, Water Parsnip and other low current-level loving plants. As they metamorphose and pupate, they actively seek the surface charms. The ascending pupa tends to be the first sight a trout would have of this potentially succulent morsel. Above the cloistered weeded surrounds lie the river currents which can whisk away the weakly swimming pupae, in some cases, quite considerable lengths downstream. Trout will be only too well aware of this and will conduct their feeding in this mid-water level.

It would be misleading of me not to express the importance of the surface film in terms of midge pupae. John Goddard was quick to press into service his devastatingly successful stillwater pattern, the Suspender, on rivers, particularly chalk streams, its self-buoyancy making it fit the role of emerger perfectly. However, I am still a little uncertain as to whether this or indeed any other chironomid emerger pattern, is taken for midge. They could just as easily, given the trouts' liberal attitude toward nymph inaccuracies, be taken for caddis or upwinged. A trout has taken the fly, and that is what matters; but sometimes, especially on the drive home from the river or during the winter abyss, it is pleasant to know why something happened, otherwise, we fish on in ignorance.

In summary, I would urge the chalk stream angler to look extremely closely at the midge; it is not an unseemly villain but a welcome interloper. The final adult stage, from emergence to the return to lay eggs, has enjoyed enormous appraisal recently on reservoirs, whereas for so long the 'dry' midge (adult) had been disregarded.

Two-Winged Flies

Although their value on rivers is, I believe, rather less than it is on stillwater. Other two-winged flies (*Diptera*) do have a role to play: black gnat, hawthorn fly, Smuts, even daddy-long-legs, are candidates for the attention of both trout and our fly boxes. Here I would err to small sizes i.e. Griffiths Gnats in size 18–24, or Malcolm Greenhalgh's Tichy Midges 18–24. Although probably the same thing happens with the adult as happens with the emerger – the fly being taken for something completely different – nevertheless the fish has been fooled. There is a certain inner glow from that knowledge, even if we are a little uncertain why.

Shrimps

There are two distinct types of freshwater shrimp, and I often think their aquatic forms have parallels with those of the squirrel! On many river systems, especially those of Hampshire, there is a quite definite colonization of grey crustaceans, which vary from a grey olive tone to opaque flint grey, all displaying the colour characteristics which suggest that the American *Crangonyx* sp. is present rather than our own *Gammarus*. Where this happens, the poor old indigenous olive/pink/tan *Gammarus* tends to be ousted from control, thus paralleling the plight of our beloved red squirrel, which has been supplanted by the grey squirrel from America.

I carry various colour combinations of shrimp, although encased in the same basic shrimp design.

Of course, carrying shrimp patterns is not a jot of use if you happen to be tethered by a dry-fly-only ruling. For this, I can only sympathize, as you are

Freshwater shrimp
(Crangonyx *and*
Gammarus *Sp.)*

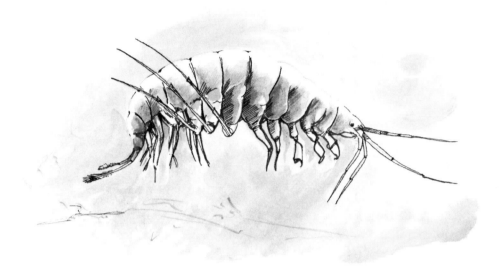

missing a great deal of demanding and fascinating fly fishing, although, strictly speaking it is not fly fishing, neither is it, as some authorities would have us believe, bait fishing. Perhaps 'imitative' fly fishing would be the best term.

The hard facts are that the majority of trout feed below the surface and, on chalk streams, a deal of this feeding revolves around shrimp. The shrimp, owing to its ubiquity throughout chalk streams and its overall existence, offers trout year-round feeding opportunity. In many ways, the shrimp is a metaphorical loaf of bread, always to hand, an ever-ready source of nutrition and palatable enough to serve until the hors-d'oeuvre and main course arrive. Their lifestyles exist around the faster areas of stream and through to the slower, but generally in and around weed-beds (their sanctuary in times of threat). People tend to overlook the shrimp's astonishing turn of speed; it can swim forwards and backwards, upright or on its side. The frequently hunched position in artificials would suggest this crustacea is permanently in a state of rest. This, in my experience, is seldom the case, and so my patterns tend to be longer and thinner, echoing the moving state rather than inert.

Another important aspect of the shrimp is the method by which trout feed upon them. Certainly the trout will often let the river do the work for them, in the same way that it does with hapless nymphs floating on the current to the trout's ever accommodating mouth. However, sometimes trout will actively hunt shrimp, and feasibly other aquatic forms in the process. They do this in a vastly different way to any other method of feeding known to me. Two distinct variations exist.

The first is 'tailing', which seems to be associated with shallow runs of between 2–4ft deep, and entails the trout literally standing on its head with its nose buried in either weed or stone crevice in a similar way to bream, carp or tench, ferreting out shrimps. Often this also coincides with plumes of silt or disturbed bottom debris. When first seen this is a perplexing sight as it is not one instantly identifiable with trout. By casting above the area of activity and allowing the shrimp to drift to the bottom into the very heart of the disturbance and allow it to remain there for as long as possible (as long as a downstream pull on fly line and leader allows, that is), the inert artificial is generally picked up. However, there is the risk of being accused of ledgering!

The other instance I have noticed most regularly on the River Itchen, which involves quite dramatically athletic movements on the part of the trout, is that when it is faced with a bank of starwort (I have yet to witness this phenomenon on *Ranunculus* or other chalk stream water-weeds), it will literally swim quite fast into the actual weed-bed, nose diving, then drift back downstream, often tearing at the weeds with its mouth as it repositions itself immediately behind the area of disturbance, from which nymphs and, in particular, shrimp flee in panic from the savage assault, getting caught up in the river's flow and swept on to the trout now lying in wait, with the cunning of a practised hunter. Trout in this situation, do seem markedly less guarded than at other times, often oblivious to all around them except the task in hand and their immediate feeding zone. Given this situation, the angler is required to do little more than cast sufficiently above the activity to allow the shrimp (or nymph) pattern to drift into the starwort's back edge, and await the trout's response in usual feeding fashion.

Of course, the shrimp has other uses. Its natural shape allows (if one wishes) a good deal of lead or other similar ballast to be incorporated which, in turn, allows it to be used in river areas and fast-water situations such as deep fast runs and hatch or weir pools, which would be impossible for other patterns to fish effectively. Also shrimp imitations can excel in providing shock tactics, i.e. casting immediately behind or to the side, and back of a trout. The plinking or plopping noise triggers a reflex action which spins the quarry around so that it is confronted by a succulent shrimp. This is an 'alternative' yet sometimes effective technique, which is extremely useful if you cannot cast above a fish, for instance, when a tree or other obstacle obscures the way upstream.

Caddis Flies

For years I felt the use of caddis in an imitative sense to be, if not a waste of time, then very restricted, only really having the role of attractor. There can be few better dry flies at times of near or total darkness than a large succulent sedge pattern but, then again, it could simply be because the fly is large and offers a

Elk Hair Caddis.

Caperer.

The reflex turn. Casting a shrimp pattern behind the trout in a lie that is made awkward by a bridge and a tree. The difficulty is in getting the fish to turn and take.

great red sedge

large cinnamon

caperer

grey flag

sandfly

cinnamon sedge

grannom

Welshman's button

small yellow

brown silverhorn

small red

Major adult caddis species.

food-like target. Perhaps it is even taken to be a moth. Indeed, there are few better 'search' flies than an Elk Hair Caddis or similar buoyant fibrous artificial. Although I still feel that the direct imitation is very much secondary to other forms in chalk streams, nevertheless Roman Moser, Taff Price and Dr Harry Orr have been instrumental in my reassessment of this roof-winged insect. This shortfall in my entomological and tactical armoury was reviewed from the standpoint of how this insect was going to affect my approach particularly, and will it improve results? First, I had to understand its various lifestyles within the scope of the water I was likely to fish.

Old diaries were scanned for occurrences and specific references. There were not many, but the first went back to 1965 when, at the age of thirteen, I scrawled an entry in the joint journal that my father and I kept, which made specific reference to caddis cases in the stomach contents of trout. Thereafter, there was little else save the odd tactical ploy of bushy buoyant patterns fished beneath trees or 'waked' at twilight in order to trigger a feeding response. The only real sign that I should possibly be more aware of this creature was a mention of a day on the Upper Avon immediately below the piscatorial water. I was fishing for grayling and trout in late September, and I caught a number of both species, it recorded, on Eyebrook Caddis, which is one of Gordon Fraser's weighted nymphs that imitates a case caddis of, I suspect, the Lymphilidae clan.

Two years ago I began in earnest making a study on the Stour of the importance of caddis. This involved autopsies, browbeating fellow fly fishers on the syndicate for information and repeated excursions to the river with my broom-handled seine net. The results were surprising.

I thought the *Rhyacophila*, or sandfly, was of primarily north country origin – not so. There they were, lots of these bright green free-swimming larvae in my net. Of course, anyone who has seen the almost carpet-like areas of various cased species, can only feel overawed at the prospect of fishing an imitation. It is rather like using a single star to lure the moon on the Milky Way. Nevertheless, I have found an artificial of *Rhyacophila* to be a sound investment when requiring a general nymph pattern for use in and around both layers, especially those devoid of weeds. I am now firmly of the opinion that trout in chalk streams feed far more on caddis pupa than we imagine. There are a number of instances which would suggest that a great deal of feeding takes place just beneath the surface, within a band of about 1ft. Often I think we misinterpret this as emerging mayfly/upwing activity, a conclusion drawn because the fish will accept upwing emergers and nymph patterns quite readily in some circumstances. However, if one looks at them, certain similarities exist between species, especially the smaller species such as the Small Red (*Tinodes waeneri*) and Small Yellow (*Psychomyia pusilla*) and the sandfly (*Rhyacophila dorsalis*).

What is also not known is whether specific imitations work any better than general nymph patterns. I carry a few pupa patterns (Roman Moser's type for preference) in olive, amber, insect green for *Rhyacophila* and chestnut brown in sizes 12–16, and also a few Invictas and Balloon Caddis. As most species hatch during the late afternoon and early evening, I have found that the doldrums period between midday and 4 o'clock is an ideal time to experiment with caddis pupa imitations, a case of nothing ventured . . . Results have been interesting, but certainly not conclusive.

The adult is a positive enigma. I expect you have witnessed veritable dancing hordes swanning up and down the river with trout taking not a jot of notice, the most noticeable of these being the black sedge (*Silo nigricornis*), the black silver-horn (*Mystacides azurea*) and the grey sedge (*Odontocerum albicorne*). Trout, it appears, do their level best to ignore this multitude, and yet, during late evening and approaching darkness, an imitation can be deadly.

I believe there is some reason for all this: the species are largely ignored except for the pupal stages and perhaps at egg-laying periods. Yet there are other less numerous species that 'came out to play' during these low light levels (and these tend to be longer and lighter in colour) – the sandfly, the caperer, great red and large cinnamon, all of which are longish and of amber/brown colouration in a loose sense. It may well be that their taste is a good deal more palatable (similarly to midge, some species are actually ignored by trout during times of plenty, for this reason). Whatever the case, trout actively feed on large sedges.

The fly-tying journals and books of yesteryear tended not to be given to sentiment about fly patterns, each having a specific role. Grannoms, Lunn's Caperer, Little Brown and Red Sedge and Sandfly, as well as other localized patterns such as the Kimbridge Orange Cinnamon, display just how important their originators thought the adult to be on chalk streams. A Caperer cast at a rising fish that has refused everything, often tempts the trout into a fatal mistake.

I am still puzzled as to why the yellow band, which is presumably the egg cluster of the female caddis, is positioned midships and not to the rear. However, it does work.

That said, the modern caddis *à la* Troth, using elk hair, the Moser Delta Wing employing polypropylene as a wing material, and other innovations, have afforded more durable and buoyant imitations, and I can think of few better dry flies than an Elk Hair, as the river changes hue to deep indigo on those silken July evenings.

Yet, on occasion, a more direct imitation may be called for. Here I have found the tent wing caddis – a mottled or similar quill wing, varnished or lacquered on the underside, then clipped to a sedge (roof-winged shape) – to be admirable. As indeed are the Voljč Sedges from Yugoslavia, if you have the patience. These were popularized by Taff Price and use a ladies' nylon stocking stretched across an embroidery frame. The selected wing material is coated with a PVC glue and adhered to the stocking, allowed to dry, released and clipped to shape. I do not use this style myself, but I know people who swear by its effectiveness and wax lyrical about its durability. These realistic dressings, *sans* antennae or with, can fool some very fussy trout who may have spurned a close copy dun or spinner.

If you feel experimentation in adult forms worthwhile, you may care to consider the two categories by which I work. These are static/dead-drift types and water movers, the latter referring to that engaging ability of caddis adults to run, hop, skip and jump along the river surface. This factor has lead to many dastardly deeds by eminent people who flaunt the upstream only rule, but maintain they are doing so in the name of imitation – quite so! In order to get your fly to behave naturally, you have to throw it across the stream and allow it to swing across and down, perhaps helped by the odd twitch on the line. Whether you view this as actively breaking the code, I leave up to you.

Static/dead-drift: Moser Balloon Caddis, the Voljč series, Tent Wing, Lunn's Caperer, and other traditional types.

The stages of development of caddis (Trichoptia).

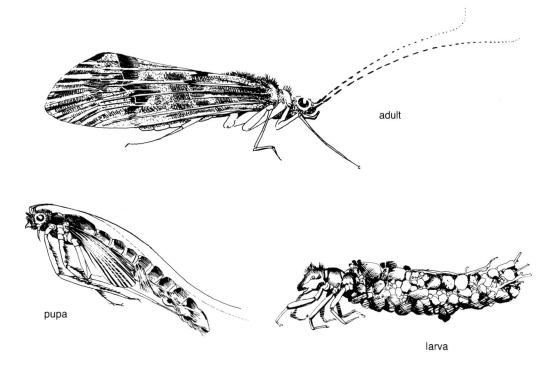

adult

pupa

larva

Water mover/buoyant patterns: G & H Sedge, Elk Hair Caddis, Nelson Caddis, and the Walker's Sedge series.

There are, of course, instances of ovipositing and spent females, yet the instances of spent or ovipositing caddis predation are remote. Any fly activity has to be viewed in the light of what is abundant on the stream and what is acceptable to the trout. Certainly, caddis is a major food form, yet viewed in the light of other aquatic forms, it has to be seen as second division.

Black Gnats and Hawthorns

The black gnat (*Bibio johannis*) was a special favourite of my father's, his 'confidence' fly which was fished at wholly inappropriate times and yet caught legions of trout.
the general dry fly sense; although specifically it should be fished during the spring when naturals are abroad.

The black gnat is often the 'hidden hatch'. Given a good continuous mayfly hatch, very often the sheer, orgiastic feeding sates the trout towards the end, and so mayfly imitations during this latter period are totally ignored. Enter the black gnat, which, being dark, is often overlooked by the flyfisher. It is often taken in an hors-d'oeuvre capacity, rather than as a main meal.

I mention the black gnat's relative, the gangly-legged hawthorn (*Bibio marci*), in April tactics, its short duration coincides with blossom, bird-song and spring. It is an unmistakable emergence rather than a hatch, as both creatures, although of the *Diptera*, are terrestrial. Great black colonies hover around bankside shrub blossom. Their effect on fly fishing is mixed, wholly depending on the weather. During periods of high wind, or even stiff breezes, when the weak flying insects

83

can be blown on to the water, they are indeed important, but in calm weather, they are not that significant.

Other Flies

If one is to mention the *Bibio*, then I suppose one also has to acknowledge the bluebottle, which is a late season offering. Tony Deacon, the editor of *Fly Dresser's Guild* magazine indeed suggests that these are a very important factor on chalk stream, although I do so only grudgingly.

The daddy-long-legs or cranefly is similarly undeservedly overlooked. I have enjoyed some wonderful days' fly fishing on the Upper Avon with this fly and I see no reason why it should not be used with equal success elsewhere.

The *Plecoptera*, or stoneflies, do undeniably exist on chalk streams. I have known a great many yellow sallys hatch on the Test during May and early June, and there are generally a few Spanish needles and willow flies on the Itchen during the later part of the season. However, in fly fishing terms they are, I feel, of little consequence to we southerners. They are justifiably the preserve of the northern rain-fed streams and not really worth imitating on the chalk to a large extent.

Terrestrials

This whole area I term 'drop-offs' – things which fall out of trees – ants, spiders, beetles and so forth. We fly fishers can get awfully snooty about them. However, beetles and spiders, especially around tree-lined banks, are a very important food form. The largest trout in the river system reside in these secret, shrouded areas and a little black and peacock spider, tied with black cock hackle, often clipped in a 'V' underneath to make it flush to the surface, in sizes 14–18, is probably the best line of attack in hostile, often jungle-like conditions, where accurate casting – even 'bow and arrow' style is difficult but equally important.

There are, of course, a host of other items eaten by trout: *Corixae*, hoglouse, small fish such as miller's thumb and minnows, and even trout parr are sometimes avidly taken. Crayfish are relished where they exist. The main attraction may be primarily upwinged species in various stages, shrimp and caddis, but it is the off-beat creature that often inveigles a trout.

TRAPPING INSECTS

One of the most useful ways to study the fly life on rivers is to trap some yourself. Trapping the dun or spinner, or indeed any adult fly, is relatively easy. All you really need is a cheap aquatic net, which is available at most aquarium/tropical fish- or pet-shops. Obtainable in various sizes, most can comfortably be accommodated in a coat or waistcoat pocket. They are eminently serviceable in catching insects both in mid-air and on the water surface and also in the upper areas of the actual river when identifying nymphs either on the move or ecloding (hatching).

Unfortunately, you will need a more specialist net if you are to uncover and search out the bottom dwellers. Nets of this type resemble seine/trawler nets and I believe can be bought in America and soon will be available at Orvis (UK) Ltd.

Home-made seine net. The two broom handles are separated by a 2ft-wide sheet of white, fine-mesh net curtaining stapled to each handle.

However, they are very easy to make: attach a yard of 4–6ft deep plain, strong nylon fine-net curtain to two broom handles, with a staple gun – *et voilà*! You have a serviceable deep-water nymph catcher. You can, if deft with a needle, create two tubes for the handles to slip into, but staples should suffice. It is also possible to strengthen the bottom with a length of wire, although this also is not necessary. To use the net, simply wade into the river pushing it upstream of you. If you are in an area of large stones or thick weed, a cut-down garden rake to agitate the bottom immediately in front of the net can be advantageous.

If you want to retain nymphs, larvae, pupae and adults, there are quite a few options. In my waistcoat live two sets of forceps – one flat-ended, one fine-pointed – a collection of test-tubes and a small box with tiny perforations in the lid. In at least three of the test-tubes is a rubbing alcohol solution to preserve nymphs for future study. One problem with this method is insect colour-loss, which can be important. To alleviate this, I carry in the car a small, strong, clear plastic bucket (a tin is just as good) and an oxygenation unit complete with an air tube and stone (Shakespeare make one for pike fishermen which runs on either battery power or the cigar-lighter unit of a car). A word of warning: always use river water and not tap water as the chlorine will destroy the little creatures. If further study is required, they go into one of my aquariums. Be watchful; segregation is important. Many times, a rogue dragonfly nymph or diving beetle has mysteriously crept in and eyed me with a self-satisfied stare, the nymphs I wished to study having met an ignominious end!

If you do wish to continue your research, it is strongly advisable to ask advice at an aquarium shop, which can offer valuable information and a set-up that costs comparatively little. Do keep aquariums out of the way of usual family occupancy. I once opened the door of my 'inner sanctum' to be confronted by a blizzard hatch of sedges. Flies will hatch out, and domestic harmony can be strained to breaking point.

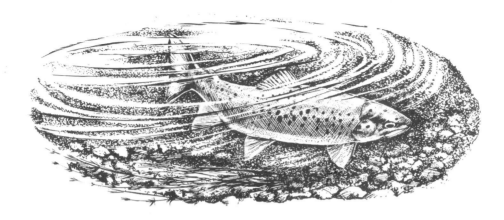

6

Their Downfall

CLOTHING

Clothing has a vital role to play in fly fishing including chalk stream fishing. This fact is very often overlooked in the wake of all the gadgetry and tools of the fly fishing trade. A myth has grown up which pigeon-holes we anglers of the chalk into a betweeded existence that few of us truly deserve. Years ago, during my 'office' days on the Test and Itchen, Americans would be quite taken aback at my non-conformist mode of dress of jeans, loose shirts and jumpers. I firmly believe they had in their mind's eye a Halfordian era of little change when plus-fours, crisp shirts, painstakingly knotted ties and Saville Row elegance was *de rigeur*. Time marches on! Comfort, of course, is essential, as indeed (given our untrustworthy climate) is the ability to stay dry and warm.

Camouflage

The ability to blend with and fade into the surroundings is, in my opinion, equal in importance to the delivery of the fly to the quarry. One only has to consider the lion stalking a herd of wildebeest or zebra to see that stealth, camouflage and concealment are at the centre of any predatory animal's plan of attack. With us it is instinct to creep rather than run, to fold a twig back rather than snap it off, to merge with the shadows under cover rather than brazenly stride about. The fly fisher is a hunter, a predatory animal stalking quarry, nothing more nothing less; correct clothing gives us the edge.

Common sense should prevail: white jumpers, shirts and trousers, and fluorescent yellow and fire orange rainwear, may have a place, but that place is *not* on the chalk stream bank. Conversely, dark clothes can sometimes be detrimental to our efforts with a fly rod. An extreme example of this would be the Kimbridge stretch of the River Test in September. When I was there, I found that, very often, the most practical, prudent and productive bank was the right-hand side of the stretch. The green strip of mown grass swept along the whole beat creating an avenue and leaving marginal cover. Behind the angler lay the broad Test Valley floodplain, home to generations of farmers utilizing the rich alluvial sedimentary soil. At this time, the fields were golden with corn. This feature meant two things were vital: firstly, a high back cast – anything else resulted in annoyance and embarrassingly frequent journeys to search for a fly in a proverbial cornstack – and, secondly, a change in dress code. A dark shape crouched or erect would give trout, hovering in the crystal-clear water, the impression of a monolith bent on destruction. The answer was to dress in tan, fawn or golden shades in order to harmonize and fade into obscurity against the sea of stalks. We caught a great many more trout as a result.

By and large, most chalk streams occupy wide valleys that have shrunk in size, leaving floodplains in their wake. These tend to be flatlands often devoid of trees. From the trout's vantage point, its window shows often an unbroken vista of sky occasionally blotted by tall bankside obstructions such as sedge, flag iris or grass. Logic tells us that a dark shape will be more readily visible than a lighter one that echoes the hues of the sky. Of course, keeping low is also a prerequisite.

Just as wide open spaces require a lighter-coloured attire, so the reverse is true in tree-shrouded areas, where the angler would obviously be well advised to err to darker, more solemn shades.

Hats

Let us tackle things head first: hats more than any other article of clothing are synonymous with anglers. Folklore has been woven around them and I, for one, have a passion for them. The casual onlooker may view these as ostentatious, but they are born out of necessity (although, admittedly, on some occasions, they are more symbolic than practical).

When choosing a fishing hat, regard should be given to the following criteria: it should have a wide enough brim to exclude unwanted light rays from reaching the eyes, in order to give better vision across and beneath the water; it should be unobtrusive in colour; and it should keep off the rain and provide a means whereby body-heat loss is kept to a minimum on colder days (a very high percentage of body heat is lost through the head, which is a chastening thought when the April north-easterlies march up and down the river valleys). Also, often overlooked is their ability to keep at bay the detrimental effects of harsh sunlight on hotter days. Partial or moderate sunstroke *is* an ever-present problem, which is generally disregarded in the heat of the chase, the vulnerable neck region being an easy target for villainous rays. The result is generally headaches and fatigue. If a hat meets all these requirements, it is a winner. Most do not, so the sensible fly fisher has two, one for winter and one for summer.

Of those I have encountered, there are several that I can recommend. There are few better styles for warm weather conditions than the archetypal safari hat, modelled on the Australian soldiers' slouch hat, although you may feel you resemble a white hunter stalking rhino in this. The venerated traditional British peaked cloth or moleskin cap is a brilliant design for fierce wind and a good all-rounder but lacks neck protection in strong sunlight. The English trilby, which is mostly made of felt and costs a fortune, is very nearly perfect. Dermot Wilson wears these and cuts a dash that humbles most fly fishers to tatty oblivion. Considering his uncanny ability to beguile trout, the fish must like them as well.

Brian Clarke is almost inseparable from his visor – which is similar to those used by golfers – as is Art Lee, the great American fly fisher. The only drawback to these is the lack of protection to the crown of the head. Art Lee, with customary ingenuity, wears his visor in conjunction with a round, woolly hat (with the bobble despatched) thus offering him warmth and heightened vision in all conditions. I must confess to doing something similar and looking bloody odd in the process. Indeed, the American peaked cap is almost the answer to a fly fisher's prayer and, being generally made of cotton, it is comfortable and cool. A stage further on is the 'Up-Downee' so loved by bone and Tarpon fishermen in the tropical coral flats, which has the added benefit of neck protection. (My wife goes into hysterics at the sight of me in this design. However, practicality outweighs the damage done to my ego.)

The tweed version and deerstalker types, I find not to my taste, yet this Victorian design has become the stereotype for headwear in country sports. They are, of course, immensely practical, but I find the coarse tweed so often used tends to chafe and irritate my forehead, especially on warm days, and an uncomfortable angler cannot fish to the best of his ability. Hats *are* important.

Shirts

That shirts should provide warmth during the spring and coolness during the summer months and also offer a degree of camouflage might appear the only requirements, but there are others. First and foremost: comfort. Any article next to the skin needs very careful consideration if it is to render you in a fishable state all day. There are stalwart folk who are able to wear wool and wool mixtures next to their skin, but they make me feel as though I am infested by virulent fleas. Nylon materials are unable to breathe satisfactorily, making life uncomfortable during the heat or cold of the day. My choice is cotton. Loose items generally perform better than tight. This is a vital consideration around the shoulder area, as the casting arm needs freedom of movement. Also consider the neck area during cold days, as a great deal of body heat can evaporate from this tiny region. It is not from any formality that many Scottish gillies habitually wear ties but sound heat-preserving common sense.

However, I tend to forsake the tie in favour of a cotton knotted handkerchief or small scarf, as these do not just preserve warmth, but also, in periods of extreme heat, can be dipped in the water, and reknotted around the neck to cool the body system. They do come in handy for doing other little jobs as well, such as drying off flies or wiping ones hands after landing fish. (This function can cause consternation to companions in confined spaces.)

Trousers

To be imprisoned in thick tweed inside a pair of waders on a hot day is to suffer a penance similar to wearing a hair shirt. Why do people do it?

For years I shunned the idea of traditional styles of trousers in favour of jeans and corduroys – a sort of inverted snobbery – how silly I was, for breeks in moleskin, cord or cotton are very practical. A large percentage of my fly fishing

Angler casting on the stream.

is bank-bound, calling for wellingtons rather than waders. Walking for sometimes miles in trousers that have been stapled to the legs with over socks can be tediously uncomfortable. Breeks solve that problem. Also, if one elects to wear shoes and then encounters a boggy, marshy area, trouser bottoms take forever to dry and flap listlessly about the ankles in their sodden wetness, whereas if it is only your socks that are damp, they will dry out quickly.

Wading is another story and for this I opt for thin cotton trousers, or even cotton long johns.

Jumpers

Thin layers, I have found, are much better than one bulky item. Days of guiding and their resultant lack of activity when someone else is doing all the fishing, can make river banks cold places and I have occasionally donned four thin layers. The weight of a thick cable-style jumper can be considerable and restrictive, and if the day should brighten up, or if you are suddenly very active, you are left with the poor choice of that or only a shirt, whereas thin layers can be shed or added to at will.

Waxed cotton bears the hallmark of practical tradition and it continues to respond to the evils of our climate, yet it has faults, mostly when there are extremes of either cold or heat. Certainly one of their biggest drawbacks is their lack of pliability in cold weather; the garments' creases almost set in formed shape, especially around areas most used such as the crook of the arm. This rigidity can hamper casting and other movement. In warm weather, the airtight material tends to create a vacuum-like effect between the body and the coat, giving the wearer an uncomfortable feel of dampness. These shortcomings aside, with frequent rewaxing, such coats remain serviceable and at least very waterproof.

Goretex in its many guises, although costly, offers the wearer a pliable and comfortable coat that breathes, and the better models are very waterproof indeed.

Footwear

Footwear, of all the clothing available, has been most resistant to change. Waders have altered little for generations, certainly in style. Indeed, rubber has been with us so long that it would appear to be in an unassailable position. However, technological progress is now finally challenging this domain, with the introduction of neoprene, the material of wet- and drysuits for yachtsmen, divers and sailboarders.

This material has the ability to hug the body like a skin of insulation which allows both freedom of movement, whilst protecting the body from cold-water hardship. Its shortcomings used to lie in the thickness of material, making it less than comfortable on hot days, but this has been improved by the availability of different thicknesses of material. Neoprene has another large plus factor: its buoyancy. Most of us suffer from falling in rivers from time to time, and chest waders fill up dangerously quickly. Neoprene tends to close about the wearer creating a tight, reasonably water-free vacuum.

Having spent a large portion of my working life trudging the river bank, I have learnt that it is necessary on many occasions to take two pairs of socks and waders and change half-way through the day, as the moisture build-up – especially on warm days – is immense. This tends to result in a slippery, almost slimy sensation in the boot area, chafed ankles, discomfort and sometimes blisters. This build-up of heat also had the nasty effect of permeating through the system.

As feet become hotter they tend to swell in size, rendering that glove-like fit felt in the store an uncomfortable experience of steel band-like restriction. I always go for a half size bigger than your usual shoe size to accommodate this factor. However, do not overdo it, as a loose-fitting wader is just as bad as an over-snug fit, and a certain cause of blistering.

Cleated rubber, by and large, is fine for waders, especially over silt, mud, small shoals of gravel and similar, but it is suspect where slippery stones, chalk deposits, boulders and algae exist. Felt is, perhaps, the best material around, especially if a wide variety of water is to be fished, ranging from the blowy salmon rivers of the north to the gentler glides of the Home Counties, but it is not cheap.

Studded soles, I feel, should be avoided at all costs, with the one exception mentioned below. The hard metallic grind and scrape of studded soles over gravel shallows when wading must surely diminish the air of secrecy and send discordant tremors into a peaceful world, as it also will on the bankside when rock or stones are encountered. I am particularly fussy about bank noise, or more accurately vibration. There are few better ways of scaring fish. The exception is a relatively new design, which incorporates tiny tungsten studs into the cleat and is to be found under the name 'Ocean'. These have proven to be excellent and relatively noise-free. I believe that other manufacturers are adopting the same format.

However, my preference lies in another variation on the cleated theme. Instead of using tiny studs, the French firm, Aigle, have encased in rubber a series of metal fibres similar to a brillo pad. These tendrils of wire protrude from the rubber sole and the result offers some of the best adhesion over a variety of surfaces that I have yet encountered. Even on the the slippery surface of a reservoir dam wall they

Keeping low when landing a trout avoids frightening the quarry – always sink the net and bring your fish to it and do not make any sudden lunges.

have held firm. Even more importantly, they offer the wearer noise-free secrecy when stalking fish.

Traditionally, thigh, as opposed to chest, waders have been *de rigeur*. Certainly, if one is merely bank fishing and water levels of 2ft maximum are to be encountered, anything larger would be superfluous. Yet, how many times have we seen fellow anglers in the middle of the river, gingerly picking their way through the current, hands gripping their wader tops in Canute-like desperation, defying the water to break over, and often it does.

A great deal, if not all, of my fly fishing is conducted with as much secrecy and stealth as possible. I creep around and kneel as much as I can, even when wading, particularly if there is little or no bankside cover. Often the light source, or lack of it, requires you to look almost along the lay of the water surface to pin-point a cast fly or hatched insect. In my first year of doing this, I learnt bitterly the shortcomings (and I use the word advisedly) of thigh waders, after my nether regions were soaked for the umpteenth time. Nowadays, I always wear chest-high waders.

Not all chalk stream fishing involves wading and not all sorties result in wet knees. Very often the only footwear required is a good pair of wellies or shoes. Jim Hadderell, my good friend and fishing companion for many years on the Test and the Itchen, once made a most valid comment. A fresh intake of neophyte anglers had arrived for a course we were holding. He eyed the assemblage with deep-rooted country scepticism. They were all in the essential countrywear (London and Home Counties sporting fashion shops had obviously made a killing) and, on noticing their footwear in pristine green with designer monograms, he wearily murmured in secretive tones: 'You know Charles, a wader or wellington is only as good as the first barbed-wire fence'.

Most wellingtons are ill-conceived as fishing items. Many come with a pair of superfluous side buckles, which have an uncanny ability to catch your fly line like

91

a greedy child in a sweet shop; cut these off. The majority do not even allow for basic leg anatomy: the calf muscles curve outwards but this simple fact seems to have eluded most manufacturers. The most comfortable, in my view, are those designed by Aigle.

Never overlook the merits of shoes. The cheaper styles of walking/orienteering boots are very useful indeed and comfortable too. During summer the humble training shoes are blissful and practical, if not the accepted uniform of the river bank. Due to the sole's construction they also offer sound grip in most bank-bound conditions and quiet stealth when stalking nervous trout. They have even provided on occasion a wading shoe when using the nylon style of stocking-foot wader.

No doubt the beloved waxproof with elbowless ventilation and baler-twine belt will still be seen in the light of old companion. I, like everybody else, have favourite hats, particular socks, trousers and so on, each with a story to tell and a fish landed. All I have attempted to do here is to offer some practical advice, because a well-dressed (not necessarily sartorially elegant) angler *will* catch more fish and gain the maximum enjoyment from a day at the waterside.

GADGETS

(The essentials and sometimes non-essentials we feel we must carry.)

I felt compelled to place this section after clothing, purely through recalcitrance. It is devoted to the 'tackle squirrel', that part of ourselves, which I know lurks within most fly fishers, the need to put as much clutter as possible into our pocket, bags and other recesses, often with no likelihood of them ever being needed – but they might!

I have purposely left the obvious essentials, rods, and lines, to the end of this chapter to follow logically into Chapter 7 on Casting.

Fishing Waistcoats

Fly fishing bags have been largely usurped from their dominant place by the American vest or waistcoat. This foreign body has quickly found favour with the British. It is for me one of *the* essentials of fly fishing tackle. Waistcoats come in a bewildering range of styles, with anything from six to thirty-six pockets. I, of course, opt for the extreme. Some models include a set collar and a webbing yoke across the shoulder region to support the downward pull of weighty equipment. Deep wading is the preserve of the wearers of the American 'shorty' type as opposed to the longer English and Continental styles, which are best suited to bank-bound tactics.

On a recent trip to Austria, during the 1989 season, I came across yet another variation on the waistcoat/portable tackle garment theme, which can only be described as a chest pouch. Two straps supported a series of zippered and Velcroed pockets to the fore whilst a wide nylon webbed belt held it in position midships. I found it workable, blissfully comfortable and it could be repositioned from the waist to just under the chin in seconds ensuring pouch and contents remain completely dry when one is wading very deep. The Hoss Kiwek Designs Fly Fishing Pouch has now become an indispensable item of my tackle and has also done me a great service, which waistcoats have failed to do, that is limit what I can take with me. It will take only two fly boxes comfortably, together with the less bulky essentials and perhaps a spare reel, which in reality, is all one needs. Another advantage is that every item of tackle is reachable. Finally, I can secrete it into the car. Bags are noticeable – certainly to the hawk-eyed sentries in my house – and they can also be cumbersome during a day's fishing, although they are easier for transporting bulky items such as Thermos flasks, food, rainwear and so on about the place. What I tend to do now is to take a bag and store it in a convenient place. The one instance when a bag undoubtedly transcends a waistcoat in transportation is to carry the catch. Anyone who has had to carry a brace of trout in the back of their waistcoat will testify to this logic; the smell, even after washing, is fearful.

Nets

I seldom use a net these days, having been almost totally converted to catch and release. However, there are occasions when one would have been useful. Only a few months ago I was fishing that delightful chalk-fed series of lakes, Rockbourne in Hampshire, and arrived minus my net. Fate took its usual course and granted an eventful day with an abundance of takeable fish. Having tussled with a 3½lb spirited rainbow and managed to subdue it satisfactorily enough to grasp it by the shoulder just behind the head area, I felt dangerously confident. The same system of extraction chanced a similar three pounder out and I was positively radiating. However, on Spring Lake I met my match. A cluster of rainbows were noiselessly

Catch and release. Hold the trout into the current. This must never be downstream but, if possible, release the quarry in the water as the shock of being out of the river for any length of time can cause extreme stress. Wherever possible try to avoid contact with the trout with hands, especially if dry.

exploring an overgrown corner, two substantially bigger than their fellows. I despatched a pheasant tail in their outer vicinity, upon which the two larger specimens gave chase like lions after a gazelle, and the cavernous white maw of one engulfed the tiny offering and I drove the hook home. There I was encased, tomb-like, by alders, with a ledge and a drop to the water of some 1½ft, and one extremely reticent rainbow trout at the other end. The tussle dragged on and on as I was abiding by the theory of 'Let's exhaust her first and worry about the consequences of landing her when I get there'. Finally she rolled, offering her white underbelly, 'Now', I reasoned, 'was the moment of truth'. This entailed me lying prostrate in the mud, making wild orchestrations with the left hand to search out the gill covers, which were opening and closing in exhausted fan-like movements. I managed to slip an index finger under the bony carmine-splashed plate and ease its silver form to the margins, whereby I discarded the rod, with a gesture irreverent of its cost, and grappled with my prize below. We both shot out of the water in a cascade of mud, spray and resignation.

From this I discovered several things. My favourite watch is not waterproof; ridding oneself of stalwart mud is a devil; 7lb trout feel a great deal weightier when they land on top of you and one should never, but *never* fish a stillwater without a net!

If you do feel naked when stream fishing without a landing net, there are several designs worth considering. But decide on your requirements first. Are the fish going to be large? For instance, in the 2–3lb class with the odd four or five pounder as the occasional proverbial icing on the cake. If so make certain your net will accommodate them easily. Are you likely to need a length of handle to cope with high banks or tricky overhangs? In this case make certain your net extends sufficiently to enable you to reach the quarry comfortably. Will you be doing most of your fishing by wading? If so you might make ease of use and transportation a priority for your net.

For years I have used two styles: the telescopic 'bow' style when on bank-bound sorties, which will, I know from experience – praise be! – land fish into double figures, and the American tennis racquet style when wading. Mine was made for me by Ian Warrilow of Birmingham, and is just a frame and a short handle. The whole caboodle is transported neatly on the back of my waistcoat via a fixed eye in the net's handle, which is pinioned to a round key retainer with a spring-loaded extending metal chain that allows for easy and tidy retraction when not in use.

Make sure that your net has a fixed metal frame. This variety fixes itself above most villainous vegetation and debris, whereas the collapsible armed variety, with a chain or thick nylon corded front, tends to hang nearer to the ground. Perhaps more important are the advantages of the fixed style over the collapsible variety when actually landing fish. Chalk streams, unless you happen to be fishing a particularly genteel stretch, are filled with water weeds of all types and it probably will not have escaped your notice that trout muster every muscle and sinew in the body to embed themselves in this verdant jungle. Very often we anglers are required literally to dig them out. Collapsible armed nets have a nasty tendency to fold on impact; the fixed metal frame, on the other hand, can be manoeuvred and steered through quite heavy growth. Being strong, it also enables the fly fisher to lift masses of hazards out of the way, thus offering a far better chance of reaching the enshrined trout. The non-net policy I will reserve for a later chapter.

Fly Boxes

To my certain knowledge I have owned in excess of hundreds of these essential 'non-essentials', ranging from tobacco tins to items of wealthy magnificence and just about everything in between. I hoard tackle, much of which I would never use in two lifetimes, and lovingly admire its design, aesthetic charm and function. It could be, of course, that each item brings us closer to the womb of our sport when forced to be a waiting vessel looking towards a new season. Fly boxes summon these pangs of recall and anticipation. As I write, within reach are at least a dozen different styles, all bursting with feather, fur and longing.

In dry fly terms, I feel it to be important that, firstly, there is sufficient room for flies to nestle happily side by side without crushing the delicate hackle fibres and wings and, secondly, individual boxes or portions are a good idea for codifying different styles, species and types. It is through bitter experience, especially in fading light, that I have learnt the need for a disciplined cataloguing of the patterns, to the extent that I religiously have one box devoted to spinner/imago patterns, one for dun/sub-imagos and one for emerger/floating nymphs. Where possible, I vary the design or colour of the boxes as well so that, at a glance, I know I have the nymph or the dun box to hand. You would be astonished at just how quickly changes can be rung even in near darkness. This all sounds terribly fastidious, and I suppose it is, but during the evening rise it makes a great deal of sense.

Dry flies have minds of their own! If you do not believe me, open a fly box in near gale conditions. It is a most distressing sight to watch a winter's hard work be picked up out of the box like flecks of thistledown and be deposited throughout the water-meadows. There are measures that can be taken to counter this potential catastrophe. You can use Richard Wheatley's renowned 'Rolls Royce' fly boxes with sprung individual lids or a cheaper variety, gleaned from Art Lee's book *Fishing Dry Flies For Trout On Rivers and Streams*. Unfortunately, although common in America, this simple divisioned pliable plastic box is rarely to be found on our shores. You can render boxes partially windproof yourself by cutting a slit down the centre, with a sharp Stanley knife, creating two hinged halves and so allowing one half to be opened at a time. At least that way you may lose only half your flies!

A few Christmases past, my parents bestowed upon me the ultimate fly box: a double-sided version with thirty-six spring-lid compartments. It was a joy, a thing of true beauty but, rather as a Christmas tree pales after the jollification, its true colours were shown on the river bank. Often the lids would suddenly spring open with such force that bits of my hard-tied flies would catapult into the sky like creatures on a trampoline. Once I knocked it over, and the confusion of flies jumbled together resembled an ants' nest. It was heavy too. However, I still carry it from loyalty rather than practicality, and keep it permanently installed in the car with reserve stocks of fresh flies for replenishment and future use.

Perhaps the most important thing about fly boxes, be they humble tins or gleaming alloy, is always to ensure that a fly is totally dry before replacing it in its compartment, otherwise it will rust the other hooks. Nymph boxes similarly suffer from the problems of rust. Therefore, one insistence is that the leaves or surface are made from water-repellent Ethafoam and that the box is reasonably watertight. The ridged ripple-foam style is best of all. I remember watching a

prized Wheatley once fluttering through the water layers like a vast silver leaf. The contents, after retrieval, looked somewhat bedraggled, not to mention the sleeve of my jacket. If you wade a good deal then a prerequisite is that both dry and nymph boxes float.

Fly Floatant and Leader Sink

These are perhaps the two most important items that I carry. I would prefer to leave a fly box behind, rather than either of these two ointments.

Floatants come in a multitude of forms. Time was when Mucilin, in its hour-glass bottle, was the accepted essential. Dipping that tiny fly into the small recess just above the cork waist, rescrewing the top, and then, with eager little hands, dousing the fur and feather in rapid tilts was, for a small boy, the quintessence of trout fishing excitement. Time has marched inexorably onwards and given us aerosols, which I have always felt deposited 95 per cent of the waterproofing into the atmosphere and 5 per cent onto my fly.

There are now also state of the art semi-solid silicone pastes which, at a temperature of about 95°F melt into a liquid. To say they have improved the quality of my fly fishing would be an understatement. If you perhaps require just the front hackle to float you can place the ointment on to that exact area, or, say, the thoraces of lightweight nymphs, thus immediately changing their capacity to that of an emerging pattern breaking through the surface film. The anointing is blissfully easy. You merely squeeze a drop on to the index finger, then agitate it back and forth with the thumb until body heat melts the substance. Then one simply strokes it into the fly. This ease and speed of operation has proved to be a blessing when trout are busily feeding everywhere and require a high-floating pattern or a different type of fly immediately. Liquids seem to take forever to dry and, as those precious minutes slip by, so does the opportunity of exciting fly fishing.

Leader sink, unlike floatant, is a relatively new innovation and we should thank the late Dick Walker for his ingenuity and foresight in bringing it to the fly fishing world's attention. Essentially, it consists of soap-based washing-up liquid, fuller's earth and glycerine, bound together to coagulate into an earthy paste. There are other varieties on the market but this, the original, remains the best in my opinion, and is very easy to manufacture at home. The mixture can be stored in a necked tub.

I cannot extol the sinkant's role enough. Nylon shines, glistens and has an exasperating habit of floating, all of which are potential hazards when trying to outwit chalk stream trout with either nymph or dry fly. When casting on a sunny day, the nylon leader, even if it is matt-finished, will resemble, from most angles, an electrically charged filament, discharging a visible aura as it travels through the air, which is surely a deterrent to catching fish if ever there was one. A few strokes of sinkant mud, especially along the tippet area where it counts most, will nullify these tendencies.

As an experiment, drop a section of nylon in a bath or basin of water, with a source of light somewhere in the vicinity. You will see how the dents, when the nylon adheres to the surface film, harden to become quite sizeable shadowy blobs. This shadow is further exaggerated when seen from the bottom, so that a 2lb tippit starts to resemble a modest hawser. By anointing the leader with sinkant, the leader or tippet will be positioned *below* the surface and not in it, counteracting any cause of shadow and thus further rendering the nylon much less visible to the quarry.

Continuous reanointing – at every other cast in many cases – is vital if your leader is to cut through the surface and become less visible, especially on quiet areas of the river where the meniscus or surface film can become very dense. Even on more agitated areas of chalk stream, such as shallows or riffles, sinkant should be applied to the basin end after about every six casts.

Glasses

The legendary fly fisher, Major Oliver Kite, is on record for disparaging this item, as marginally 'unsporting', giving the angler an unfair advantage. Be that as it may, to this lesser mortal, polarized glasses are utterly indispensable in almost every instance in chalk stream fly fishing. Heaven knows, the trout has advantage enough, if we look at its design, camouflage, eyesight and knowledge of the river. Surely we deserve some crumb of comfort.

Polarized glasses afford the edge by dispelling some of the more mischievous and intense light reflections, which can often cast a veil of shimmering intensity across the whole river. Therefore, you may be able to see the quarry before it sees you. However, not all polarized glasses are good and the most expensive are not necessarily the best. The photochromatic variety should be avoided at all costs; these are simply not good angling glasses.

Which glasses are most effective partly depends on the type of river and the time of day. For example, grey lenses should be used when the light is at its strongest and amber on duller days or when fish spotting and nymphing are paramount.

I cannot extol the virtues of glasses enough, especially from a safety point of view. A wayward fly, even for experts, is not an unknown factor and your eyes are a precious blessing. A hook can be lethal. The following tale, from my guiding days, is a prime example of this flirtation with danger.

Holding courses on the Test were, for Jim and me, a monthly and sometimes bi-monthly occasion. On Friday evenings, a string of victims of various ages, abilities and aptitude would sidle through the mill doors. One of the high spots was always the afternoon sessions spent fishing on the river. It was difficult to temper the enthusiasm of the group, especially the young. Rather like naive rookie soldiers going into an adventurous conflict, they threw aside any qualms or reservations.

Normally children of ten to twelve years of age were allowed a fairly free rein. Jim Haddrell and myself recommended – nay insisted – that everyone wore glasses for protection. Mostly, small people clamoured for 'a pair like Jim's wearing, please daddy'. As most had doting parents, keen to encourage them in their own favourite hobby, they often soon became the proud owners of polarized glasses with pop up frames.

On the second day of this particular course, all was well and going according to plan. One boy (who is probably bigger than me now, so no names will be mentioned) insisted on fishing the top pool, an area of hatch pool which was fast and deep, requiring specific tactics and heavy flies. However, it was a 'blank saver', that is predictable. I finally gave in to his continuous clamour.

Normally, it was I who got the terminal tackle and fly line out, before handing

the rod over to eager hands, as it was not an easy place to fish and was definitely *not* for beginners. This lad insisted on doing things his way, having watched me in action the day before. (Twenty minutes of reasoned argument did nothing to placate or convince him.) I gave in and surrendered the rod. This was my first mistake. The heavily weighted Mayfly nymph dangled like a cream-coloured match ready to ignite at the boy's feet. I continued a mild protest, but he said, 'Look! Like this – you see, I can do it'. Somewhat incredulous, I agreed, yes, he could do it. My second mistake.

The next cast went woefully wrong. I was peering transfixed at the water where the cast should have entered, when from my side came a wail. I swung around. My third mistake that afternoon was in not ensuring that he had closed the visor-like spectacle frames. His two hands were clasped over his eye. My legs seemed to have turned completely to jelly, causing me to totter like a new-born foal.

After the awfulness of the initial shock, with trembling hand I eased open the boy's clamped fingers. The nylon leader dripped like a sinew between the gap; my worst fishing nightmare was upon me. I peeled his hands away trying to pacify the boy in his plight, and eased the glasses off his head. From the soft fleshy skin covering the supercilium – the muscled, bony eye-shield – hung the size 8 Mayfly on a sliver of skin, his eye miraculously saved by a fraction. He did not do it again, nor perhaps ever shall. A cautionary tale, and one that is sadly enacted each season.

However, there are occasions when glasses can be counter-productive in angling. You may see a fish simply too soon. This tends to happen in particularly good light when dry fly fishing. Almost as if in slow-motion sequence, you see a fish rise, open its mouth, tilt in the surface and engulf the fly, and you strike – nothing. If, and only if, this seems to be occurring monotonously, you might try fishing without glasses, although you run a dangerous gauntlet in doing so. You should be guided by your standard of prowess in handling a fly rod, as if you are proficient, then a bad cast can either be aborted or circumnavigated, depending on the circumstances.

I must thank that master of the dry fly on reservoirs, John Moore, for the introduction into my fly fishing armoury of another style of glasses altogether: rather than banishing light, they intensify it. The article I refer to is the bright-yellow-lensed shooting glasses. Although initially difficult to adapt to, these have the ability, during times of extremely overcast conditions and failing light, to enhance vision to such an extent that a good half-hour of extra fishing time can be added during late evening sorties. They enable the wearer to spot a diminutive dry fly 'running' the far bank to such an extraordinary degree that I now consider them almost essential to low-light dry fly fishing.

I also like to carry a purpose-designed spectacle cleaning cloth. Like most people I have squinted my way through layers of grit, dried water droplets and greasy matter that did nothing towards achieving optimum vision, and so now have become very fussy about cleaning my lenses.

There are some very expensive and agreeably efficient filters of light intensity about, but not all provide good underwater vision.

One word of warning: whichever variety of glasses you choose, do *not* wear them all day long, but take them off at intervals; many a headache will be averted as a result.

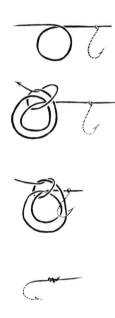

The turle knot. A useful knot for up-eye hooks nad emerger-type fly patterns.

Nylon

Tippet nylon, an Americanesque term for leader material, can extend the life of a shop-bought leader almost indefinitely and, by careful stepping down of various diameters, can create a far longer and serviceable length of nylon, capable of coping with wide varieties of b.s. tips. Therefore, spare spools of nylon can both prove cost effective and offer an armoury of tactical permutations.

Always start the season with fresh stocks of nylon. I have frequently encountered anglers who are proud of the fact that they have made one spool last for years. This is utter folly. Nylon rots – ultraviolet light sees to that – and the deterioration, especially during periods of strong light, is alarmingly rapid. A new fresh tippet length should be knotted each time you embark on another day's fly fishing. Nylon also weakens when braided or chafed, kinked or moderately knotted (wind knots). If this happens, tie a fresh length. It is time well spent, I assure you. To lose a fish through old nylon is just plain bad fly fishing, and not exactly conservationally responsible, which leads me to an extremely important point regarding nylon waste. Always, but always, when ready to discard the old tippet or leader, cut it into small ½in sections. Water life along the river bank is precious; death through entanglement is brutal and ignoble. Respect, I entreat you, the creatures that share the chalk stream bank with you.

There are three kinds of tippet nylon: stiff, semi-stiff, limp, and the recently introduced polyanids, which are extremely limp or soft, and low in diameter. This is because different situations require different nylon properties. The ultra-stiff nylon is, for the most part, not advisable for tippets, but it can fulfil a vital function in leader make-up.

Semi-stiff does have a role and certainly can form the staple diet of tippit renewal. The properties of this nylon primarily suit continually windy conditions and large bulky hackle flies, the stiffness being a valuable counterbalance against leader twist, which occurs when a wind-resistant fly is sprung through the air during the cast, causing the nylon to spiral upwards towards the fly line. The relatively springy nature of semi-stiff nylon also gives it the ability to snap a fly over – presentationally-wise – in a head-on wind or breeze.

Semi-limp/limp nylon is perhaps the most popular all-rounder, having some of the virtues of the above whilst allowing small delicate flies of say sizes 16–20 to be presented with thistledown gentleness upon the water surface.

Ultra limp/reduced diameter per b.s. nylon (the polyamide type) has, to some degree, revolutionized our approach with a fly rod. Being of such a small diameter per poundage breaking strain, it allows tiny patterns to be fished on as much as 3lb b.s. tippet strength. Before its inception, this would have resembled a piece of fluff being attached to a hefty piece of wire. Using this nylon can undoubtedly give you the edge, especially when matching small-fly hatches, fussy fish or a wicked combination of the two.

Nevertheless, there are problems attendant to this polyamide type of nylon. Firstly, it has a low stretch factor, which, if not used in conjunction with a buffer zone like braid, power gum or an elastic nylon, can lead to breakage on the strike or during the fight, if a trout seeks sanctuary in an obstacle and weeds itself. Secondly, it is shiny and will require a great deal of degreasing with a sinkant. Thirdly, it is intolerant of bulky flies and can, if matched with an unsuitably large or heavily heckled pattern, lead to inordinate leader twist and poor presentation.

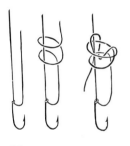

The George Harvey knot. A favourite with American fly fishers.

(Overleaf) Damned knots.

This, of course, is relative. You can up the breaking strain to nullify this problem, but it does remain a shortcoming none the less. However, I would say that the advantages outweigh the disadvantages.

Nylon can only be as good as the knots you tie, and considerable care should be taken when tying a fly or replacing a tippet. Never hurry a knot; too many or too few turns or a momentary lapse of concentration causing you not to moisten the nylon in order to counteract the material's self-cutting and friction-producing tendencies, and it will be your downfall rather than the trout's.

The number of nylons that you need to carry at one time largely depends on the types of river being fished, the hatches of insect to be imitated and the size of fish likely to be encountered, although the latter is the least important. Sensibly, you need only carry five at most and, very often less, once you get to know a river. I would recommend the following: 5lb b.s. for large Mayfly (danica) patterns, heavyweight shrimps and quick leader maintenance and extension; 3lb b.s. as an excellent all-rounder; 2lb b.s. for very fastidious fish; 1½lb b.s. for micro-flies and rarified instances; and 4lb b.s. (optional).

Ironmongery

I remember having to enrol myself on the register of a new dentist and, on his preliminary investigation of my teeth, he said, with uncommon alacrity, 'I see we have a fisherman on our cards'. Steve Rourke turned out to be a good fishing friend and companion and, as he prophesied, my teeth have indeed lost their cutting edge. I tend now to favour the nail-clipper variety of nylon cutter, rather than scissors as, being clumsy, I am forever impaling bits of my anatomy on the sharp points.

Forceps are, again, an essential. It is best if they have smooth, rather than grooved, jaws because not only will they deftly remove hooks from fish's mouths but also debarb them, should the need arise or rules insist. Finally, you should have a hone for repointing blunted or knurled points on hooks.

Stomach Pumps and Priests

I do not have much use for a priest or a marrow scoop as much of my fishing is done by catch and release. I used to be left with little alternative but guesswork when it came to food forms. Until, that is, a chance meeting on the Test some years ago with an American angler who showed me a way of both sifting through recently digested foodstuffs, and releasing the trout afterwards completely unharmed (although it is a bit unfair, I confess, to divest a trout of its meal). The device is a simple stomach pump comprising a large syringe body – of 9cc or more – attached to soft plastic winemakers' tubing. Its manufacture is very easy, requiring only that the syringe aperture is wide enough to accept the tube. If it is too tight a fit, merely heat the tubing, allowing it to become pliable and place it over the end. This is a remarkably efficient method and – dare I say it – far better than the revered marrow scoop.

Like it or not, I believe priests must be covered, as one never knows, even on catch-and-release water, when their assistance may be called for. A badly hooked fish is rare but occasionally one is in such bad shape that its return to the water would only prolong the final outcome. The quarry should be respected, and it is

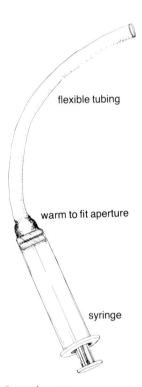

flexible tubing

warm to fit aperture

syringe

Stomach pump.

essential to despatch trout quickly, cleanly and humanely. A well-designed, heavy priest does this. Please avoid stones or bits of wood; they do not work quickly or effectively enough.

Amadou

The other item that I, at least, consider to be essential is something to dry waterlogged flies or patterns, which have become covered in mucus from a recently caught trout. For the past decade I used Orvis Dry'n'Float. These separate silicone crystals are shaken on to the fly, allowed to soak up the moisture, then brushed off. It was a system that worked well. However, last year, whilst tying flies at an exhibition in Belgium, I spied what I had only heard about in legend: Amadou, the dry-fisher's fungus. Amadou was a vital component of the bespoke chalk stream fly fisher during the early part of the century. Thereafter, I had thought, it became too rare to produce. Having now used it for a season, I know what all the fuss was about; the way moisture is soaked from the fly borders on the miraculous. To my knowledge the only supplier offering this is Rudi Heagar of Traun River Products. It is expensive but, I believe, worth every pfennig.

Of course, I could load you further, with tape-measures, scales and a hundred other collectables that few of us can resist. On more than one occasion, I have resembled a corpulent Christmas tree trudging down the bank. However, you can do as the masterly John Goddard and keep all your essentials on a lanyard round your neck and just have a box of flies in your pocket. But then he has double my thirty years experience. No doubt, in time, I shall learn!

Fly Reels

If I have one fad, it is fly reels. It matters little whether I am told by leading experts that they are arguably the least essential item of tackle. I ignore their theory that reels exist solely to store fly line; for me they remain instruments of beauty, functional, precise and an integral part of a fly fishing system. One only has to look at fly history to see I am not alone. Over the years, chalk streams have echoed with the purrs and noises of finely tuned engineering.

It was the intervention of the stillwater boom during the 1960s that altered opinions as to the role of the reel. With the ever-growing demand for greater distance and speed of retrieve, and the different standards adopted concerning tackle and tactics, the reel's operational value was reduced to a mere mechanical contrivance on which to store line. Fish were played by hand, and still are. Constant casting rendered constant line retrieval on the reel obsolete, and stripping baskets, line trays and coils of line, at an angler's feet, became the norm.

Chalk streams present a different set of circumstances, as indeed do rivers *en masse*. Loose coils of line, even when wading, are inviting disaster. As soon as a trout takes or is hooked, a loose coil of line invariably becomes entwined with your feet, snagged around a twig or stem or similar vegetation or embedded around water-weeds such as trailing tendrils of *Ranunculus* or mare's tail. By using a reel sensibly, a good percentage of these problems can be nullified.

Whenever possible, I play my fish off the reel. This position logically places my fly line neatly out of danger, but it does necessitate various criteria: a smooth and utterly reliable check/ratchet mechanism; a spool free from friction, torque or imbalance; an easily accessible handle; sufficient line capacity and, ideally, an exposed rim to aid control and braking. Sadly all these bear the hallmarks of high prices and renowned manufacturers, but I feel it is money well spent. As to the present infatuation of anglers and manufacturers with weight reduction, I have added what I hope are a few pithy observations in the casting chapter.

Your reel should be treated with respect. Periodic cleaning, regreasing and the occasional wash maintain its serviceability. Indeed, view a fly reel in the same light as a good sporting gun. My abiding horror is the sound of an angler stoically winding a fly-reel handle with the cage and spool arguing the contest with particles of sand, grit and neglect. Reels deserve better than this, as indeed do the trout.

Backing

In thirty years of chalk stream fishing, the number of trout which have taken me 'down to the backing' can be counted on one hand. Yet I consider this item of equipment necessary none the less. Fly-reel spools are narrow at the best of times and line pinch and tight coils are endemic. A quantity of backing can negate the effect to a tolerable degree. As my reels also have to function on stillwater (where backing really is essential), I always insist that a reel's capacity allows for a minimum of 50yd, plus the fly line.

If nothing else, backing gives you a sense of confidence and reassurance should a fish of a lifetime be hooked. One important feature is the junction (knot) between fly line and backing. This must be made both smooth and secure. The last thing you want to have is a perishing knot which steadfastly refuses to pass through rod rings.

Rods

The progress of fly rods during the last decade, has been meteoric. There are now few truly bad implements, it is a game of subtleties rather than out and out erroneous decision. By and large, carbon fibre, or graphite if you prefer, has usurped all others. That is not to say split cane (bamboo), or indeed the occasional hollow fibre-glass model is to be considered redundant, as both are sometimes eminently serviceable. However, it is normally prudent to choose one in this rocket fuel by-product's domain.

My formative years were full of split cane and dry or wet fly action. Later I came to believe that dry was the perfect example and wet tended to be the reject of the same. Whether or not this is true I do not know. We have come a long way since those indecisive times, although in the process – as with so many things – have lost some of the values of craftsmanship. Mass production has created an agreeable cloning and precise formula, but most offerings lack personalized character, which is the hallmark of a fine cane rod. Nevertheless we can now categorically say that the a fly rod is either middle to butt action, butt/middle to tip or purely tip actioned.

Effectively for chalk stream fishing one can eliminate the tip or extremely fast-actioned rods as being rather brutal as their role of pure distance casting, makes them not best suited for the short ranges often needed. Butt and middle to butt or slow-actioned rods, so loved by a past generation, again can be largely

Rod handles. The uplocking reel seat of the Western is an advantage for the longer rod, adding balanced weight and reel security.

overlooked as they are rather soft and lacking a certain discipline and control when casting and, although being extremely delicate in presentation and generally 'forgiving', can be inaccurate, especially in gusty, downstream windy conditions, there being little reserve power to spear a line headlong into and through an oncoming breeze to deposit the fly on target.

This elimination leaves us with two options: middle to tip or middle with an inclination to butt. I use both, but in differing circumstances. For general fishing I opt for the middle to tip, but for delicate or subtle tactics and tiny flies on fragile tippets, I plump for the softer middle to butt.

There is actually a very easy way of deducing just what kind of action a rod possesses, even without casting with it. (Most tackle shops will let you do this just so long as you are careful, and indeed you should insist that you do so before

Rod actions.

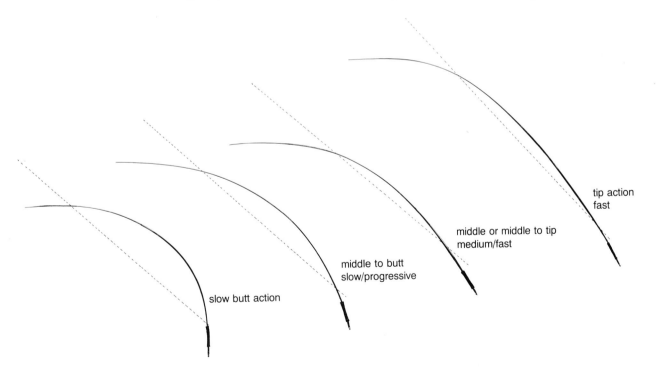

slow butt action

middle to butt
slow/progressive

middle or middle to tip
medium/fast

tip action
fast

purchasing.) Place the tip of an assembled rod, with the rings facing you on the floor, hold the handle in line with the shoulder and *gently* press downwards on the tip. The rod will now have the semblance of a hoop and display a tendency to stop and go straight just below the tip, say 6–12in (fast action), slightly further down (middle tip), bend at the ferrule (middle to butt) or continue to hoop into the butt section (butt or soft). A fast and extremely accurate judgement can be made that way.

The next consideration is length: 8–8½ft has, for years, been the accepted norm, and serviceable it is too. My preference is for somewhat longer than this. The majority of my stream fishing is conducted with a 9ft rod, but last season I often used a 9ft 6in one. Both lengths have afforded me control of terminal tackle, which would have been impossible using shorter weaponry. The light weight of carbon fibre (in most instances being about 4oz or below) allows for the additional length to be used in complete comfort for the entire day.

There are occasions when a shorter rod would be sensible but, through the kind help of Neil Patterson, the unsung hero of the chalk streams, an easy answer is to hand, literally. In a 9ft rod, you have – as long as it is a two-piece – two rods in one. All that is required is to unclip the top section, put the butt section together with the reel (having pulled off sufficient line) into your wader top, and then you can cast with the top section – an instant 4½ft rod.

On the first occasion I tried this, I had been invited by Peter Lapsley to his delightful 'Lilliputian' stream at Rockbourne fisheries (now owned by John Cain). I had been 'set up'. Peter urged me, 'Try this stretch, I think you'll have fun for an hour or so'. The trap was laid. I pondered my task. The entire stretch was alder and willow canopied, and the headroom (if it can be described so) appeared to be no more than a foot or so. 'This'll be interesting', I thought. Wading obviously gave me the advantage of being lower. Then I remembered the half-a-rod dodge. By doing as N. Patterson Esq. advised, I was able to cover water, not nervously, but with alacrity.

Peter's practical joke was not yet over. The 18 Adams danced down the current and vanished amidst a dark blip in the surface. Up swung the top section and contact was made. The fly line then hissed across my finger at the speed of a lightning bolt. Ten minutes later, having performed a crazed ritualistic dance in order to rejoin the two portions of rod back together, and to at least offer some degree of control over the creature somewhere in the distance, I was making an exhausted breakthrough: the prize came within grasp. It was 5½lb of extremely tenacious and unforgiving rainbow. Peter had purposely omitted to mention a recent escape of large and supercharged rainbows from one of his stews.

Half rods are both practical and occasionally tactically advantageous, but perhaps best suited for smaller brethren.

Arguably the best all-round choice for both large- and medium- sized rivers is 9–8½in loaded with #5 and for brooks and streams, 8in loaded with #4.

Fly Lines

Few of us could have foreseen the vast choice that has been made available in the last two decades in this essential area. Even if rules permitted otherwise, the only sensible choice is the floating or 'dry' type. Therefore, level lines and shooting heads should not concern us further. There is one other line which I very occasion-

Various rod rings. While the 'single leg Fuji' is made of silicone carbide, etc., the snake is made of chrome or 'hard' tungsten – though more fragile, a good choice due to the wide aperture.

ally carry but I shall reserve its mention for the contentious and rarified instances of its usages described later in this book.

When choosing a fly line, you need to ascertain which line profile is best suited for the task it is to perform. The choice once lay between double taper or weight forward. My choice used to always be the weight forward, although, traditionally, chalk streams are seen as the domain of the double-taper varieties. The advantages of a weight forward are their shooting abilities, a higher line speed build-up and the resultant ease with which it can puncture oncoming winds. These far outweigh any disadvantages of marginal loss of control and an inability to roll cast smoothly or hold more than 30ft or so of line outside the tip ring of the rod, during false double/single haul casting. However, for the past few seasons I have used what has become known as the long belly. This brings together in one line the advantages of both without any of the disadvantages, at least as far as I have found.

The weight of line you choose is dictated by so many factors: the sort of river, the distances to be covered, the size of fly, the nervousness of the trout and so forth. It would be presentationally ludicrous, for instance, to attempt to fish a Mayfly pattern (*danica*) over a distance of say 10yd with an AFTM #3 or 4. No matter how adept at casting you may be, frustration and tangled leaders will be your epitaph. Arguably, the best all-round line is a AFTM #5 with a #6 for big rivers, air-resistant flies and blustery conditions, and a #4 for micro- flies, short ranges, 'educated' trout and bright conditions. There are lighter varieties – #3, #2, even #1 weights – but these can best be seen largely as fun lines and not as serious stock in trade.

Problems are simply magnified when a well-meaning friend or shopkeeper insists that a #7 or #8 flyline is the cure. These are the heavyweights and will not help you to achieve chalk stream deftness, precise and accurate casting or increased catches. They are simply too thick and cumbersome for the majority of our rivers and, if chosen, will lead to upward spirals, knots, bigger reels, stronger nylon, bigger flies and fewer trout.

Also, the thicker the line, the wider a shadow is cast on the bottom. Bearing in mind that most chalk streams are clear, this is potentially disastrous. Watch any trout going happily about its business, and if suddenly a large bird or a plane passes overhead and fleetingly casts a shadow silhouette, or even if there are moving bankside objects (ourselves not exempted), panic will ensue and sanctuary be sought at this discordant and dangerous note in an otherwise tranquil world. This phenomenon of distrust of shadow was explained to me by David Attenborough. He suggested that it was a response rooted deep in natural history, a throwback to prehistoric times when danger came from above via the wings of pterodactyls. The solution is to use as light a line as possible.

Now for a dispute that has raged for ten years: which colour? The late Dick Walker was a firm believer in dark-coloured fly line and, with customary mis-chief, split the fly fishing fraternity in two. Later John Goddard and Brian Clarke further fuelled the argument with the same notions. The question is still emotive. I confess to a certain dichotomy. Whichever colour you choose (even turquoise with big fluorescent pink spots), if it lands on top of a trout, he will not take the fly. This is irrefutable. No fly line, regardless of colour, is beneficial to presentation if it is endlessly wafted over a river. A dark colour, although less reflective, still offers a surface that reflects some light. Therefore, the best colour is not colour at all – trite but true.

THEIR DOWNFALL

For years I have used fluorescent lines, either green, orange or yellow. These aid my nymph fishing, as I am able to detect takes by watching for line movement. They also help in locating the fly in failing light, by running my eyes along the drifting length to the tip to the leader tippet. Even 9–14ft away, I know that there is a fly, and so a rise in that vicinity is immediately acted upon. Curiously, I also find they appear to shoot better, although there is no logical reason for this.

However, to every argument there is another side and I encountered one when fishing the delightful Lathkill, a tributary of the Derbyshire Wye. Phil White, the head keeper, had managed to secure me a few hours by kind permission of the Duke of Rutland. As we walked the water-meadows, Phil's words rang a familiar note: 'They won't be easy, they're fussy and educated and, whatever you do, be accurate, delicate and precise'.

I was enthralled when I gazed at the verdant crystalline stretch and, by the afternoon, was to become bewitched by the river's gentle charms. However, the water offered perhaps the most frustrating experience I have ever encountered. I, of course, should have known better. After half an hour I had managed to fox what turned out to be one of the largest trout that season, a pristine cock fish of nearly 3lb. Thereafter, I was swept away into oblivion at each rising fish (and there must have been dozens). The same thing happened: a cast of inch precision, landing often like thistledown, a hatch-matched fly, a disdainful look from the trout followed by its aloof ponderous descent to lower depths. Each fish I tried, I spooked. In wearisome frustration, I sought Phil's counsel. His delightful Wilt-shire burr soothed my hostile state. 'Well, it's your line Charles, in it?' 'Lines have nothing whatsoever to do with it', I countered. 'They have', said Phil, 'Look, try my rod.' I did and started to catch fish – his line was dark!

On reflection, I realize that the overall vista of Lathkill was dark; trees shrouding a quite narrow valley, whereas most of my fishing had been in wide open surroundings of sparkling sky-laden water-meadows. In these secluded avenues, my light-coloured line clashed alarmingly with the vegetation.

This instance considerably altered my opinion concerning line colour. Now, if I am fishing an unknown water, I always carry an olive line, as well as the normal type. In order to obtain the right colour, I dye my own in a Dylon solution, 'Jungle Green'. It must be an exact science; any mistake and approximately £30 is at risk. The procedure is as follows:

1.   Rinse the coiled line in warm water with washing-up liquid added.
2.   Immerse the line in Dylon dye, mixed double strength, at about 180°F or less, and allow to soak for four hours, during which time the dye can be allowed to cool.

'When I dye lines, I pour boiling water from a kettle into an old saucepan and add Dylon and stir. Then I reduce the temperature of the water with an egg cup full of cold water to reduce the dye bath's temperature. I usually leave the line to soak overnight. It works very well like this.' (David Fynsong.)

Never boil any fly line in the dye bath, as this will wreck the line.

3.   Remove the line, rinse and examine. If because of touching turns, dyeing is incomplete, uncoil and re-coil the line, and replace in the dye for another four hours.

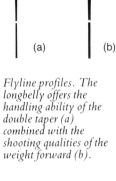

(a)   (b)

Flyline profiles. The longbelly offers the handling ability of the double taper (a) combined with the shooting qualities of the weight forward (b).

108

4.   Remove and rinse the line, hang up to dry and, when dry, rub down with a dry cloth.

NB   If a floating line is being dyed, it must be submerged in the dye; a jam jar full of water or a saucer or side plate placed on top of the line will ensure this.

The passing of silk lines is to be lamented (there are a few still made but these are hideously expensive) for, not only were they more delicate in presentation, they were also matt – non-reflective – and a drab olive in colour.

My last point on fly lines concerns quality. A floating line must float not in, but on, the surface. Speed of pick-up is essential in both dry and nymph styles. The lower-grade varieties simply do not behave as well as their up-market brethren. Not only should they float and ride high in the belly section, but also in the fine tip area. Even on the highest-quality line, this reduced-diameter section causes some concern, as meniscus, debris and algae all contrive to sink this vital portion. Therefore, regular use of Mucilin or Permagrease to keep it high-floating is essential to effective fishing. To illustrate this point, let me take you to the lush banks of the Itchen at Ovington. This particular stretch is uncharacteristic in as much as there is little if any bank-bound fishing. It is generally tackled by wading – it is clear, wide and unforgiving of all but the most fastidiously presented fly.

One particular evening I was fishing as the guest of the late Philip Pardoe. His advice to wear chest waders was invaluable. Stealthily, I picked my way through the current and waving fronds of *Ranunculus*. Before me swept the Itchen in all its grandeur, the surface punctuated by the fleeting blips and upheavals of its wild brown residents. First here, another over there, they came: spurwings, like little grey, spiralled yachts, pirouetting and coursing, with the current mounting in intensity. Cast after cast we made, close to the water parachute style, in every conceivable permutation I could muster, but still I failed. I was rising fish – some good ones – but not one could I secure.

The Bush Public House lays but a cast away, and there I took merciful and libatious release from my task, in order to ponder the situation. My line was OK, my presentation sufficiently good, the pattern I was using had to be all right, otherwise the trout would not be rising to it, and the same applied to leader and tippet, so what was it?

Having mustered at least some shreds of confidence, I returned to my penance. Same scenario: risen fish, missed fish. Night was closing in and, going through the check-list again, I realized my oversight – the fly line tip. I quickly smeared Permagrease on the fine section and immediately its profile lifted high and dry from the surface. In the next forty-five minutes I secured and brought to the hand half a dozen brownies, wild and aggressive and released to fight another day. I had learned a very valuable lesson: test 'pick-ups' as floaty lines catch more trout.

No fly line lasts forever, at best you will receive a season's hard work from one, occasionally two. As soon as cracking sets in, discard it for a new one. Cracks and general wear and tear are detrimental to performance and it is simply not worth it.

As to maintenance, a warm bath of soap-flakes in hand-hot water should be considered mandatory every month or, better still, fortnight, drying the line off with a towel thoroughly before re-spooling on to the reel. Watch out for little black spots and nicks, as these are symptoms of a future cracked line. Also, always try to get the best fly line you can afford, you will be repaid a hundredfold.

Single-actioned fly reel with an exposed rim.

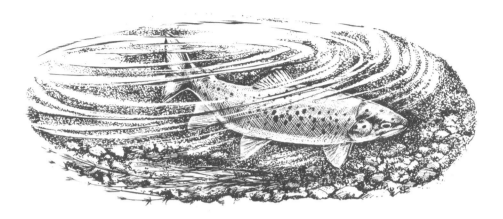

7

Of Casting

It is a constant surprise to me how this one facet we choose to call fly casting can encompass such diversity. There would appear no right or wrong way of doing it, although I am of the opinion that there is an efficient and an inefficient way. This, together with some ruses and variations, I hope to explain in this chapter.

I have for many years walked the banks of our rivers and reservoirs and also bobbed across the waves on occasion and have been witness to just about every style, action and human casting endeavour imaginable. For any student of fly fishing, watching fellow fly fishers is a sound policy, to gain certain understanding of the criteria required for effective casting. How well I remember the late maestro Jack Martin saying to me, 'If you want to understand casting, my boy, take yourself to a reservoir dam wall on a busy day and pick out anglers throwing a good line. Then set about improving on their style and efficiency.

Of course, watching will not help a jot, if you do not know what you are looking for! So, forgive me if in the following words I seem rather simplistic, but my earnest thought is to describe the casts with clarity, causing as little ambiguity as possible. I hope to be able to put casting in its proper place, as being a means to an end: getting the fly to the right spot, at the right distance, with the minimum of fuss.

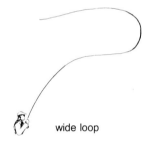

wide loop

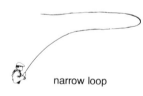

narrow loop

Wide and narrow loops created by different rod actions. Wide loops tend to be formed by soft-action rods, and are much less accurate. Narrow and tighter loops are the product of fast-action and middle to tip, and are better for more controlled, precise casting.

THE GRIP

It is often a good idea to reassess your grip to see how your casting can be made more effective. There are three basic styles of gripping the fly rod.

1. Thumb along the top part of the rod handle.
2. Forefinger along the top.
3. The handshake grip.

110

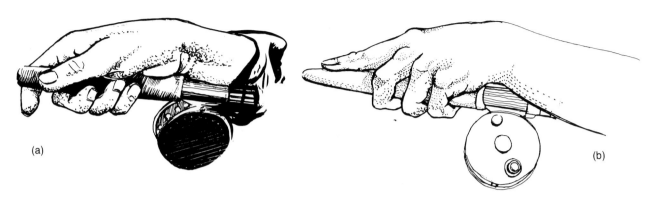

(a) *The familiar and advised handshake grip which suits most casting styles.* (b) *The forefinger style used in conjunction with short rods and oval loop styles.*

I favour the handshake form but, before explaining why, I ought to outline the other styles.

The thumb uppermost is perhaps the least used as it can lead to inflexibility and result in the wrist compensating for the rigidity by breaking back, which is an anathema to casting.

The forefinger up method might appear controversial to British eyes. Many would deem it a 'fault', and I might too had it not been for a chance meeting with the great Austrian fly fisher Roman Moser. He showed me a style which had much to commend it. However, although similar to our own method, it did have intrinsic differences (more of which later). But, and it is a big *but*, it would appear that the forefinger is best applied to the 'oval loop' style rather than our own familiar overhead techniques.

Perhaps with this in mind, it would be a good idea to explore the handshake style's possibilities. The first thing I would advise anybody to do is to allow the rod handle to fall across the palm of the hand. You will note if you do so that the reel will cantilever the butt section cosily up and into the forearm. Only when this happens should you place the thumb either to the side or on top of the rod. This sequence will comfortably lock the rod and the forearm together. Immediately, a certain amount of restriction is placed on the wrist movement, which is a sound policy for effective casting. If you grasp the rod in a rigid grip, with thumb in conjunction with fingers, the handle, reel and butt section will veer out at an angle from the forearm. This is the first phase of 'wrist break', with its resultant problems, and should be avoided.

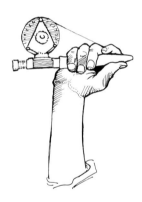

Wrist break – the scourge of precise casting.

I cannot stress strongly enough the need for careful vigilance when picking up a fly rod. It is, without doubt, the first and one of the most important links in the casting chain. If the initial movements are smooth, it seems to permeate through the subsequent casts. Attention to detail brings about its own rewards so, by getting both yourself, tackle and movement fluidly co-ordinated from the outset, better and more efficient casting results.

The overhead cast

(Overleaf) Itchen drama.

Once you have the correct grip, with the rod butt snugly resting in the forearm, the line running *straight* in front of you for 10–20ft, the serious business of casting can begin.

The real cast, in most peoples' eyes, develops from the initial upwards motion of the rod. This juncture is critical. Indeed, I would go as far as to say that this area, more than any other, will determine success or failure – it is *that* important.

As you no doubt know, the beginners' first thoughts often revolve around sheer muscle-bound effort, combining a vicious hissing of water and a ponderous ascent of fly line, the whole power stroke dissipating in a tangle of line, half-flexed rod and 'bluish' oaths to long-suffering gods. The mistake is a common one – nay, an inbuilt one: mainly the urge to throw.

Certainly one of the most poignant illustrations I offer a beginner, or when demonstrating, is to attempt with all my might to use the throwing action literally to propel the fly a distance away from me. I wind up and lever back from the shoulder and, again from the shoulder, pitch the fly line as far as I can. Usually it falls in a crumped heap at my feet, or if fairly lucky, a series of wiggles of very doubtful use and lacking any presentational quality whatsoever. The whole episode has been utterly futile and contrary to fly casting. Yet this movement is not only re-created instinctively by beginners with a fly rod but by many seasoned fishers when striving for distance. The vital flaw in this approach is quite simply the fly fisher using himself and not the purpose-designed tackle.

So what should one do, so as not to use a throwing action? Like so many things, it is a great deal simpler to say and illustrate than do, for the right movement deceptively appears to be a very basic one. The line must be *straight* in front and trapped by the forefinger of the rod hand on the cork handle. (This is important as you need a reaction on the line as soon as the rod tip is motioned upward; curves or slack areas between rod point and fly obviate this.) At this juncture, stance plays an important role. If one is right-handed, then the balance should be weight to the right-hand side, almost obliquely to the angle of the rod (slightly sideways on); if left-handed, vice versa. By standing too square, the temptation will be to go into a throwing stance, resulting in the cast being made with a shoulder bias.

With the right foot slightly forward, the rod tip at water-level and the line straight in front, we can begin. It is here, as mentioned, that one imagines that superhuman muscle explosions are necessary; they are not. The movement of the rod is made by lifting and bending at the elbow, *not* the wrist or towering of the shoulder and should initially be done slowly, almost as if you are stroking the line off the water with a feather. You will notice the reaction on the line as the tip of the rod prescribes a more acute angle. The fly line dutifully follows the moving rod tip until a point is reached on a 'casting clock' of 10 to 10.30. Then the acceleration is made upwards, and not behind. It is worth going into this crucial stage in some detail.

All the time that the rod tip has been slowly drifting from water-level to the 10 to 10.30 position in front, line has been taken off the surface and is clear of the meniscus that can impede – especially in the thicker 'belly' area – a clean lift off, with the result that the finer section offers less resistance accelerating upwards. Obviously the initial movement is not sufficient to energize and load the rod with the necessary power it requires to make the forward cast. Hence the need to accelerate at the 10 to 10.30 position. It is a precise area for, by leaving the power stroke too late, the wrist (and indeed arm) might be forced back past the vertical phase stopping nearer to 2 o'clock or, worst still, 3 o'clock at the back. By starting the power stroke at 10 to 10.30, the elevation is upward, making the vertical position that much easier to achieve. This is primarily an elbow movement, but I

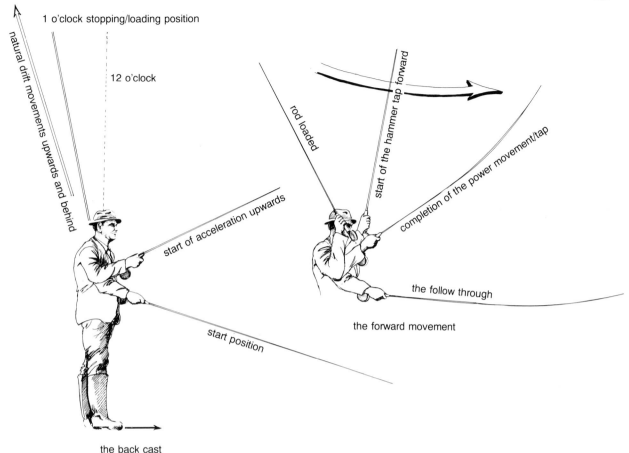

natural drift movements upwards and behind

1 o'clock stopping/loading position

12 o'clock

rod loaded

start of the hammer tap forward

completion of the power movement/tap

start of acceleration upwards

the follow through

start position

the forward movement

the back cast

The basic overhead cast. The right foot should be facing forward if the right hand is holding the rod.

have found that in recent years I have harmonized this with a certain amount of what I term 'natural drift', that is to say the elbow floats upwards with the accelerating rod, thus achieving a relaxed rhythmic action, still working from the vertical platform. But why stop at the vertical or, at least, near it? Quite simply, it is the point at which we load our rod with the power to make the cast. Rods, rather like springs, need a firm or fixed base to work from and, by stopping, or at least aiming to stop, precisely at a 12 o'clock position, this power base is effectively created.

This can be scientifically explained by centrifugal force. This is a force that appears to cause a body (the fly line being moved by the rod), which is travelling around a centre (ourselves or arm movement, the elbow lifting the rod), to fly outwards (or in our situation, upwards) and off its circular path. Quite simply, in casting terms, the circle, rather than being flat, is upright.

Get this movement right and a good up cast will manifest itself (I abhor the word back cast as it smacks of flies on barbed wire fences, caught on grass stems – need I go on!).

It is once this initial movement is complete that natural drift comes into play. If the rod stopped suddenly at 12 o'clock above us, the chances are that a poor or 'stuttering' cast would occur. However, the natural drift of the rod arm tends to smooth any of these sudden messages out. Indeed, 12 o'clock, in reality will mean

12.20 to 1 o'clock. This should cause our movement with the rod to be one of flowing power/force.

Having outlined the arm's movement from the water-level point, when it is slightly bent at the elbow with the arm and rod in perfect line with one another, one merely needs to bend at the elbow to start the movement which will chain react with the upper arm close to the shoulder. In fact, some anglers (and good ones too) will actually hold the elbow slightly out to the side and dissect an oblique angle in front. This perhaps, is the ultimate action, but in reality fishing tends to keep everything on the same plane.

There are now two routes practised by professional instructors. The first is the plane/arm moving straight up to the bridge of the nose. Once the caster has seen the base of the thumb in line with his eyes and the bridge of the nose, the first phase has been completed. Incidentally, this style is not dissimilar to that of a darts player, and creates pin-point accuracy which can often be utilized to great advantage in many practical fly-fishing situations. The second is in line directly between the ear and the shoulder. Although more open to indiscretion, such as overt wrist break, it is this one I favour. It is more relaxed and free from the imagined fear of covering the face with a fly line, leader and all (in truth this is very unlikely to happen, but the fear exists).

Therefore choosing the latter, with the rod pointing at water-level, the lower arm is lifted by the elbow, gradually easing out from the body very slightly as the rod begins the movement upwards; the accelerating by sharply lifting the elbow whilst the forearm remains perfectly still in direct upwards motion to the side of the head, the movement stopping when the base of the thumb is to the side and in line with the eye. The fly line will follow this path and be projected upwards.

This obsession with a high up or back cast is because of gravity, or more precisely, the need to load the rod with sufficient power to project a good forward cast. This may be contrary to scenes witnessed on our trout fisheries where much emphasis, it would appear, is applied to the forward movement, the back being almost cursory. However, my suggestion is supported by the adage of Charles Ritz 'High speed – high lines'.

The line, having achieved the upward path, with the rod hand stopping at the vertical (12.30/1 o'clock, in reality, is given further impetus and speed by the other hand moving upwards in unison. The rod hand should never venture above the top of the head, as this causes the disruptive influence of the shoulder to come into play.

I have explained the need for a high back, because the line travelling backwards loads our rod with power. It will, of course, then start to drop earthwards, and once the fly line falls below the upright tip of the rod, the power will be lost. The angler is left with no alternative but to go into a throwing/shoulder movement to compensate, widening the loop and, by so doing, setting up problems. However, the high back or up cast is maintained, one can get over gravitational pull, allowing for a time lapse when the fly line will be fully straight behind, but still providing a power base for the rod. This is generally indicated by a tugging sensation on the rod tip or perhaps a shift of emphasis in the rod hand. This *is* the time to make the forward cast.

You can give a sideways glance over the shoulder in order to ascertain whether the fly line is 'on the up', but resist a full-blooded turn of the head, as this will only result in shoulder casting and a swivelling of the body, both of which can undo a lot of good work. Remember that a flyline will only follow the plane on which it is set. In other words if it drops behind and the fly is positioned in line with the angler's shoulder blade, ear or head, that is generally where it will end up! As it will if it drops in line with tussocks of grass or barbed wire fences. This, in turn, relates to the rod angle, by keeping it stationary on the 12.30/1 o'clock platform all will be well. Allow it to deviate to 2 or 3 o'clock and we are back to uncomfortable sensations behind us.

Next time you use a fly rod, place a bit of wool on the tippet and allow your wrist to break, sending the rod back to the level on the back cast, *then* make the forward cast. I guarantee that you will become a devotee of the high line and stopping near the vertical.

Once it is up there and behind, that is the time to get the 'beast' out in front, where the fish are. In a perfect world, the line flowing upwards and behind, loading the rod, should carry sufficient force. Sadly, this is not so; we casters do need to exert some effort.

It is wise, at this juncture, to recap on the basic overhead phases:

1.   The fly line should be straight from rod tip to fly, with the rod tip stationary at water-level.
2.   The casting hand is brought slowly up to approximately the 10/10.30 position, lifting the elbow and forearm (the wrist should be firmly controlled and not breaking).
3.   From this position, accelerate smartly, lifting the line on the arm with a decided upwards movement, finishing on the vertical or coming to a stop at 12 o'clock.
4.   At this point, allow natural drift of the hand to continue upwards with the velocity of the rod. (Charles Ritz suggested that you press on the rod handle with the fingers to achieve this.) The fly line outside the tip should be continuing on a semi-vertical plane upwards and behind.
5.   The line is allowed to go backwards and straighten (not to do so would result in a whip crack, or the line tangling behind. When fully straightened, it is brought forward (do not allow the line to drop as critical power loss from the rod will result in a poor or shoulder-bias cast).

THE FORWARD CAST

The forward cast is actually simple by comparison to the previous movements. Imagine a window or wall in front of you at eye-level. With the thumb, push imaginary putty into the crevices, or tap a nail into the wall. This will produce the correct movement for redirecting the fly line forwards. It is honestly as simple as that. From the vertical position (where the hand ends up on the final stages of the back cast) you merely tap with the rod handle a smallish nail with an average hammer (not a 6in nail and a sledge-hammer!) into the horizontal imaginary wall in front. Imagine that the hammer head is about 4–6in up from the handle and into the blank, the power movement forwards, coming not from under the hand, but above it. If this is correctly timed, you can actually sense the power oozing forwards and gathering momentum in the fly line as it projects forwards.

This movement requires flexibility in the wrist. The Americans call it a 'snap'.

The snap or hammer tap, whichever you choose to call it, is sufficient in a variety of circumstances to get the back cast in front and out to where you will be fishing. However, it is not over yet. Like all good strokes, be they for maximizing the power obtained from a cricket bat, golf club, tennis racquet or fly rod, a follow through is essential to make the operation clean, controlled and precise. This is simply achieved by the angler, after the application of power forwards, allowing the rod to drift with fly line speeding outward in downward projection, finishing at about 8 o'clock to the angler's front. The basic overhead cast, with all its ramifications, has been achieved.

It might appear that I have laboured the point and directed far too much importance to just one particular cast, but get this discipline right, and the other variations, which are based upon this theme, fall into a logical pattern of progressive links in the chain.

The following are things that can go wrong:

1.   If you come up too slowly or all at one speed, not accelerating at the 10–10.30 position when doing the basic up back cast, the fly line in front will merely fold towards you and fail to get into the air.

2.   If you start too quickly, the fly line is ripped off the water with gusto from the water surface. Peculiarly, this movement stops abruptly at the point you should have accelerated from (10.30), the line usually jumping athletically in the air, crumpling in front or festooning the perplexed angler in loose coils. The remedy is to start slowly, building up to the point of acceleration.

3.   If you notice that you are having to operate a throwing action in order to get the fly out in front; or that there are various tugs from behind and portions of grass impaled on the fly hook; or you are forced to retrieve the fly and tippet forlornly dangling from a barbed-wire fence (or similar) or you have impaled yourself or coat behind, then this means your wrist has broken. Instead of allowing the rod to load from a stationary platform at or near the vertical 12.30/1.00, where the wrist is kept as stiff as possible, it has broken back, dragging the rod backwards, so that the loading area is between 2 and 3 o'clock. Gravity pulling the line further downwards leads to even more problems. Again the remedy is simple: keep the wrist as controlled, steady and stiff as possible at the upright phase of the cast. If this is very difficult, buy one of those Velcro fastening ties used by footballers and rugger players to keep up their socks. Place one around each wrist and the lower part of the rod handle (by the reel fitting). This will keep the arm and rod in harmony whilst allowing for natural movement in an acceptable manner.

4.   If you deliver what you think is a good cast, but the line's profile as it is shot appears wider, more rounded than it usually is and, as it starts to turn over, it inexplicably blows back towards you, the whole cast collapsing in front of your eyes, once more, wrist break tends to be the culprit. This can often happen when there is a slight wind. The rod is driven from a near vertical plane to a near horizontal, the line has followed suit and is still dropping. Luckily it does not catch on anything and is brought forwards. The power source has altered from the rod's influence to one supplied by the angler, generally in the form of propelling the low-lying line upwards via the movement of the rod tip. This almost bowls the line out in a rounded loop or shape offering much more air resistance than the tighter loop afforded by the high line. On hitting air, this wide loop tends to be at

its mercy, having very little penetrative power, resulting in generally an indefinite path forwards. To overcome this, merely adopt the same policy needed for 3, i.e. maintain a firm wrist.

5.   If the same wide loop/unsteady forward cast occurs, although you are positive your back cast was near perfect and your wrist firm, it is probably because your hammer tap or snap was aimed too high when coming forward. This normally combines with the line dropping slightly behind, causing the angler to readjust or compensate, resulting in the initial upwards movement being made from behind. Therefore, the forward cast is aimed on an upwards trajectory and, having reached a point when the line loses its power (inertia), will comb back down the plane or path it was sent, rather like going uphill, running out of steam, then going backwards down the same, gaining similar momentum. Gravity will tend to pull the fly line down on to the water in a series of useless wiggles and unfishable curves in and around the vicinity of your good self. To overcome this, always make sure the hammer tap is made on the eye-level horizontal plane in the basic cast, and snap out from this point. (There are instances when marginally higher or lower trajectories are needed. Therefore, specialized casts will be dealt with later.)

6.   The most audible problem is when one looks right and left to see who is taking pot shots with a rifle. This is known as whip crack and, oddly, seems to be less prevalent than it once was; I cannot tell you why. It occurs when the back cast (up!) goes behind and, as the loop straightens, a small percentage of line and leader are still left looped or not quite straightened. This is suddenly brought forward by the 'tap', and the result is similar to a bull whip and just as deadly on tackle and flies. The remedy is, in the words of the legendary Lionel Sweet of Usk, 'Wait for it, wait for it!'

7.   The problem of catching the rod tip with the fly is more annoying than disastrous and quickly sorted out. Essentially caused by creating too small an area for either the back or forward cast to develop in, the line correspondingly produces an extremely tight or narrow top, and although lightness is a requirement in this area, one can overdo matters. Simply open the acceleration area from the 11 o'clock to 10–10.30. If this fails, the chances are that you are being jerky in the various casting movements, so try to make everything smoother, which is how it should be anyway.

8.   Catching the fly on the fly line or leader when casting to the front usually happens when an angler is striving for a bit more distance, or a rising fish, or when it is felt that speed is of the essence. Generally the angler tries to gain precious inches by pushing outwards with the rod arm. Bearing in mind that the cast relies on a fixed base or platform to load, spring and work from if this is suddenly taken away, then the fly line has little option other than to fall down.

THE ROLL CAST I

On rivers, cunning trout lie, happy in the knowledge that their positions are impregnable. However, they often fall for a deftly executed roll cast. Its uses are many and yet it is often overlooked. It is a simple manoeuvre to master, if taken slowly. Some people claim that it is 'splashy' on touchdown, but it can be just as delicate as any forward cast.

    To start, I assume that there is something like 10–15ft of line already on the

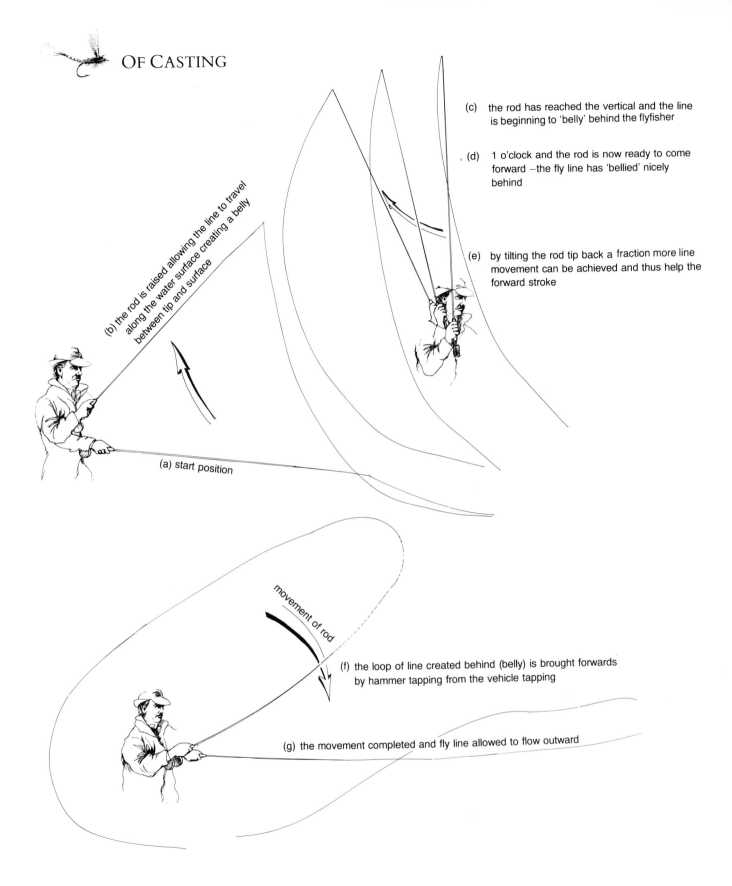

OF CASTING

(c) the rod has reached the vertical and the line is beginning to 'belly' behind the flyfisher

(d) 1 o'clock and the rod is now ready to come forward —the fly line has 'bellied' nicely behind

(e) by tilting the rod tip back a fraction more line movement can be achieved and thus help the forward stroke

(b) the rod is raised allowing the line to travel along the water surface creating a belly between tip and surface

(a) start position

movement of rod

(f) the loop of line created behind (belly) is brought forwards by hammer tapping from the vehicle tapping

(g) the movement completed and fly line allowed to flow outward

120

water in front. Have the rod tip pointing at the water's surface and keep the fly line as straight as possible. As soon as the rod is moved, an impression is made on the line and rod. From this 7 o'clock position, the rod arm (bending only at the elbow), is moved steadily upwards and to the right-hand side. This can be done either with speed (if you wish to shoot line), or slowly for a more gentle presentation.

The rod arm should be taken to 12 o'clock, although a certain inclination to 1 o'clock can be desirable. Then the rod arm is punched downward, stopping at 9 o'clock. By adjusting the trajectory, either higher or lower, you can determine how the fly will be presented: higher – say at 10 o'clock – and a wide loop will be fashioned, suiting a team of flies when drifting broadside; lower – at 8 o'clock/8.30 – and a tighter loop will develop, enabling one to master either a head wind or a tight space.

The fly line should be brought slightly away from the body during the initial move. This is a simple matter of drifting the crooked right arm away from the body at the moment the upward movement commences, so that a gap develops beneath the armpit on the right-hand side.

Another matter of safety concerns the fly line, which drifts over to the left when casting right-handed or when there is a strong wind coursing from right to left. Both are potentially dangerous when roll casting but can be overcome simply by bringing the rod over to the left shoulder, and watching the loop of line develop. Once it hangs in a half-moon loop, you should make your cast forwards. In brief, the sequence for the roll cast runs thus:

(Opposite) The roll cast. (a) The start position. (b) The rod is raised allowing the line to travel along the water surface, creating a belly (a loop of line) between the tip and surface. (c) The rod has reached the vertical and the line is beginning to belly behind the fly line. (d) The 1 o'clock position, and the rod is now ready to come forward. The fly line has bellied nicely behind. (e) By tilting the rod tip back a fraction, a bit more line movement can be achieved, and this helps the forward stroke. (f) The belly created behind is brought forward by hammer tapping from the vertical down to 3/9 o'clock. (g) The movement is completed and the fly line is allowed to move outwards.

1.   The line is in a straight line in front. The rod tip is projecting towards the water (7 o'clock).
2.   The first move is made with the right arm held slightly away from the body, whilst raising the rod upwards, locking the wrist and using the elbow for movement.
3.   Give a glance over the shoulder to watch the loop configuration.
4.   With the line still gliding across the surface area, and as the rod achieves the vertical 12 o'clock/12.30 position, punch outwards and downwards. The punch or hammer tap should be aimed to stop at 9 o'clock in normal circumstances, 10 o'clock for a wide loop and 8.30 for a tight loop.
5.   Be watchful for line drifting too much to the left-hand side, as this could prove dangerous.

To get the feel of the cast, initially try it almost in slow motion, gradually increasing the line speed across the surface as your confidence grows with each subsequent cast.

THE ROLL CAST II:
The Shooting Roll or Switch

In a practical sense, the roll cast has fairly limited potential; certainly those out-of-the-way areas can be fished, but at a cost, as the result can admittedly be a splashy touchdown. Even if the trajectory of the cast forwards has been sufficiently high to facilitate a soft landing the other associated problem is the lack of

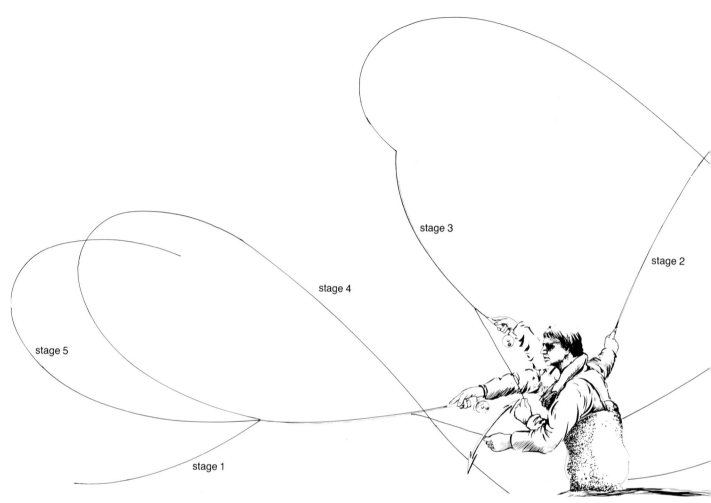

stage 3

stage 2

stage 4

stage 5

stage 1

Shooting roll/switch cast.

distance which can be effectively achieved. A roll cast in the accepted manner will seldom shoot any line at all. If some does manage to struggle through the rings, it is a half-hearted desultory affair – certainly not enough to inspire confidence or indeed seek out admiring glances from neighbouring anglers. But, all is not lost.

The cast I am about to introduce is a long way from being an easy option; to master it, at least well enough to enable one to take a relaxed attitude during actual fishing, requires hours of practice. Timing is vital to all casts, but in this one it is doubly so. However, I consider it to be one of the most important casts I have learned in recent years.

It was the Austrian fly fisher, Roman Moser, who introduced me to this cast's subtleties, and it was on the banks of the Traun, I first saw it employed. The river, having a history of paper manufacture, still has tow-paths in some areas. It was whilst standing on one of these that John Goddard and myself watched, in a state of awe, as Roman covered a group of trout some 20yd distant, constantly rising just above a vast weir in the slick, gliding water, which these obstructions often create on their upstream side.

Now there is nothing particularly devastating about casting some 20yd, but there is when there is literally a solid wall of beech trees and branches behind, making a back cast of any proportion completely out of the question. Roman not only achieved the required distance but landed and presented his artificial like thistledown, drag-free. We could only watch in admiration.

I made up my mind long before the first rainbow was foolish enough to be beguiled by the fur and fibre concoction, that this cast, known in Austria as the 'switch cast', must be learned. It has taken me a long time to feel even half-way comfortable with it. Every angler will develop his own interpretation of the switch, or shooting rolls or double haul roll. The choice of grip is entirely yours, the true Austrian way is with the forefinger along the top and I find this most comfortable, but the cast works equally well with the handshake style.

Proceed as you would if roll casting, with the rod tip at water-level, raising it gently and remembering to keep the line on the water, which is essential, as you must have that pull provided by surface tension or current. At this point, when the rod approaches the 10 o'clock position – the usual acceleration point for the overhead cast – the variation to the normal roll cast procedure begins.

Without breaking the rod's upward momentum, you must now flick the rod tip upwards, which in turn will drive the line. Some speed underneath the rod will condense, narrowing the travelling loop of line. Some portion of the flyline *must* still be on the water during this operation. Whilst the rod tip provides the line speed, the line hand pulls downwards in an opposite direction (the first part of the double or single haul); this will allow the further line speed necessary.

The rod is stopped at 1 o'clock or 1.30. At this point the loop of line should still be moving with a portion of fly line and the leader still sliding across the water's surface. Almost immediately, the forward cast with rod hand can be made – the weight of the loop of line combined with the line hand's haul will have loaded the rod sufficiently – differing only slightly from the usual movement employed with the roll cast. The hammer tap is aimed quite high, at 11 o'clock, the high point of release and maximum forward power enabling a high trajectory, which in turn allows for a greater distance to be covered by the shooting line.

From the bank position of 1 o'clock or 1.30, as the forward movement is about to begin, the line hand, which should at this point be just by or below the reel and the rod butt, hauls downward. This is quite a long movement, which further injects speed into the travelling loop. Again, it is imperative that some fly line and the leader remain on the water. Maximum distances seem to be achieved by having approximately 30–40ft of line outside the tip ring, thus achieving the designated AFTM rating weight between line and rod.

The most suitable rods seem to be those with a fast-action tip, which can achieve quite remarkable distances once the cast has been mastered, or middle to tip (semi-fast) if soft delicate presentations are required at middle distances. Certainly the best form of line for this style of casting is the long belly. This, of course, does not preclude double tapers or weight forwards; it is just that the long belly appeals to function best of all. The Air Cel Ultra II provides the best in terms of loop control and shooting capabilities.

Once mastered, hitherto unknown vistas will open up to you. Tree-shrouded areas, pockets and holes that are impossible to get at given ordinary overhead casting, and deep wading and long, controlled casts using minimum effort are the hallmarks of the switch, shooting roll or spey cast.

(Overleaf) Rainbow trout, River Test. Harvesting midge pupae.

 OF CASTING

THE SINGLE/DOUBLE HAUL TECHNIQUE

Most anglers, at some point during their trout fishing careers, become besotted with distance, urging their fly constantly to the far bank of a river or making herculean efforts to reach the reservoir's opposite shore (probably half a mile away). Naturally, a well-executed, delicately controlled cast, delivered at comfortable range will generally outfish a badly contrived effort touching down like a jumbo jet further afield, yet, trout, perverse as ever, have an infuriating habit of setting up a pattern of rises generally 10yd out of normal casting range. This and other considerations, such as a headstrong wind would suggest we do need to broaden our casting approach.

Having laid the foundation of a good overhead basic cast, it is time to address perhaps the ultimate of single-handed fly rod applications, the double haul. Rather than outright effort on the angler's part, it requires applied power, harmony between angler and tackle, and not a little style. It is not merely the preserve of reservoir fly fishers, all of us, whether fishers of small brooks, chalk streams or lakes and lochs, will at some point benefit mightily from the double haul cast and its infant, the single haul. It matters little whether you use a #1 or #2 weight system or a #8 or #10 outfit. Indeed, it is possible for a good fly caster to cast a great deal further with a D.T. #5 than a poor practitioner with a #9 shooting head.

By learning both the single and double haul, distance can certainly be achieved, but also neater, tighter wind-piercing line loops will emerge, as will the ability to cover rising trout expediently. Like all good stories, the cast has to start somewhere, and for this we look to a sound accelerated lift-off or single haul. The execution of this cast is simple. The line hand does the work rather than overburdening the rod hand. It is also a practical cast in its own right and is especially useful when increased line speed is necessary to effect a tight loop, and in a wind when a swift change of direction is considered necessary, as it offers the ability to cover trout cruising at a fair rate of knots when hunting pupae in the surface film, or those shoals of fish one often sees ploughing through the waves when broadside drifting. Our fly rod springs more positively over a shorter area, thus more power is projected into the forward cast, with both a lighter wind-piercing loop and greater distance achieved.

Correct stance is essential to both single and double hauls. Do not be hoodwinked by the often seen 'tournament stance' or open stance, with left foot well ahead of the right: tournament casters may only cast in this position for five to fifteen minutes in a day, so this explosive use of power can be directed into a short period; we humble anglers may be out there for some twelve hours and, to fish effectively, need to be almost as fresh in the later stages of evening as in the first adrenalin-charged hours. It is better to opt for a closed stance with the left foot pointing in the direction of the cast towards the water and the right foot at right-angles behind it (or vice versa if left-handed). Of course, this stance does not limit the cast's usefulness when fishing from say a boat or when kneeling, but initially it will restrict some body sway and excessive movements from the trunk, which could prove ruinous to the manoeuvre unless worked at.

With feet correctly positioned, it is time to begin the cast. If you are not familiar with this cast, or indeed any of the other casts, I would urge you to practise first

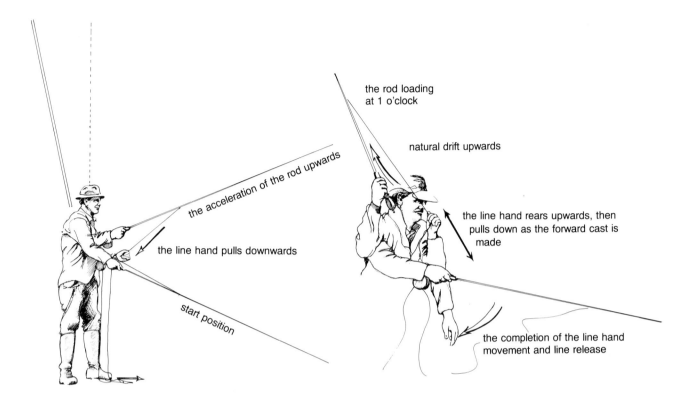

the rod loading
at 1 o'clock

natural drift upwards

the acceleration of the rod upwards

the line hand rears upwards, then
pulls down as the forward cast is
made

the line hand pulls downwards

start position

the completion of the line hand
movement and line release

*Double and single
haul casting.*

on an area of grass, as water, especially if containing trout, does little to aid one's concentration when learning a cast! Standing in the advised stance, with the rod tip familiarly placed at water-level (or grass), you can begin. With the fly line straight in front some 20–30ft, you should gently grasp the line by the butt ring with the line hand and, as the rod is raised in the usual manner, slowly to begin with, the line hand pulls down slowly to the opposite side of the body. The last pull should be as the rod accelerates up to the vertical, the line hand finishing at the waist or a shade lower. The long draw is the essence of this manoeuvre, generating the line speed, and should not be hurried. Try it in almost slow motion: you will almost load with the rod. Whatever you do, do not hurry the line hand movement or make it jerky, merely see it in the same context as the basic overhead cast – a gradual build-up of speed and power.

For the single haul, the forward cast is made in exactly the same way as previously described. Do not try to add more power at this stage, your line hand has already done this and by adding more with the rod hand you will cause a problem, with the rod sending the line out so quickly and forcibly it will most likely recoil on itself, setting up shock waves and instability and causing a less satisfactory landing.

Once the single haul has been mastered, it is time for the double. I have always likened this manoeuvre to rubbing the top of your head in one circular direction whilst patting your stomach. The timing and counter movements necessary for this cast are beset with problems to which there are no short cuts, only time and practice will provide mastery. Hopefully, these few words will help, especially if

read in conjunction with the casting photographic sequence and a prior knowledge of the single haul.

In essence it runs like this: the rod tip assumes water-level, and again the line hand is positioned up to the butt ring. Pull the line smoothly to the corresponding hip as the rod hand goes through the familiar arc in front, not forgetting about natural drift at the vertical. This almost nonchalant stab upwards with the rod tip helps, I find, with this and many other casts' effectiveness. The line should now be travelling almost vertically from the rod tip, this movement, compounded by both natural drift and the line speed of the single haul, providing tension. The line moves upwards to such an extent that the line hand is almost encouraged and pulled back up to the butt ring by the line's momentum upwards and behind. This single haul is repeated. Now comes the departure. The line hand, rather than remaining at the hip, floats back up to the butt ring of the rod which now assumes the casting position of 1 o'clock.

The timing required to affect both the downwards, single haul and then, in the same movement, to float back up to the butt ring, must be precise, unhurried and smooth; any jerking at this point, either with line or rod hand, will simply set off a vibration along the line, loading the rod behind and causing significant loss of power just when the rod should be absorbing it.

You will notice that, owing to the increased line speed, less time is required for the fly line to straighten, so, unless extreme lengths are developed in the back cast, as soon as the floated line hand has reached a position of nose level or by the side of the rod hand reel face, it will be time for the conclusion – the haul downwards in conjunction with the rod's forward movement. The rod hand should, at this point, add no more power and merely operate in exactly the same manner as for all other casts, providing a power snap or tap forwards in order to propel the line behind in front, finishing with a gentle follow through.

The line hand should move in conjunction with this movement, smoothly and forcefully downwards to the hip area, where the first haul finished, in other words, making a 'V' configuration, trembling down the last side of the 'V', finishing at the sharp angle. The point of release should harmonize with the power tap. As the tap forwards is made, the line hand should have reached the hip, either releasing the line at this point or repeating the exercise for a further sequence.

If I was asked to crystallize this cast (and goodness knows, stripping any cast down to its bare bones is difficult enough, especially when equipped only with words), I would quote the American casting *aficionado*, Mel Kreiger: it is a 'down-up' movement with the line hand, although modifying this to a down-up-down movement then release. If you consider that whilst imagining a 'V' – the base being the rod, the final manoeuvre clamping down the slope finishing at the 'sharp end' – you have the double haul.

LINKS IN THE CHAIN:
Getting your Line to Shoot

The more exasperated angler may well see this as an invitation to pepper the fly line with buckshot – refrain, I urge you. Getting line to shoot is the end result of a good back cast. Indeed, one needs hardly any more power other than what has become installed in the rod behind. Rather than allowing the line to be trapped by the non-rod hand, and allowed to fall waterward, one merely releases the line as the tap or forward snap is made. Lo and behold, the line will travel through the rings and carry on moving until finally coming to rest.

The temptation, as with most casting movements, is either to apply too much force or to misdirect the aim, going too high or too low. As I have explained before, the rod is already loaded or stored with power, so applying very much more can be detrimental rather than beneficial and, as the power snap or tap is made on the forward stroke, the line is released a split second *afterwards*. Before, and the result will be at best hesitant, at worst a chaos of line plummeting suddenly downward. This is best explained by a 'building' analogy. In order to keep a dwelling upright, solid foundations are essential. Take the foundations away and everything falls down. The parallel for this is wrist break, allowing the rod to drift too far back. The same effect can result when the line is released either behind or before the tap forwards is made. Suddenly the rod, loaded under the pressure of the line weight has the travelling weight taken away, the rod recoils back to its existing unloaded shape, sending shock waves along the line, which is also now at the mercy of gravity (there being nothing holding it up), and an earth-bound tangle is the only result possible.

Aiming either too high or too low is a fault but at, least, it is easily assessed and rectified. By tapping and releasing at a big elevation, greater distance should be covered. In reality though, what happens is that because the eyes are set on a higher plane of trajectory, the back cast, which should be projected upwards, is pitched downwards, a self-defeating exercise, resulting in the fly either catching on the back cast or collapsing through lack of power established in the rod.

FALSE CASTING

I often wonder to myself just how many trout are swimming about our water-ways with a jaunty cavalier attitude, being acquainted with the humans' often manic attempts at seducing them with a fly rod and tackle. The trouts' snooty and sometimes abject dismissal of our best efforts, is often due to one particular fly casting phenomenon: false casting, i.e. piscators who, for some reason become mesmerized and bewitched by lines travelling back and forth through the air in graceful (and sometimes not so graceful!) loops.

In its basic shape, false casting is seen as holding the line in the air without it touching either the water in front or bank behind. What is often overlooked is the point of it. If distance either near or far is the criterion, line must be released, and this is where problems can occur. Before going into this, let me first explain the basic movement, crystallized, it is a pull and then tap or snap movement of the rod hand, in that sequence, again a high line above and behind is essential. As the line begins to flatten out behind, the forward cast is made. Be careful that this is not too abrupt as it will send shock waves down the line. Also, do not work in too tight an arc overhead, as this will cause the fly line, or more precisely the tippet and fly, to catch on the rod tip. The ideal overhead arc is 1.15–1.30 behind, tapping through to 11 o'clock in front. This will allow the loop to project forwards and straighten. When trying the movement for the first time, it is a good idea to cast directly over the shoulder, glancing behind to check the height and loop, and then, still watching the cast materialize, tap in front and repeat as often as your strength

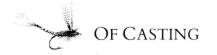

will allow. This, I hasten to add, should not continue into fishing trips, but form a practice base only.

Having mastered merely holding the line in the air, now is the time to release it to gain distance, although, initially, only a short amount. This must be done *in front*, a split second after the tap or power snap forwards has been made. Not to do so will cause acute loss of power with the familiar problems. If the angler attempts to compensate for lack of power in the rod by utilizing a throwing action, this will result in a widened loop, more effort and a pedestrian line movement forwards.

The real trick of false casting is to hold the line after it has been shot, so that it does not touch the water. Only practice will reveal the mystery of this beast and it does require the fly fisher to know how much line he can handle outside the lip ring at any given point. Be careful not to overload the rod by unforgivable margins. Once a line reaches the critical 30ft area, the line sizes in real terms increase, as more line (of the same weight) is extended. Holding 40ft of line in the air, may render the rod a soggy, under-responsive shadow of its former self. Therefore, if continuous long casts – using double taper lines especially – are to be your chosen method, in conjunction with extending false casts, I entreat you to go a line size lower than that which properly flexes and loads the rod on the first 30ft. For instance, a rod comfortably performing with a D.T. #6 at 30ft should be harnessed with D.T. #5 if frequent casts holding 40ft of line in the air are to be made.

By remembering that it is a definite pull/push, tap/snap movement and by carefully watching the loop configuration overhead – making it sufficiently open so as not to catch the rod tip coming forward – allowing it to travel forwards, shoot a little, holding it in the air, then repeating the process, gradually a rhythm will develop. Once mastered, three false casts (occasionally four) will be all you need to clear the whole fly line and, more importantly, to deliver the fly in an expedient and controlled manner, obviating the potentially hazardous, fish-scaring attributes of line and rod flash, so familiar with the 'ten false casts aficionados', who become quite mesmerized by the line going backwards and forwards.

AWKWARD WINDS

Primarily, wind is seen as the tormenter of lake, loch and reservoir anglers, but there are many occasions when a delicately worked dry fly, pitched elegantly upstream, has suddenly either been unceremoniously dumped some feet off target or wafted like thistledown in a trice on a downstream journey. Defeating the winds' influence is curiously easy, especially if a sound working knowledge of the cast has been acquired. All one need do is to aim slightly lower on the forward cast, having brought the line overhead rather more quickly than normal.

To explain the reasoning behind these minor adjustments, let me transport you to a windswept bank on a river, with the wind tunnelling downstream. The first thing that will become apparent when casting is just how speedily the line goes out behind due to the wind's influence, thus flexing the rod far more quickly and perhaps with more power than on normal days. This means that everything happens more quickly, so there is much less time to make the tap and snap forward. This can be put to good advantage, as even without single or double haul, considerable line speed has been formulated behind in the back (up) movement. This requires the angler to use less effort with the rod hand coming forwards.

Having made the back cast, you can consider the forward movement and, rather than tapping forwards at eye-level, look straight ahead, lowering the eye-level to a point just above the wave tops or ruffled water. Therefore, rather than making the forward cast at, say, 11 o'clock or 10.30, it is made at between 10 o'clock and 9.30 and, during real 'hooligans', 9 o'clock! This will have an effect of aiming the loop slightly downward in trajectory.

Even during the hardiest of blows, there appears to be an area of slack air just above the water surface. This is what you need to search out. Quite what causes this I do not know. It could be warm air evaporating from the surface, causing a minor vacuum. By allowing your line to flow across this slack space, surprisingly effortless casts can be made.

Oddly, wind coming from behind the angler poses more potential hazards. Putting aside those nice tranquil breezes, laden with summer scents, if one is drifting, or indeed fishing a bank, where the wind is very definitely blowing, the forward cast can sail flatteringly inordinate distances in front, but the power source behind is under natural threat. The cast will also be controlled by the wind direction, rather than you. A wind that is 'backing', which is not approached in the correct manner, will result in there being loose line without a proper power base (the flexed/loaded rod), at the mercy of the wind which causes several problems. The first of these is inconsistent loops behind, indeed, if very severe, the lighter and more unstable line, tip and leader will be enmeshed with the heavier tapered areas thus causing wind knots. Secondly, an unstraightened line propelled forward, whilst still unfurling from the back cast movement, and being unstable, at the mercy of gravitational pull, will drop, clipping the rod tip coming forward. Indeed, what often happens is the whole unfurled loop is projected in front, either catching the angler or dropping in disarray some distance in front on the water. Thirdly, the line, not driven back with sufficient force, 'backs up' against the wind, producing a concertina effect of waves in the back cast which lacks power or the sufficient 'proper' speed to be driven forwards.

For all these, line speed and delivery behind should be increased so that the line straightens back against the wind, but without breaking the wrist, as more problems would then be heaped upon the existing one; again, a cast of high speed behind.

It is at such times that a thorough working knowledge of the back or up cast movement is required, possibly in conjunction with either single or double haul technique. The essence of defeating a wind blowing from behind is to drive the line back with sufficient force to make it straighten and load or flex the rod, yet still overcome the element blowing in the opposite direction. This can only be done with the line speed generated by the fly fisher.

Side wind can also pose a few succulent problems, with the line being blown suddenly in the opposite direction. There is a simple remedy. The initial movement is the same as usual, with the rod tip at water-level. It is from that point that the cast deviates, and rather than being taken and accelerated upwards to the right hand shoulder (if right-handed), the rod hand in line with the ear, the cast is made instead across the body in *exactly* the same manner putting in exactly the same acceleration points as one would do ordinarily. Indeed, it is even possible to maintain both single and double hauls whilst doing so. Therefore, the casting hand ends up on the opposite side in line with the opposite ear or corner of the eye.

THE SIDE CAST

This gives the ability to 'reach the parts that other casts cannot', to use a well-coined phrase. Trout enjoy a lifestyle hell-bent on making life intolerable for the fly fisher. I have hung upside down in trees like a beleaguered Amazonian sloth; crept, disenchanted through nettles, cowpats and thorns; argued the toss with bees, wasps and the occasional bull, just to get my fly where I believe trout may care to see it. Such is the nature of the beast. Trees are, without doubt, notorious villains in the river fishers' utopia, just as well, really, or fly dressers might go out of business.

If it is impossible to achieve a high-line back cast because of branches, the remedy is straightforward: one merely casts in exactly the same manner, applying the same acceleration, loading points and forward movements as for the overhead, but on horizontal planes. However, it must be remembered that the rod has to stop in order to flex and load with the power to make the forward cast. Therefore, when side casting, do not use too much body sway or movement and allow your rod a loading platform or base and tap outwards from that point. Indeed, with sufficient practice, you will find both double hauling and single eminently possible when using the side cast technique.

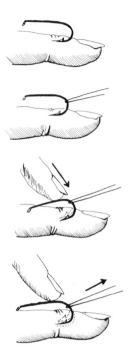

Should disaster happen with a hook, this simple depicted procedure is effective.

ODD CASTS – ODD PLACES

One of the more problematic areas of river fly fishing is the presentation of a fly in a drag-free state. Often at that critical moment, the artificial is whisked away, creating fish-scaring furrows in its wake. By and large, this has been caused by the angler not allowing for the variance of current between himself and the quarry. Seldom is the river benign enough to be moving at an even pace across its width.

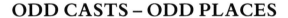

The simplest method to master is the 'slack-line pitch', the cast being made in the normal way, the only variation coming in front *just after* the tap forward has been made, as the line speeds towards its destination. The rod hand pulls back on the handle slightly, allowing the rod tip to move backwards towards the angler momentarily, and this will allow the leader and fly to travel to their destination.

However, the line will now have a series of shock waves rippling along its length, which tend to remain until the line lands on the water where a series of waves or irregular half loops will alight, allowing the fly a longer drift, until they are gathered up by the river's flow. Sometimes, especially in the case of very fast current deviations, I will send an even more drastic series of curves in the line. Although using the method outline, it is once more that I look toward the line hand to assist the cast.

On making a normal overhead delivery behind, I allow the back cast to drop just a fraction. This will allow a slightly wider loop and higher trajectory to be fashioned in front. On the forward tap, rather than aiming at a horizontal eye-level of about 11 o'clock, I tend to look up a shade, so the rod is projected almost on the vertical, this will then bring the fallen loop from behind, still on a straight plane to the target and slightly upwards in elevation. The fly line will straighten just beyond the chosen target area and very gently climb down the path you have set. This sets up a manufactured concertina in the line, further emphasized, if deemed

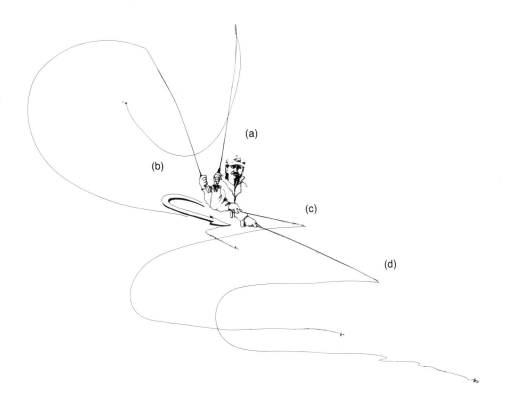

The reach mend.
(a) The first movement: an ordinary forward cast is made.
(b) The rod is then moved sideways either to the right or to the left whilst the fly line is travelling forwards.
(c) The rod is then swung in an opposite direction to that at (b).
(d) The completion, with the manufactured bend in the line.

necessary, by a pull downwards by the line hand as the tap forward and upward is made.

This cast is ideal for fish upstream especially in fast water, and is almost essential if going in for the European and American 'Art Form' downstream dry fly fishing (which, although questionable in our ethical terms is, in fact, very difficult to do, given that the same criterion of drag-free floatation exists).

Lastly, the Reach Mend. The expertise of American fly fisher, Gary Borger, is known to many and it was he who first showed me this cast. Essentially, it is a slack-line cast with a difference, that difference being the effect of delivering the fly very accurately to its target, whilst creating a large slack bend across the water, without the need to disturb the water as would be the case in normal mending procedures, the cast doing up or downstream mend in mid-air. It is one of those casts that looks alarmingly difficult, but in (and with) practice, becomes easy to master and can become almost second nature where certain types of water are encountered.

The standard high line back cast is made to load the rod. The power tap or snap forwards is made in the usual manner and, immediately afterwards, the rod is folded over to either the left- or right-hand side by tilting the elbow to a horizontal flat plane in line with the chest, and then brought back straight away to the start/finish position.

This semi-circular movement will be duplicated in the line, causing it to curve either one side or another but, more importantly, allowing through the initial cast

133

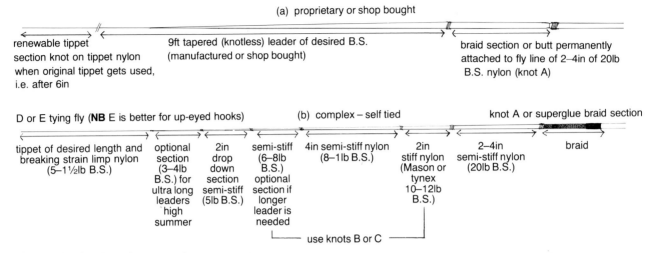

(a) proprietary or shop bought

renewable tippet
section knot on tippet nylon
when original tippet gets used,
i.e. after 6in

9ft tapered (knotless) leader of desired B.S.
(manufactured or shop bought)

braid section or butt permanently
attached to fly line of 2–4in of 20lb
B.S. nylon (knot A)

D or E tying fly (**NB** E is better for up-eyed hooks)   (b) complex – self tied   knot A or superglue braid section

tippet of desired length and
breaking strain limp nylon
(5–1½lb B.S.)

optional
section
(3–4lb
B.S.) for
ultra long
leaders
high
summer

2in
drop
down
section
semi-stiff
(5lb B.S.)

semi-stiff
(6–8lb
B.S.)
optional
section if
longer
leader is
needed

4in semi-stiff nylon
(8–1lb B.S.)

2in
stiff nylon
(Mason or
tynex
10–12lb
B.S.)

2–4in
semi-stiff nylon
(20lb B.S.)

braid

└── use knots B or C ──┘

Leaders.

forward, the fine diameter leader and fly line tip to go straight to its destination, whilst the thicker line belly, held up by greater air resistance (due to the thicker diameter) is allowed to bow.

It would be remiss of me to close this chapter without saying something about climatic effects on casting. I remember, years ago, the late Dick Walker speaking of the inability of the lines, during evening periods, to shoot any distance. I have found this to be so and not just at the end of the day; grey, overcast, muggy conditions seem to offer the same problems. Lack of wind is not the sole problem, (though it does help) it is also the actual atmosphere being very dense and wet at the same time.

As the forward cast is made and allowed to unfurl and shoot, the fly line penetrates a mass of heavy air, and the tiny molecules of water adhere to its comparatively wide surface area, causing extra weight, sag and the eventual debilitation of movement.

The only antidote I have yet come up with is, in many ways, largely self-defeating, and that is a heavier line system, opting for a #7 or #8 instead of my more usual #6 lines. The problems are of course obvious: less delicacy and an even thicker surface area to have atmosphere attach itself to. Perhaps the real answer lies in a modification of line profiles. We are still bound to systems developed years ago and, in the age of sophisticated carbons, borons and kevlars, surely line tapers are next for the revolution?

Unlike other angling matters, casting as a subject is not best served by literature. Even the video, an ideally suited medium, has fought shy of casting. Yet the would-be fly caster does have a saviour, the casting instructor. An hour under the guidance of an instructor, qualified either by the Association of Professional Game Angling Instructors (APGAI) or the National Anglers Council (NAC) could prove essential to success.

As with any sport, you get out of fishing what you are prepared to put into it, and after thirty years of practising, I like to think that I have gained some understanding. So why is it, I muse, that I still manage to get the odd fly lodged into an opposite tree branch or spook a trout with a heavy touchdown? Perhaps the next thirty years practice will provide the answers!

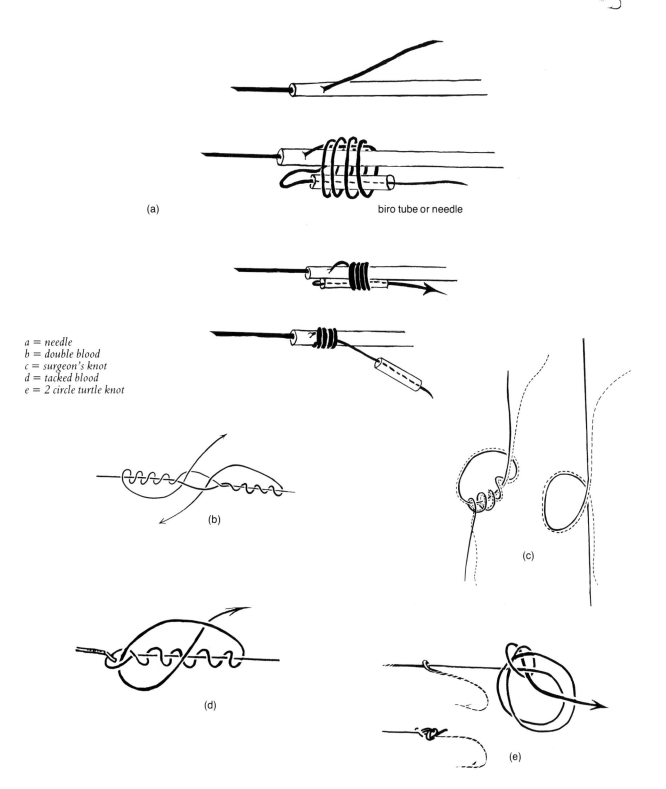

(a)

biro tube or needle

a = needle
b = double blood
c = surgeon's knot
d = tacked blood
e = 2 circle turtle knot

(b)

(c)

(d)

(e)

8

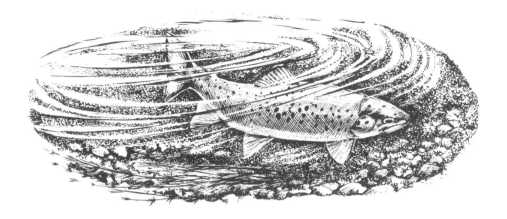

Fly Tying

DRY FLIES

A few years ago, well about 1,700 to be specific, a group of purists hovered about the streams in Mesopotamia and, just like subsequent anglers, wondered how on earth they could deceive the 'speckle-hued fishes' who were preoccupied with the wasp-like bumble-bees which incited the rises. Someone had a bright idea: off they scurried, secured some red sheep's wool and a few of the 'feathers that grow beneath a cock's wattle and are the colour of wax', and 'tied' a fly, which today bears some resemblance to a Hackle Point Red Sedge. The result was that they caught fish. Aelian, the Greek biographer of this event, could never have imagined, in his wildest dreams, what he had seen started.

After so many years, the dry fly having mirrored each generation's fad, fancy and/or peculiarity, how are we left? What have we learnt? Perhaps very little, save that trout are just as awkward and obtuse as they have ever been. We like to think that we know a little more of what we are imitating, but this is suspect, as is the reason why trout mistake a floating bundle of feathers for the real thing.

Certainly, much of today's understanding and principles owe a great deal to both F.M. Halford and G.S. Maryatt, the elder statesmen of the dry fly at the turn of this century, without whom upstream fishing would possibly not have evolved, nor indeed, the chalk stream strictures that are still adhered to today. However, more importantly, it was their approach to the artificial floating fly, and especially Halford's, which fashioned a minor revolution. Even as far back as 1889, there are references to 'detached India rubber bodies' and calculated matching of certain hatches.

Halford's fly boxes must have been prodigious. There would no doubt have been at least ten or more upwings and five caddis naturals for him to imitate. Given his preoccupation with both male and female dressings, and the odd general pattern such as the Pink Wickham, or G.R.H.E. and, that he would probably

hackled

traditional wing/hackle

no hackle

Dryfly styles.

136

The basic tactics for dry fly fishing and upstream nymph fishing.

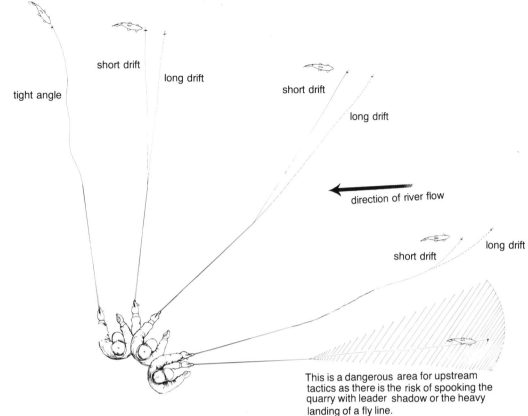

tight angle

short drift

long drift

short drift

long drift

← direction of river flow

short drift

long drift

This is a dangerous area for upstream tactics as there is the risk of spooking the quarry with leader shadow or the heavy landing of a fly line.

emerger

thorax

parachute

funnel dun

Dry fly styles.

carry three sizes and perhaps four of each size, this would create a large number of flies, not including terrestrials or spinner patterns.

If anything, 100 years on, we are becoming a little more simplistic in approach. But I doubt that there are many river fisher's fly boxes without the odd Greenwell, Lunn's Particular or Wickham's, even in these enlightened times. I will go further and mention that the approach to, and construction of, the dry fly at the vice has changed little from the Halfordian and Lunn eras, even allowing for innovation in the States and, sadly, a decline in feather availability and quality. As in other areas, we can benefit from hindsight and move forward, especially utilizing the now abundant insect-orientated books, and produce either exact or suggestive imitations of floating flies as our style and mood takes us.

The one big advance (particularly favoured in America) is the notion that 'the best things come in little packages'; imitations have, where necessary, become a great deal smaller. The idea of 20s, 22s or 24s is no longer a fad or eccentricity.

Dry Fly Dressing

I do not believe that you can be truly innovative and be serious about removing the barriers to tactics and styles if you do not tie your own flies. You do not have to tie well, as a somewhat untidy but well-designed and balanced pattern works as well as the most expertly tied. The fact that your fly's finished head may have the odd bump or two should not deter you in the least from using it.

137

poly wing

If fly tying has eluded you, get cracking and learn it. There has never before been such a wealth of literature on the subject: you could do a great deal worse than Peter Gathercole's *Handbook of Fly Tying Methods*. An excellent read, although more advanced and occasionally obscure, is Darrell Martin's *Fly Tying Methods*.

What is a dry fly anyway? What are its relevant components? Balance? Outline? How can we secure the best results from various materials in different situations? I want to start with my personal journey through the labyrinth of dry fly concoctions.

Hooks

For years, dry flies have religiously called for the use of an up-eye format. There are many sound reasons for this, the fly sitting sprightly on the water being just one. However, let us look at this logically: given any situation, the fly tied on an up-eyed hook is in either a state of emergence or imminent take-off, and this in many instances is desirable, for example with floating nymphs or 'high'-riding sedges. Indeed, the micro-spinner pattern may benefit by an optimum area of 'gape'. By and large, though, a down-eyed hook will render an imitation of a dry fly more realistic, situating the flow in rather than on the surface, where a trout would expect to capture a trapped dun or spinner.

clipped hackle

Secondly, few naturals, if trapped, would be in a state of take-off. Their bodies would have either a curve upwards from the surface or at least be flush with the meniscus. An up-eye gives an upward appearance contrary to that of a natural; a down-eye hook in this situation appears more realistic.

Thirdly, we have the question of leader shadow and its detrimental effects in clear water. Again, the down-eye hooks are favourable, positioning the tippet under the surface, rather than the up-eye which tends to kick the leader into the air in a looping fashion.

hen wing

The spent spinner: types and styles.

The only common denominator is the 'wire' of the hook. Irrespective of style or eye positioning, the criteria is and always has been that the hook is light, strong and sharp in the point. These factors alone preclude the use of 'just any old thing'.

Midges/tiny Ephemeridae/micro caddis/Caenis Partridge KIA, 22–28; E1A, 20–22; L3A, 20–22; Unwin Prof. 33445, 20–28.
General dayflies/medium–small sedges/chironomids Partridge E1A, 14–18; E6A, 14–18; L3A, 14–18; Unwin Prof. 33405, 14–18.
Large dayflies/sedge/mayfly Partridge L3A, 14–10; Unwin Prof. 33405, 14–18.

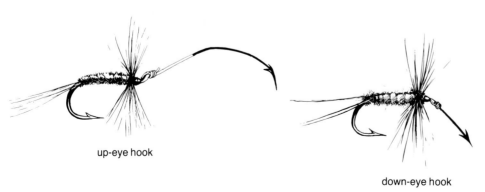

up-eye hook

down-eye hook

Up-eye versus down-eye hooks for the dry fly. The arrow shows how the nylon tippet is projected; the shadow caused by the up-eye projection may 'spook' trout.

Silk

Next on the construction agenda, and the first material to be used, is the silk. My preference is for micro-thread, for no other reason than practicality – the smaller the thread, the neater the fly. Dry flies are neat things in their natural environment, and I believe, as do many others, that a fly dresser must meet this challenge. There are quite a few options here – Sparton, Danville, Taff Price – and all these come in a variety of colours, which is essential for body matching. Occasionally I will use a maroon-coloured silk to represent many upwinged species' eye colouration. However, if a light body abdomen is called for, always use a light silk/thread.

Tails

Now for the first true imitating portion of a fly – the tail. Agreeably, caddis and midges do not have tails, and one of the most successful dry flies ever devised has also managed pretty well since 1854 without one. However, Greenwell's Glories aside, tails do have a function on dry flies; firstly to support the overall weight of the pattern; secondly, to complete the fly in masquerade of a natural. Very often, though, the point is overstated, with as many as 20 or 30 spiky protruberances destroying the imitative illusion. It is far better to err on the sparse side. Indeed, nowadays, I opt for the naturals, with two or three tails made from comparatively stiff (but tapered), nylon oil-painting bristles, although good-quality cock hackles can be equally viable. No fly should need more than eight such whisks, unless one is constantly fishing fast currents and turbulent streams. Then it is quite logical to opt for deer hair, moose mane or similarly buoyant bulky hair tails. However, even so, it is seldom necessary to tie in more than eight and often only three or four.

Dubbing

If I browse through my fly boxes, I suppose a mere 5 per cent of the flies would be what I term hard or harsh, the other 95 per cent are soft dubbed. There is a reason for this, a sedge, dun (sub imago), spinner (imago) or midge (chironomid) has a podginess and succulence about the abdomen, which is not, I feel, best served by stripped peacock quill, plastics or even (dare I say it) seal's fur. Hare, rabbit, mole or stranded soft poly 11, all serve the illusion better, together with colour blending and an interplay between materials.

I am aware, of course, that most anglers concern themselves with body trans-lucence. J.W. Dunne painted his hooks white, Goddard and Henry overwrapped them with PVC, Peter Lapsley underbodies with mylar and tinsel (for nymphs only, I believe) and dubs over. This may have some interesting possibilities for dry flies and is well worth experimentation. Personally, I am drawn back to my coffee grinder/blender and a selection of fur with which I can comfortably re-create any colour that the natural imbues, in the trout's floating foodstuffs. If one looks hard at a newly emerged dun or sedge or midge, tone and colouration are not only soft but drab and only semi-reflective. Even the spritely effervescent spinner has a softness about it and, if we look at this in terms of water and trout perusal, this is an advantage as the silhouette can, with such soft fur, be calculated to a more exact taper, and give off a reflective surface almost identical to that of a natural. Of

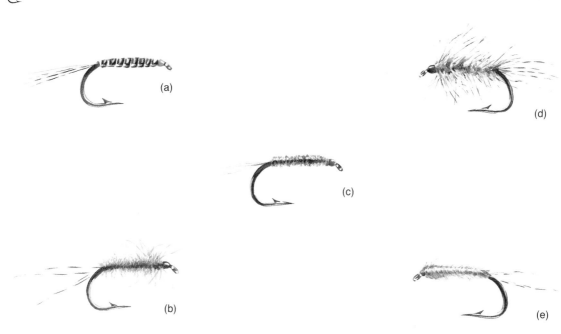

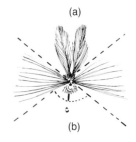

course, this is as it appears to our eyes; we can only guess as to the trout's perception of it! Of course, there is the exception: the ubiquitous Beacon Beige. This proudly contradicts everything I have said, but is in my fly box and is not only a favourite, but devastating in its effectiveness, and its body is stripped peacock quill!

Even floss, in fast water situations, has a role; the dastardly Humpy proves that. However, I still believe that a soft-dubbed body will outfish all others. If one needs a certain sparkle, one need only to blend in a few fibres of Antron to the original mix and immediately a fly will fizz with reflections. Feather fibre may be another option, but it should be a fragile one, which necessitates ribbing (the next item on the agenda). As to actual dubbing methods, with such soft furs it is seldom necessary to opt for anything other than the conventional finger and thumb, clockwise-only routine. However, if experimentation is considered viable, look no further than Darrel Martin's *Fly Tying Methods*. However, I cannot reconcile myself, in a dry fly sense, that any advantage is gained by its inclusion. If, as we are lead to believe, it denotes the insect's segmentation, how will a length of copper, gold or silver wire achieve this?

Dubbed correctly, a fly will automatically assume light and shade banding, as will a stripped peacock or cock hackle stalk. Lightness of dressing is our criterion; wire will not help the cause. If you feel (and it is a big if) that a rib is essential, choose instead a flat thread such as Danville's Muro-Cord. If durability is your goal, a layer of varnish under the dressing run along the hook shank is a much better option. There are only a few exceptions, the Elk Hair Caddis being one, where the palmered body hackle may need trapping, although, even on this pattern, if the hackle is tied in at the bend by the point and wound up, wire can be excluded.

Body styles of the fly. (a) Hard – peacock quill stripped or stripped hackle stall. (b) Harsh – Seal's Fur (Antron sub.). (c) Semi-hard – feather fibre. (d) Soft – hare's mask or animal dubbing, including guard hairs. (e) Very soft – hairtran or rabbit fur mixed with 'soft' Antron (pure).

Trimming the dry fly. By cutting at (a) and (b), a low riding profile can be achieved with any fly – also a semi-parachute effect.

140

Hackles

Greenwell's Glory.

In discussing hackles, I shall first explain how my whole floating fly philosophy has been changed by a recent theory: the importance of the 'soft pattern'. I have for some time thought that normal hackled dry flies are incongruous, yet they work and so I was loath to change a winning combination. Still, the uncertainty prevailed, because trout caught with a dry fly tend to be hooked in the outer limits: the neb, the scissors edge of lower jaw, etc., rather than in the mouth. This factor suggests that the trout found it inviting enough to try but not quite so convincing as to commit itself wholeheartedly.

Whilst fishing with Roman Moser on various trips to the Traun, one feature that I noticed about the majority of his surface patterns was their softness. They were squidgy with bodies comprised of soft dubbed deer hair and Antron mixes, for example, polypropylene and Antron wings, and very soft hen hackle tails. 'Grayling', he explained, 'are often lost or missed by virtue of the springiness of a cock hackle tail'. This echoed and clarified my feelings. Most of our patterns of dry flies are hard and springy. We search for a stiff cock hackle because tradition tells us this 'looks right' and because it is good at floating. Dick Walker, years ago, urged the use of hen hackles in a variety of dry flies. I belatedly second that.

Hare's Ear emerger.

For the last two years, I have used one style of dry fly almost exclusively, in a variety of waters in several countries, only changing the size and colour; it works, and convincingly so. The fly is not overly special, but nearly everything about it is soft; the wings of *cul du canard* readily collapse, yet still form a shape when doing so, especially when wet. This pattern is now my most used and first choice when either emerging upwings or duns are about. My unshakeable confidence in it stems from the fact that approximately seven out of ten trout that are caught require the use of forceps in order to retrieve the fly from inside their mouths, often dangerously near the throat passage. I do not think that my timing has been altered dramatically, so the fly must be accepted without reservation, which is proof enough for me.

Kite's Imperial.

The Duck's Dun (*see* Appendix) has almost total supremacy in my box; it is, for me at least, a near panacea. However, this makes me a little sad, as I have no wish to become a 'one fly' fisher. Therefore, I still carry a horde of various dressings, seldom used, but loved for this reason. I also realize that there are a good many occasions when this fly does not work, terrestrial and spinner feeding being two.

Mention the word hackle to some American *aficionados* and they will either laugh you off the stream, faint, or fish somewhere else, the next state if possible. Others, on the other hand, will clasp your hand and speed you off to view their newly acquired Metz or Hoffman cape (and make you green with envy). In this country, I do believe that we overstate the case a little. People tell me a hackle represents legs. Most streamside insects have six of 'em, twenty or more must look strangely incongruous to trout, even allowing for the water surface's veiling effects.

Lunn's Particular.

By and large, if you decide to use hackle, hackling a fly falls into four separate categories:

1.   Fast water, where a fly needs floatability and perhaps heavy hackling offering both high riding and visible qualities.
2.   Moderate currents, such as shallows, ripples and glides, where visibility, combined with good body support are required.

141

3.   Streamy, eddying currents, where less hackle is needed, but sufficient to support the fly amid its pirouettes and deviant routes, and present a good impression of legs/dimples in the surface film.

4.   Calm/semi-still water, where even less hackle is required. A trout will have much more time to scrutinize the object for defects throughout its slow, ponderous drift.

There is only one style, to my knowledge, which accommodates every instance, and that is the 'parachute' hackle. Either heavy or sparse, it will fit most occasions. However, the standard winding technique suits category 1 and 2 fairly well, but less so 3 and 4. The thorax method (another favourite style) suits 2 and 4. There is another style, which fits into 2 and 4 and, although not personally tested, is favoured a great deal in certain circumstances by both Neil Patterson (who devised it) and Peter Lapsley, which is recommendation enough. It is the Funnel-dun method. This has a large advantage over many methods as it utilizes longer hackle fibres than are ordinarily called for in dry fly manufacture. It also uses the up-eye hook to good advantage – contradiction is rife in fly fishing!

I have illustrated all the hackling techniques and, of all, the thorax style hurts the most, barbarically clipping a 'V' shape underneath a fly (and also on top for spinner patterns). Seeing Metz barbules tumble in profusion is worth an occasional sob and a tear!

Hackles will always remain an emotive issue. However, one factor remains: the floating insect we set out to imitate, and generally this creature spends its most 'available to the trout' moments trapped in the surface film. Therefore, any hackle will, if not carefully applied, destroy this illusion.

What is needed in the way of capes? Surprisingly few in respect of the insects one has to cover. You can get on with a red/brown, a black, a white or cream, a grizzle, a blue dun (light) and a light or golden olive.

Always get the best hackles/capes that you can. There are sadly few options: Indian, Chinese and 'Please, Mr Bank Manager, can I buy a genetic cape?' Of the three, the genetic offers you best value for money although the initial outlay is mind boggling, followed by a good grade 'A' Indian. Chinese is generally far too soft in the fibre to be of any use.

Wings

The final flourish to any fly, in a natural sense, is the wing, nature's delicate master-stroke. How often have we, the dry fly fishers, chosen to ignore this key and most obvious recognition point in a trout's world? In order to present this case, I have illustrated a typical trout's window when observing a floating fly overhead, together with a fully hackled representation and a winged parachuted/thorax tie. I leave the deduction to you as to which, in most circumstances, must be the most effective. Suffice to say that a good 70 per cent of my dry flies are winged, the notable exceptions being the Beacon Beige and Funnel Dun and, oddly, spinner patterns (Ephemeroptera imago). After years of hen wings and poly- winged types (some of which I still carry), I feel that the hackle versions, clipped both top and bottom, allowing just the hackle to protrude at right angles from the thorax only, are the most effective, merely hinting at wing indentations in the surface film and not offering a solid wing silhouette.

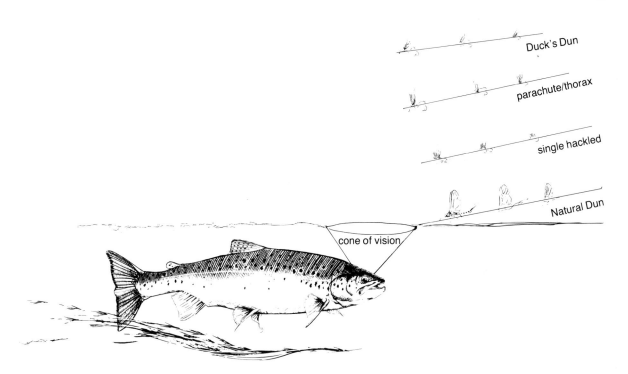

Duck's Dun

parachute/thorax

single hackled

Natural Dun

cone of vision

Fly coming into a trout's line of vision – the importance of wings.

Thereafter, I utilize every conceivable form of wing to justify particular ends, even the Halfordian/Maryatt split quill has its role. Most are augmented by hackle, yet others, such as the no-hackle, comparadun and poly's, rely solely on the charms of the wing alone.

When winging a fly, or indeed at any part of the construction of your imitation, try mentally to picture the fly you are imitating, its stage and the water the artificial will eventually land on. Such mental pictures will dictate whether it is to be heavy, hackled, deer hair, buoyant dressing (for turbulent water), or a delicate wisp of tail, wing and hackle (for slow stretches), and the permutations in between, be they upwinged, roof-winged, flat winged or spent – the world is your oyster.

NYMPH PATTERNS

I constantly find it curious, if not downright irritating, that one can spend hours and take infinite pains labouring over a dry fly dressing – aligning wings, carefully turning hackle, delicately spreading the tail into lifelike separations of two or three, accurately tapering the body whilst contriving a colour match and mimicking size accurately – only to have it rejected by the trout, and then be told by countless people that a good many of Oliver Kite's fish were deceived by a bare hook nymph! (There is little consolation in the fact that it was not actually a bare hook but incorporated the lifelike charms of a few twists of copper wire.) This demonstrates the often illogical and unfathomable characteristics of the method we call nymph fishing.

It might be wise to give the nymph a lineage. Here many fall into a familiar trap. G.E.M. Skues, as profound and important as he was in pioneering the method

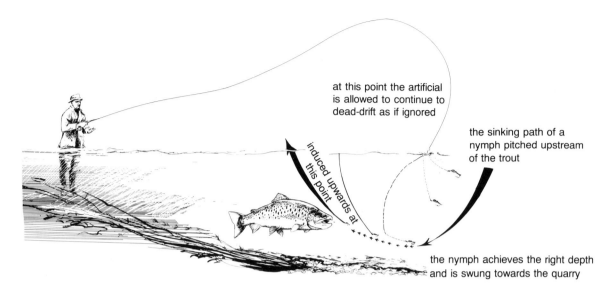

at this point the artificial
is allowed to continue to
dead-drift as if ignored

the sinking path of a
nymph pitched upstream
of the trout

induced upwards at
this point

the nymph achieves the right depth
and is swung towards the quarry

would, I think, be the first to acknowledge the importance of two, perhaps lesser-known but none the less creative nymph anglers, T.E. Pritt and W.C. Stewart, who both fished the wild and turbulent streams of the north and border areas. Although they were nineteenth-century wet fly *aficionados*, they created a variety of spider patterns to mimic hatching and drowned insects. These, in any terms, must be seen as nymphs.

Skues merely adapted these patterns for chalk stream use and, similarly to Pritt and Stewart, operated in the upper half of the river level, concentrating in and around the surface layers. The real revolution came with Sawyer and the weighted nymph. To my knowledge, he was the first man to incorporate a 'ballast' actually in the dressing. Sadly, like Skues, he was castigated for it. After Sawyer came the adaptions, States-side. Charles Brooks, Liesenring, Whitlock and many others, have created permutations on this, arguably our most potent weapon.

To understand a little of nymph fishing, I believe it is equally important to have a working knowledge of the dry fly, if only to recognize the vast differences between the two methods and the resultant variations and amendments so necessary to a successful application and conclusion of both.

Dry fly has one major advantage over wet in that the whole fishing exercise is conducted in the angler's own environment. For instance, if one's fly has been rejected, it is visual, we know what the trout has refused and we can do something about it either by looking at the surface of the water for signs of fly life, or by capturing the insect hatching and looking at it. This in turn allows us, the anglers, to deduce shape, size and colour and to relate to what the trout is seeing. After all, when a fish rises, it is entering momentarily into our dimension, from its own underwater world.

To understand the nymph in this same context, we would have to incorporate scuba gear with our familiar tackle and trappings, or revert to our amphibious past. The trout has the upper hand when feeding on the nymph. As this food item forms three-quarters of the whole river trout diet, the fly fisher has to at least attempt to unravel some of these subsurface mysteries if he is to make the most of a day's fishing.

The Sawyer of Netheravon nymph method, performed upstream, dead-drift, and then an induced take.

144

There is, however, one curious feature. Trout will and do succumb to less than accurate representations of nymphs. The fact becomes even odder when one realizes that this is in the fish's own dimension – water – where they are not only fitted with phenomenal eyesight and reflexes, but are used to feeding on and looking for, almost exclusively, nymphs. So why do sparse parodies of insects such as Sawyer's Pheasant Tail, Grey Goose and Killer Bug (a mere cigar-shaped lump of darning wool) work at all? Here, we must look at major flaws in the trout's design.

Firstly, its inquisitiveness – anything that looks tasty is worth inspection – and, secondly, aggression. A fleeing object in a feeding area provides too good an opportunity to pass up. These two points are the fly fisher's saviour, but they only accommodate certain aspects of nymph fishing.

The fly tying fly fisher must go, figuratively, beneath the water's surface and survey the problems from a trout's point of view. After all, the ubiquitous Sawyer Pheasant Tail was not a spur of the moment whim, but represented hundreds, possibly thousands, of hours of careful and studious study of the things trout eat.

Nymph Tying

Before discussing the various parts of the nymph, I shall chart briefly the kind of nymph patterns that are suited to four basic water types.

Water Type 1

(Fast water, boulders, riffles and stony bottom, no weed)

Pattern shape   Largely flat, muscular looking, short, stocky bodies, leaded if to be fished near the bottom; lightly leaded and curved if to be dead-drifted; unleaded for near the surface.
Colouration   Generally mottled, a predominance of brown shades but also dirty yellows and golden.
Profile and appearance   Hard looking, i.e. heavily ribbed. Dubbing should be spiky and also hard, i.e. seal's fur (sub), hare's ear and musk guard hairs or very tightly wound sparse softer dubbings including guard hairs. Heavy hackling is pheasant window feathers and rump, heavily marked partridge.
Insects to be imitated   March brown (10–14), stonefly (18–16), autumn dun (12–14), olive upright (14–16), etc.

Water Type 2

(Fast acidic water, some weed/moss, rock/pebble bottom)

Pattern shape   Slightly longer and more lithesome than for type 1. Quite hairy, soft-looking bodies, more round in appearance, less flat. Weighting lead (heavy) for near the bottom; leaded and curved for dead-drifted; unleaded for near the surface.
Colouration   Dappled olives ranging from light yellow through to almost black. Some browns, generally red and golden tinged and mottled.
Profile/Appearance   Soft and less armoured, i.e. dubbed mole and rabbit,

occasionally seal's fur and other natural furs such as beaver or fox. Less heavily ribbed, light hackle (i.e. cock, partridge, snipe, woodcock etc.).
Insects to be imitated Blue-winged olive (14–16), yellow evening dun (14–16), turkey brown (12–14) and claret dun (14–16), etc.

Water Type 3

(Medium current chalk/freestone/limestone flowing weeds over pebble base)

Pattern shape Dapper active-looking nymphs, fairly small, built for speed. Predominantly three tails, flowing legs. Pronounced thorax and wing pads. Weighted with copper wire (or lead in thorax only), all should be straight, not curved.
Colouration Mostly olives, appearing in some instances translucent, often dappled, many pale colours.
Profile/Appearance Soft-looking and sinewy, i.e. mole, rabbit and feather fibres are especially good, also natural furs with guard hairs, dyed appropriate shades, and Polyblends (Orvis). Sparse hackling (soft feathers such as partridge and woodcock, kept short).
Insects to be imitated Mostly *Baetidae* – pale watery (16–18), spurwing (18–20), olives (various) (14–20), etc.

Water Type 4

(Slow/silted currents, long straggly weeds)

Pattern Shape Cylindrical, generally unleaded unless depth is required, when copper wire would be used, straight format.
Colouration Pale fawns, yellows, tans, soft greens, (also midge colours, clear through to black).
Profile/Appearance Soft and feathery, often with dark segmentation, i.e. long flued feather fibre – goose (heron sub), ostrich, peacock herl or any delicate dubbing like rabbit under fur.
Insects to be imitated Mayfly (*danica*, *vulgata*), *Caenis*, broadwings, and chironomids, etc.

This has been an enormous oversimplification of an almost infinite area, but does demonstrate that a logical approach will enable the angler to give himself a head start and certainly cut a few corners if samples are not readily obtainable (and who wants to ferret about in a river, turning over stones, in February?).

Colour

In many ways, I am lucky being an artist – my business is colour. Green to me (and I firmly believe to the trout's eye), is not one solid colour, but a fusion of several, giving an overall tone. An olive in an artist's terms (and possibly in the trout's) is a blend of blue (Prussian) and yellow (cadmium) and a little red (vermilion). This will give a certain tone and, by adding a fourth colour or altering the amounts of any of the other three, I can either lighten or darken the colour at will.

In fly-tying terms this is just as feasible. For instance, my blend for a Demoiselle Nymph (yes, I do fish stillwater!) is seal's fur or substitute in the following proportions: 40 per cent light olive, 20 per cent lemon yellow, 10 per cent blue (royal), 10 per cent cream, 10 per cent orange and 10 per cent amber. This gives me a rich light golden olive. It should be taken into account that a colour, when wet, is between two and four times darker than when dry, therefore my demoiselle body will darken to a dark gold olive when fishing. This is very important, for all flies, both natural and imitation, follow the same pattern of change.

Another facet of colour blending, especially when incorporating primary colours (blue, red, yellow) is their ability, when underwater, to echo and throw off refracted light transmission, altering in faithfulness to those found in river life. Every colour in water, no matter how dark or light, conforms to the primary colours and the resultant secondaries (fusion of the primaries). This is an inescapable law and can, if applied sensibly, lead the fly tyer to some very 'killing' nymph patterns. A tip when tying nymph patterns is to drop the completed fly into a tumbler of water and leave it for ten or so seconds. You will then get a good idea of how it will appear when in the river.

'But why bother?' I hear you say 'isn't a pheasant tail a simple brown colour?' Well, no, not really, is my reply. If you wind pheasant tail fibres you will see, on close inspection, a whole gamut of variety. Within the turns will be reddy browns, black flecks, fawn, golden brown, even dark green and blue tinges.

Shape

There are other considerations apart from colour, not least of which are size and shape. The shape of a nymph can tell both trout and angler much, often what species, what family, what type of water, and where in the river it lives. By nymphs, I mean the upwing dayflies of the Ephemeroptera group and stonefly, as opposed to larvae – sedges/caddis, alder, midge, etc.

Hooks

There are, of course, other factors, similarly to dry fly, that will and do affect our representation of nature and the first is hooks, the vital 'iron'. So few anglers give this ultimate fly tying requisite much more than cursory notice; the 'it's sharp, it'll do' syndrome. By and large, especially in nymph fishing, any old thing will not do. Because of the nature of rivers, hooks receive a great deal of punishment, often being bounced on rocks, or tumbled across boulders. Only one hook, to my knowledge, tolerates this hard labour: Partridge. The chemically etched variety are superb for surface film and floating work but are fragile; a hand-tempered point can be repointed, and this is critical.

As to design, I personally vary little from the types previously mentioned, save for the curved nymph. Here I employ the Yorkshire Caddis (K2B) and, for larger nymphs, the Wilson Dry Fly Salmon (01). If only it were made in smaller sizes, it would, I believe, be the ideal nymph hook for both the stonefly and the Ephemeroptera species. Therefore, briefly I use Partridge E1A, K1A, E6A, K2B, and Kamasan B400, B405, B180, for fishing in the surface film, and in mid-water. For the bottom layers I use Partridge K2B and Cptn. Hamilton patterns. Large nymphs and heavily weighted types include K12ST and 01 Tiemco Larval.

FLY TYING

Dubbing

Almost as important as the material, is how it is applied. Obviously with herl it is a simple case of 'touching turns' but with dubbing one can ring the changes. For water types 3 and 4, the normal twisting/rolling method is all that is necessary but 1 and 2 can both benefit from spun/loop methods that will give a marked segmentation to the body. This method is also very useful for thorax areas and one can trap successfully the long guard hairs together with the under fur and produce legs as well as thoraxic bulges. Here I have to recommend one book, Darrell Martin's almost essential fly tying treatise – *Fly Tying Methods*. For the river angler it is a positive bible of procedures and application.

Ribbing

Generally in water types 3 and 4 I would not use ribbing, unless nature made it a recognition factor, such as a mayfly's bands. Here I would use a thread such as Danville Mono Cord in the appropriate shade. In water type 2 water, both silver and gold wire or tinsel can be used to good effect. Water type 1, however, incorporates ribbing as an integral feature and here I would strongly recommend either dyed flat nylon or, in the case of large stonefly and Ephemerid patterns, a new and excellent material: larva lace.

Wings/Wing-Pads/Thorax Covers

These are certainly important features and ones which I almost totally tackle with feather fibre, carefully matched to the colour and shape of the insect, either clipped

Colour is primarily a mix of various colours; showing how an amalgamation can create one overall tone of a different colour (this instance is olive) and how it can be lightened or darkened at will.

148

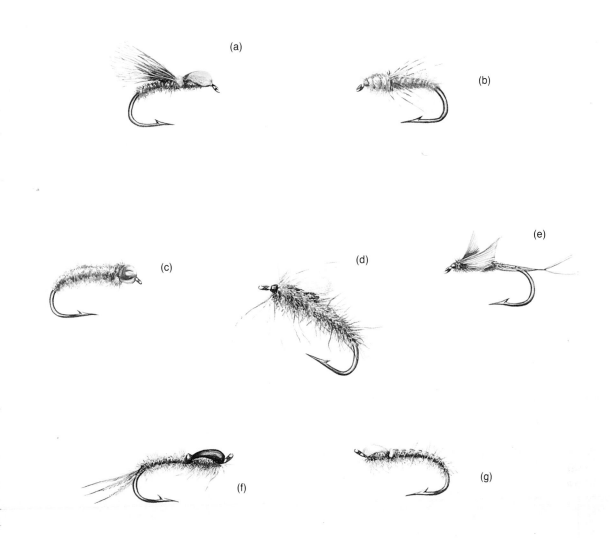

*Fly group. (a) Balloon
Caddis. (b) Sedge
Pupa. (c) Goldhead.
(d) Deer Hair
Emerger. (e) Stillborn.
(f) G.E. Emerger.
(g) E.T. Emerger.*

to shape as is the case of stonefly or pulled over the thorax as in a P.T. With emerging patterns, especially in water types 3 and 4, which may call for minute detail to imitate the immature and emerging wings of the adult fly (dun), I invariably opt for a small pair of quills, mostly mallard but sometimes teal. These are especially valuable in hatching caddis pupae patterns. Another consideration would be Traun River Products' preformed organza wings which would find many a good pattern benefiting from their inclusion, also, where emergers are called for, the thorax dubbing ball.

Hackle/Legs

These really do fall into two distinct categories: with nymphs in water type 3, during an active state, they are largely superfluous, but when emerging, cock hackles can be helpful both at suggesting the illusion of legs and supporting the artificial in the surface film. Only a few fibres each side of the thorax are necessary (usually tied in a figure of eight winding). Thereafter, it is a choice entirely based on personal and natural requirements, for instance, with a stonefly in a static or bottom-fished posture I opt for realism, even knotting fibres (such as oak turkey or pheasant tail) to render this. However, in a tumbling, dislodged, curved pattern I prefer a 'buzz' of hackle, and wind a cock hackle (of appropriate colour) through the thorax, then fold the wing pad over. Most of my patterns fall into these formats.

Weighting

Weighting is, on occasions, critical, not merely to get the fly down through the current to where fish are holding but, if applied appropriately, to accentuate the shape of the insect imitated. I have included illustrations of the types I most frequently use. Illustration (f) simulates stonefly and broad nymphs such as march brown. Lead wire is tied to the side of the hook and also around if a very heavy pattern is needed. Illustrations (b) and (e) cover the rounded nymphs well in fast water, and again call for lead; (d) is copper wire, Sawyer style, for slower currents and also illustrated is the thorax area only using lead if a quick penetration of the surface and a semi-diving motion is required. Finally, illustrations (a) and (c) are of two styles I employ for shrimp patterns. We owe a great deal to the continental pole angler, using the mouse dropping leads and olivettis. The other method is a familiar humped, layered effect with lead wire doubled and redoubled until both desired shape and weight are reached.

Tails

Similarly to thorax and wing pads, tails are an important detail. Once again, if we look closely at Mother Nature's suggestion, materials will offer themselves.

For nymphs in water type 1, I make hard, spiky tails such as goose biot (dyed an appropriate colour); stripped hackle stalks – peccary (wild boar) body bristles are excellent if you can get them – nylon (dyed and round), and mink guard hairs. Insects in this area all have pronounced and well-separated tails and your tyings should reflect this feature.

For water type 2, I again make hard and spiky tails but slightly less so. All the

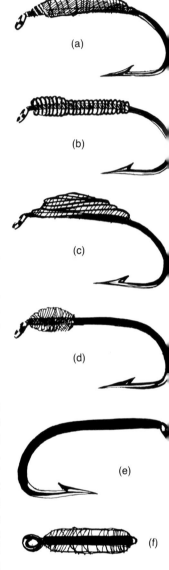

Methods of weighting a fly. (a) Olivetti, pole fisher lead. (b) Conventionally wound lead wire. (c) Lead wire bound on top of hook repeatedly. (d) Copper wire (Sawyer, etc.). (e) Heavy wire hook. (f) Binding lead wire strips to the side of the shank.

above are appropriate but include, especially for the Ephemera, flank feather fibres such as wood duck, hare mask guard hairs and whiskers, and also pheasant tail.

For water type 3, I use feathers, cock hackle fibres, and also tail fibre such as pheasant or goose and flank feather fibres, teal, mallard, wood duck, etc. It is helpful (but not critical) if these are divded into the lifelike divisions of two or three.

Water type 4 calls for a slightly different approach, and softness is a key feature. Marabou (short) is an unfamiliar yet interesting river material in this capacity as is ostrich. Rabbit 'tied in' by the soft under fur, allowing the guard hairs to project, can also be used. Icelandic sheep is another candidate – indeed anything soft and responsive can enhance a nymph in these slow-water areas.

I have earnestly tried to cover a world of infinite permutations. Nymph patterns, even more than dry, are open to any suggestion from the enquiring angler and in its short, but controversial, lifespan I firmly believe fly fishers have only scratched the surface (or bottom). There is still a vast area left to investigate and imitate.

As no single article can really do justice to such a wide subject I have asked Phil White to write about fly patterns as well, in order to get a second opinion. Phil White is one of the most talented river keepers in this country; his expertise has taken him from the Hampshire Avon to Darwell Reservoir, just outside Hastings. He is currently keeper of two of the most beautiful rivers – certainly in this country, if not the world – the Derbyshire Wye and Lathkill on the Haddon Hall estate.

I have always considered Phil to be a traditionalist; indeed, on occasion, I have been fearful of showing him my fly box, yet like so many 'thinking' anglers, he has also questioned theories, and these thoughts are now beginning to surface as very versatile patterns indeed. His words and ideas carry weight, not just because he is a superb fly tyer and fly fisher but also because he sees with the practised eyes of a countryman. These are his words:

TRADITION AND BEYOND

In Derbyshire we are blessed with some very special trout streams, in particular the Dove and the Wye, with their tributaries. My personal experience is limited to the Wye and its tributaries, Lathkill and Bradford. Once the haunt of Walton and Cotton, these Derbyshire limestone streams are arguably the home of dry fly fishing and it is the quality of this dry fly fishing that has maintained their popularity. One of the biggest problems on these waters, particularly the Lathkill, which is gin clear and slow, is that fish have ample opportunity to inspect your flies very closely, and I have found that the more traditional styles of fly are not as successful here as on many other waters. My observations of the behaviour of both natural and artificial flies over the years has resulted in a lot of experimentation, both with traditional patterns and new ones of my own.

Taking the traditional patterns first, I have reached the conclusion that the accepted norm for commercially dressed flies is far too full a dressing for these rivers. However good the dresser, it is impossible for the human hand to fashion an artifical fly to rival the natural, but some thought can allow you to get closer to a natural position, and silhouette, on the water. Just ten minutes observing a hatch

of flies without a rod to distract you, will show that natural upwinged flies do not sit high above the water but virtually on it and that they have only six legs, not a great mass of them. By carefully trimming a 'V' out of the underside of the hackling, you will lower the artificial considerably, into a more natural position, and also make it less likely that individual fibres will pierce the surface film, thus sinking the fly. I prefer this style to the parachute hackle, although parachute flies are often very successful. It must be said that trimming a hackle this way is far from new and is not my idea in any way. Further, by taking the body of the fly through from tail to eye, instead of stopping behind the hackle, and then winding fewer open turns of hackle, a more realistic silhouette is achieved, without loss of floatation qualities.

By adopting these simple variations, proven patterns can be made even more successful and take on the form of many of the better American thorax styles which, together with the 'no hackles' also from America, have become so popular over the last few years. The Gold Ribbed Hares Ear was probably the first 'no hackle' dry fly in regular use but the style never seemed to develop further until rediscovered by the Americans.

The mayfly, smaller stoneflies and black terrestrials play an important part in our fishing here and I have spent a lot of time observing them and how the trout respond. Taking the mayfly first, my observations, both on the local rivers and indeed before I moved here, convinced me of the importance of the hatching fly locked in the surface film as it crawls forth from its shuck. I have been experimenting with a pattern whose origins are in John Goddard's Hatching Mayfly and originally had great success at both Powdermill Reservoir in Sedlescombe, Sussex (where the mays are very dark olive) and Lower Moor Fishery in the Cotswolds (where they are a dark chocolate colour), using appropriately coloured versions. The basic design of the fly has a thick tail and a wound body of feather herl, dubbed fur thorax, open wound hackle and bunch wing, thus suggesting the nymphal shuck with the front of the fly out and the wings drying. This condition actually seldom happens since the fly leaves the shuck quite quickly, before the wings become upright, but the fish certainly approve of the pattern and it is by far the most successful mayfly pattern I have used.

One special point about fishing this and the next pattern is movement of the fly. By wriggling the rod top quickly from side to side it is possible to make the fly shiver slightly on the water without drag. Mastering this technique alone will improve your catches with both mayfly and sedge.

After the first ten days or so of the mayfly hatch, we often experience a difficult time for about a week when fish are hard to take, but when they seem to prefer the spinner, usually around 5.00 p.m. For a number of years, a successful spent pattern seemed to elude us on the Lathkill, until one evening when I was just sitting watching the activity on the river. There had been a good hatch every day and large numbers of females were egg-laying and drifting down spent in the surface film. Fish were rising freely and after some time I realized that they were not taking the spread-winged spinners at all but the half-spent spinners only, those that were still active but trapped in the film by one wing only, the other being still in the vertical position, free of the water. Subsequent observation showed this to be a regular occurrence and I set about matching this stage of the fly's cycle as best I could and the resulting pattern proved very successful in both 1989 and 1990, taking fish regularly when other patterns failed.

Phil White's dry fly patterns.

(a) dark terrestrial

(b) stonefly

(plan view)

(side view)

Moving on to the stonefly, which is prolific on some of our waters, I stumbled on to a successful pattern quite by accident, one which I rather ignored previously. Whilst teaching at my fly-dressing class one winter evening, I demonstrated several flies with sedge-type wings, one of which was the 'Wonderwing' style, dressed flat over the back of the hook. The hackle was trimmed flat top and bottom, and the whole fly was made to lie very low on the water. Having found its way into my box it was forgotten until one evening in early September when nothing was working for one of the guests on the water. I put it on because it was different – no other reason – and it worked. In fact we had been guilty of a most serious fishing crime, fishing in blinkers, looking at the fly box and not the water. There were numerous small stoneflies on the water and in the air but they were ignored by us. Subsequent efforts with this fly at appropriate times have met with an encouraging amount of success. Some two years later I was shown a fly by Chris Lee, which he had dressed after observing small stoneflies egg-laying on a stretch of the upper Dove, and which had proved most successful. This fly was so similar to my own in its overall appearance as to be quite uncanny, particularly as my own pattern was still on the 'secret list'. Whilst not a general pattern by any means, either are well worth a corner in a dry fly fisher's fly box.

The final pattern has evolved from a fly whose name is totally unknown to me but which did great things on the Lathkill in late June 1988 when the guest so out-caught everybody else it was quite embarrassing. He did it with a size 14, peacock body, black- hackled fly with two peacock herl 'legs', one each side. Conditions were hot, bright and breezy with no obvious hatch of fly. From then on I kept a few of this pattern in my box, which were usually successful in these conditions.

One day, when up to my middle in the river, clearing off cut weed, I spent a long time watching the fly life trapped in the surface film as it drifted past me. In addition to the duns, spinners and nymphal shucks, there were huge numbers of small black flies in the surface drift, as well as thousands buzzing back and forth over the water. These varied form obvious black gnats to the small dark flies, similar to houseflies, which frequent the meadows and sheep droppings thereon. Work started on a suitable variation of this peacock-bodied fly that evening. I adopted a black silk body, peacock herl thorax and 'wings' and a dark dun hackle on a size 14 hook. Subsequent experiments during Hawthorn falls early season and on lakes when dark sedge hatches occur have shown this to be a most successful

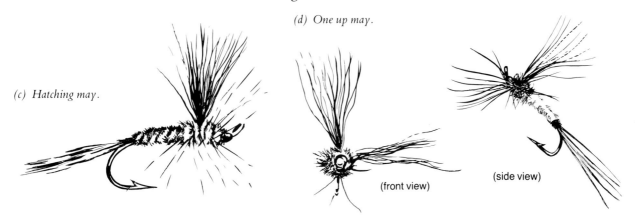

(c) Hatching may.

(d) One up may.

(front view)

(side view)

general pattern in a range of sizes from 12 through to 18, and I am sure even smaller if tried.

Fly Dressings

The dressings of the flies are quite straightforward and require no special skills from the average home tier.

Hatching Mayfly – sprite 10 hook or equivalent

Tail   Golden pheasant or ordinary cock pheasant tail fibres – a good bunch tied long for the shuck.
Body   Butts of tail fibres wound up the hook shank.
Thorax   Pale olive rabbit fur or similar dubbing, behind and in front of wing.
Hackle   Grizzle dyed medium olive, wound in four to five open turns through the thorax, then clipped underneath.
Wing   Olive texas whitetail or mixed olive and natural elk hair.

One-Up Mayfly – sprite mayfly 10 or 12 hook or equivalent

Tail   Dark brown pheasant tail, the colour of plain chocolate.
Body   Two turns of tail butts then white rabbit or similar dubbing.
Thorax   Mixed black and white rabbit dubbing – a rabbit tail gives both.
Hackle   None, but pick out thorax or dub it rough and shaggy.
Wings   Dun elk hair with a few brown or black fibres mixed in. This is bunched in two with one wing vertical and the other horizontal. It is easier if the wings are tied in first of all and the rest of the fly dressed to them.

Stonefly – sprite size 14 or equivalent

Body   Two turns of yellow floss or herl followed by dark olive herl. (Pheasant tail was used originally and is also successful.)
Hackle   Dark hackle – can be olive, dun or nat. black, trimmed absolutely flat on top and bottom. The hackle should be palmered over the front half of the fly but three to four turns is enough.
Wing   Dark hackle tied 'Wonderwing' style, very flat and a little longer than the body.

Dark Terrestrial or D.T. – Sprite 12–18 or equivalent

Body   Black gossamer tying silk.
Thorax   Two peacock herls at least half body length.
Wings   Tips of the two peacock herls left trailing over the tail of the hook.
Hackle   Dun, natural black or grizzle (called the G.T. if grizzle hackle is used). Dressed palmer fashion over the length of the thorax and trimmed top and bottom as for stonefly.

NB   Even smaller patterns can be dressed if the tips of peacock eye fibres are used for the wings and thorax.

154

PART II

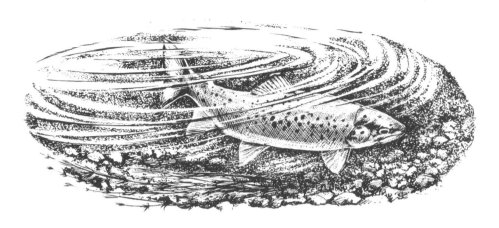

9

The Early Season

This period, encompassing April, May and June, can summon the worst and the best of the British climate, often beginning hostile and bleak, mellowing into soft, gentle and warm and finishing in a flourish of blue skies, vibrant greens and a riot of bankside colour. It can also jostle those elements into any permutation, snow sometimes being encountered in May.

Strangely, though, there is a definite stability to fly life, even if this is not echoed in the weather. Large dark olive hatch regularly in April, the medium olives in May, and the iron blue on dull days during May and June. The mayfly is as regular as clockwork as far as hatches are concerned. The one which varies the most is the hawthorn fly. Therefore, tactics also tend not to vary. Use a nymph if you must, and if allowed, but there is no need; early season is about the emerger and dry fly and so it is these which should usually deceive your trout.

APRIL

Not to be on a chalk stream in April is a sin. Everywhere life is in a turmoil, shaking off the shackles of winter, the whole scene awash with change. It is exciting. However, sadly, very few streams are open for business, most awaiting the plenty of May. The two rivers that I have come to know best have both been fishable in April and, sensibly, open to efforts with a fly rod.

Usually this month is visually more stimulating than piscatorially abundant. So much, of course, is affected by weather. The traditional showery weather and scudding clouds may make an appearance, although these, by and large, appear less prevalent than years ago. Even so, the rain-filled or cool grey days may see the appearance of that doughty lover of the cold, the iron blue, especially towards the end of the month. Those of us who live in the south tend to be held in the icy claw of the north-easterlies, which sweep like Cossacks from the tundra and icy wastes of Siberia. This does very little to help the fly life to prosper. However, over the last few years, we have experienced unseasonally mild periods more reminiscent of balmy late May.

If the weather cannot be trusted during this period, one creature which can be generally relied upon is good old *Baetis rhodani*, the large dark or winter olive. This large upwing has, on more than one occasion, represented the Seventh Cavalry riding to the rescue.

The fly fisher may labour under the misapprehension that trout in April are naïve. Although this is true in some cases, generally, we are fishing for the survivors, those that have endured. These are not fools and, in spite of the frugality of fly life, are not beguiled by any old imitation.

Let me describe an archetypal scene on the River Itchen. The lush valley, which plays host to the sliding river, is always green, but during April nature seems to have gone wild with her palette, the river banks are subtle riots of differing shades of green. Although winter frosts will still be echoed in the dead stalks of meadow-sweet, cow parsley and nettle beds, it is an overall scene of lushness. The river, similarly rejuvenated after winter floods and frost attacks, is responding with little shoots of starwort showing yellowish-green; *Ranunculus*, their ever-present lacy fronds waving unerringly in the current. Enter the trout, hungry, but cautious. The trout's quasi-spawning or the real thing, combined with a lack of foodstuffs (even accepting the chalk stream's constant temperature band, creatures do become more scarce, and wind down during the cooler months) mean that trout in April will be hungry, up and looking and decidedly on the fin. Nowhere more so than the Itchen. However, for all the uncertainty of weather, this river – above Winchester at least – can be relied upon to perform with watch-like precision. I have heard that this happens elsewhere. At between midday and 12.20 p.m., the first few large dark olive duns, with their dark battleship grey wings, swing down the current. This is the 'masque for the overture to come'. With mounting numbers, the hatch reaches a crescendo at 1.30 on a warmish day, and around 2.30 during blustery cooler weather, and will certainly be all over by 3.30 at the latest. There is absolutely no point in staying on the bank a moment longer, unless of course you are given to masochistic tendencies. During the many Aprils I have fished, I have only noted two major hatches of fly, the large dark olive and the medium.

In fishing terms, one could exert terrible damage with weighted nymph patterns. I remember fishing with Neil Patterson. It was the day I was introduced to Red Spot Shrimp, his deadly pattern. The stretch of water was not known to him, and the Fulling Mill/Kingsworthy water was humbled by the shrimp's use. Trout after trout succumbed to its persuasion. Obviously the man who was wielding the rod, line, leader and fly had some influence, for Neil is a brilliant fly fisher. Nevertheless nymph patterns seem particularly deadly during this month, fished dead-drift upstream, no inducement really being necessary. It is probably because of the almost mesmeric attraction that the weighted nymph holds that I never fish them in this way these days. Although I would advise those with less lofty ideals that they could do worse than to carry some Red Spot Shrimp in size 12, G.E. Nymph in 14 and 16 and the odd Pheasant Tail in 14, and (if you must) a Killer Bug. But April should be about the surface and that exciting, fleeting rise.

When fashioning tactics, the weather should be a prime consideration. Consulting the diary that I have studiously kept for fifteen years, reveals that, on balance,

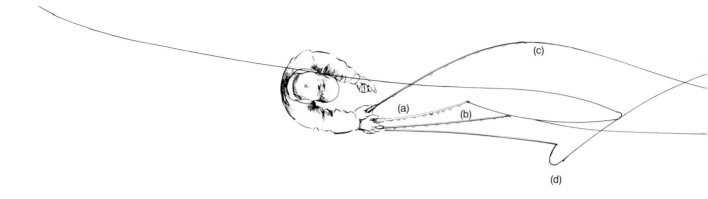

90 per cent of trips to streams in April were met with high winds, often real tree benders. Therefore, I would suggest that size 4 may not be the best line of attack! It is numbers 5 and 6 that are required. I see nothing wrong or unsporting in using an 8½ft rod for a # 6 line. Although it would be considered heavy for most standards, for piercing head winds there can be few better outfits. Delicacy can be manufactured by the fly fisher by aiming above target and allowing for a cushion of air to soften the flight forward. In order to cast into the wind, aim a fraction lower on the forward cast. A # 6 can happily direct a fly as delicately, accurately and directionally straight as any other, just as long as it is handled properly. However, I do keep leaders short, my usual 12ft cutting back to 8–9ft including tippet. I seldom, if ever, use a braided type or at least not the mono-fibre variety as these are often bulky, having a wide surface area, and not sufficient aerodynamic, and so can frequently be taken yards off target by the wind. As with all chalk stream application, the need for accuracy is paramount. Therefore, I opt for the knotted leader I outlined earlier, comprising 4ft of 15–20lb medium-stiff nylon, 2ft of 10lb stiff nylon, 2ft of 8lb medium stiff, 2ft of 4lb and 2ft tippet.

Tippets do not actually have to be that light: the large fly, gusty conditions and often the tolerance of the trout would suggest that 2½–3lb tippets to be fine. Much heavier and the fly pattern does not work through the current properly. Any dry fly or emerger must, if it is to be truly convincing, move with the river fluctuation, limp-free nylon is the only surety you have. This tackle system, a size 6 – an 8½ft rod with # 6 AFTM line and the aforementioned leader – is ideal for nymphing, emerger and dry fly capacities.

Now for what to put on the end. This would be best explained by me taking you on a particular stretch of the Itchen at Kings Worthy. The day starts at the fishing hut, a wooden shed surrounded by wattle fencing and willow withies beginning to sprout green. The vast spreading horse-chestnut on the opposite bank is still a winter filigree, but the shoots promising a summer count. Overhead the sky is a piercing azure with a hint of yellowish green to the horizon line, promising both austerity for a week or more and a chill north-easterly. Pale spring sunshine lights up the water meadows into a carpet of green, swaying in waves with the knife-edged breeze. It is ten o'clock and time for a coffee, with a suitable 'additive' to keep out the cold, and tackle talk.

The downstream dry fly. Although often frowned upon in the difficult lies, it can be the only way of getting a fly to a fish. Timing is paramount when striking or lifting into trout, as are the tactical ploys required to present a cast downstream both delicately and accurately enough to deceive a trout. (a) The initial forward cast is made. (b) The fly is on its way above the target. (c) The rod is held back abruptly creating shock waves along the lines, and then folded to one side, creating an angle to the fly fisher. (d) The rod in fishing position and the leader and fly allowed to follow the natural course.

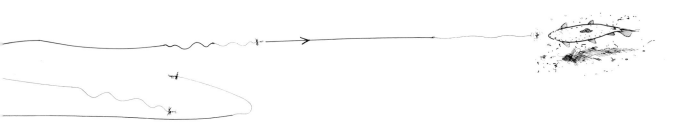

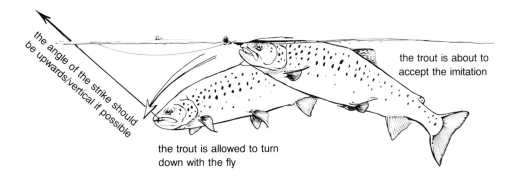

the angle of the strike should be upwards/vertical if possible

the trout is about to accept the imitation

the trout is allowed to turn down with the fly

The take. The angle of the strike should be upwards/vertical if possible.

The # 6 AFTM system having been chosen and the leader fashioned from its various sections, discussion revolves around fly choice. Experience over a number of years has taught me what to expect. I discuss the options, the coffee steam coiling up in light grey wisps in the dark entrance of the fishing hut, and you are surprised at how traditional my choice of fly patterns is: Hares Ears of various styles, Greenwells, and so forth. I say that one should never change a winning combination, unless absolutely necessary. Too often fly patterns are created in spite of their predecessors not because they offer anything innovative or advanced. I also carry very few patterns, and all are large. The size of the large dark olive is big and, as with the medium olive, there is little need to fish 18in or under. Indeed, a size 14 suffices most of the time. If medium olives are in evidence, a 16 may be called for, but this is unlikely, owing to the weather. The time has slipped by to 10.30 a.m. and, with our inner souls buoyed by the coffee concoction, it is time to try the first tentative casts of the new season.

On our way down the springy bank-side margins, pock-marked with vole holes and speckled with winter rainfall. We go to the farthest boundary some mile or so away, because of the nature and character of the river and the bottom make-up, which is silt and gravel with deepish water above, making it unlikely that the nymphs of the species in question will be present in sufficient numbers.

The lower stretch is shallower, faster and given to *Ranunculus* beds, which large dark olive and medium olive nymph love, as well as other *Baetidae* – agile darter nymphs in other words. Naturally, this is where a hatch of any consequence will take place. This is the reason for my nymph nets and notebook, where I record various species in various areas, as the nymphs of various classifications will offer the clues for future adult activity. Also trout enjoy the high oxygenation of fast flows in the early part of the season, feasibly for conditioning reasons.

As we go, I notice the ominous build up of dark-centred cloud coming from the north like billowing masses of cotton wool. The weather, unsettled at the best of times, looks set to do its worst and, with the cloud, I feel a freshness slice across my cheek, indicating a keener edge to the knife-like wind. Appropriately attired, we move downstream, careful to stay back from the immediate bankside so as not to spook trout in resting or prime lies, either tucked under the overhanging sections of bank or mid-stream.

Having detoured through the meadows, we semi-circle around and reach the bottom boundary, a red brick, low-slung bridge with central upright dividing the stream. On all fours, our knees thankfully protected from the sodden bank, our careful approach is made to the bankside sedges. I point out the light sandy shape hovering mid-water level immediately to the front of the pillar and the remnants of last month's cut weed strung in a mat around the area where it enters the river's currents.

Once you look beneath the surface, rather than stopping the polarized enhanced vision at the surface, you can see that the piece of weed moves and looks as though it is feeding – it is a trout. Although relatively stationary, the trout flicks from side to side every now and again and each movement is accompanied by a momentary glimpse of a pinkish-white mouth. This is a nymphing fish.

The time now is 11.30 and the sky has taken on a leaden look; the blue peep-holes are fleeting, uncomfortable and some enveloped by heavy cloud. One might almost question whether there is any insect activity and perhaps our joint sanity in being on such a mission. Still keeping a low profile, resting on one bended knee, I point out the first large grey wing curling, waving and pivoting down the stream. You are surprised at the large size. I emphasize how the large dark olive is quite big, but the dark wings against such a light background can be deceptive, giving an appearance of being longer than they really are.

'Not long now' you suggest, our combined thoughts turning to fly choice. I select a size 14 GRHE. It is tatty, rather dowdy, and looks nothing like the real thing, the ragged appearance to the fly being merely reminiscent of the adult dun hatching in its nymphal form in unkempt confusion. In essence, it is an emerger and should be fished in the film, rather than on top. The clipped head hackle is liberally anointed with gink, so that this aspect of hatching can be achieved. Twelve noon and the first gentle sip caresses the surface about 100yd upstream, but we wait patiently as I know from long experience of this stretch that there will be more.

Close on ten minutes elapses and the entire 300yd stretch has come alive. Every so often an audible 'blip' emanates. It is now that we can start fishing in earnest. White flakes drift soundlessly from the sky and the freshening wind ruffles the water surface into agitated movements. We both realize that casting will be a problem but, by keeping a low profile and shooting line low, reasonable presentations should be created. Although, in order to offset any likelihood of disaster, we select trout rising opposite and in mid-stream rather than chasing far-off

The figure of eight movement for controlling slack line in slow/medium moving river areas. Repeat from (a) to (c). The angler has the option of trapping the line by the forefinger of the rod hand; however, this retrieve needs practice to master, but quite a speed can be achieved with a little effort.

targets at acute upstream angles. This you do with practised ease, making certain that the back cast goes high-bellied from our low position, clearing the barbed-wire fence at our backs.

You place your fly perfectly 2ft above the target, the rise mid-stream. All that can be seen of the fly is the dent in the surface film. Drag-free, it curls and twines in the current and suddenly is lost amidst a hump and a few tiny rings rocking the surface. 'Lift', I urge, and the rod hoops satisfactorily. Right on time the wild brownie protests but is soon subdued and brought to the bank. Previously, we have flattened the barb on the hook and you slide the rod tip down the leader to the fly. A few wiggles and the fly comes loose and off swims the trout, having not even been bothered by its outside world. Fourteen inches, we estimate, about 1¼lb.

The wind, although moderate still, causes the mounting snow to swirl in flurries across the spring background, fading in to grey and obscurity. You deceive several more trout, and then suddenly the fly is refused, ignored continuously, but for no apparent reason. The switch has taken place in that period when, for various reasons, the trout diverts its attention from the surface film to the actual top and so begins to take the dun. Hastily, the now even more battered Hare's Ear is snipped off and on goes a size 14 Greenwell's Glory, arguably the finest large dark olive dun imitation of all time, although I have devised an alternative pattern, the Pieddicke Dark Olive – named after an American who fished with me, and for whom it was tied – which I use on rare occasions. Another pattern worth trying is Neil Patterson's Grizzle Mink and Funnel Duns, if they are tied in the right colours.

The snow is now falling in large flakes, momentarily alighting on the river, then swept away to dissolve. Still the trout rise, still the flies hatch. It is now 1.30. We fish the Greenwell, taking trout throughout the stretch, fishing it exactly the same way, only the surface presentation of high floating varies from the tactics employed with the Hare's Ear. At two o'clock, with our waterproofs dusted with snow and the rise winds down, only one or two trout are bothering with stragglers of the hatch. I suggest that, if we want to continue, a nymph may prove inspired, but the suggestion is overruled in favour of my mention of a dram and a fry up on the camping stove at the fishing hut; bacon winning over nymph, shrimps and trout. By the time sanctuary is reached at the fishing hut, the surrounding countryside is patchworked with snow, the horizon a solid grey wall of obscurity and white flecks; the trees, shadow figures in a quasi-winterscape. The fishing had been fleeting but fast and furious.

If I had forgotten the next occurrence, Dermot Wilson would never have forgiven me. When the idea of this book was first being discussed, I forgot it and Dermot was less than amused: 'What about the Grannom?' he politely suggested. This, our earliest sedge – or caddis, if you prefer – used to be a familiar sight on most chalk streams. If you now know little of it or, indeed, its whereabouts at all, I am not in the least surprised. Abstraction and pollution have decimated its presence on the majority of waters. As a boy, growing up in the 1950s, fly fishing trips to the Avon at Fordingbridge during April were generally greeted with a bewildering number of this sedge, often so dense, that the further bank was obscured from view. Not so these days, although the lower Test still has a few, as does the lower Itchen, I believe. I have not seen them for years on the Avon in numbers worthy of imitation, although doubtless they make an annual appearance

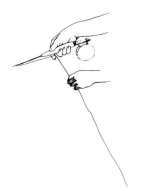

The stripping retrieve for control of line for faster areas and maintaining contact with terminal tackle and fly.

somewhere along its length. If an artificial is called for, then Pat Russell's Grannom (adult) is admirable.

If tradition does exert its influence and provide seasonal high winds and the odd damp day, then, towards the end of the month, a terrestrial becomes important: the hawthorn fly (*Bibio marci*) a close relative of both the heather fly and black gnat. This long, gangly back-legged black fly which adorns bank side blossom, in particular hawthorn and may (not surprisingly), often gets blown on to the water. Hawthorn flies will congregate in very large colonies about various bankside foliage and, being weak flyers, are influenced by wind direction, if not sheltered. Often this results in a good many ending up in the river system, where further problems exist for the unfortunate creatures owing to their long back legs becoming enmeshed in the glutinous surface film, resulting in the insect drowning. Trout greet the occasion with customary ghoulish joy, becoming almost solely preoccupied with this terrestrial.

Although basic upstream dry fly techniques apply, it is absolutely essential to ensure that the fly is fishing *in* the surface and not on it, as a high floating pattern is, at best, treated with suspicion, and at worst, utter rejection. For a pattern to work (and you do not necessarily have to have a totally accurate facsimile), it must be supported in the surface film, either by hackles or a buoyant substance in the thorax, such as Ethafoam. The leader tippet must also be sunk. This fairly short occurrence, lasting sometimes merely a couple of weeks, spans April and introduces May.

MAY

I firmly believe that if God has wanted to create a water expressly for fly fishers, it would certainly look similar to a chalk stream in May; a place of unparalleled loveliness.

Had he wanted to create an angling method, it would surely be the dry fly. Chalk streams and the dry fly are synonymous and have both given rise to many popular misconceptions, for instance, the image of a chalk stream angler in tweeds, sporting a cane rod, a large bank account and somewhat archaic principles. I mention this as I have come across many anglers who feel intimidated by the prospect of fishing the chalk, feeling it is probably beyond their means. However, there are many fine chalk streams which can be fished for the price of a day ticket on any stillwater.

Having tackled that myth, let us tackle another: the upstream dry fly proper – April being a learning process. Although the style is a long-standing tradition governed by a strict turn of the century code of ethics, upstream still remains today the most logical, practical and efficient method of catching fish on the dry fly or nymph.

It is very important to understand how a chalk stream functions, as this does affect fishing. It is both geographically and geologically different from the free-stone type of stream, its flow being dictated by underground reservoirs in the chalk downlands rather than direct rainfall. A chalk stream is rich in alkaline, a fact which not only gives it its crystal clarity, but also its rich weed growth and resultant insect population. Trout, in such an environment, thrive well and grow large on their insect-rich diets.

With regard to trout behaviour, there exists a river pecking order, with each fish finding a suitable lie – an area containing both cover and foodstuffs – which it jealously guards. Even the nomadic rainbow will usually adhere to this code. This fact naturally affects the angler, as he knows that any fish observed feeding in a specific area, will almost certainly remain there, sometimes throughout the season, occasionally for years. Generally speaking, the more difficult the lie in terms of being reached by the fly fisher, the larger the fish tends to be.

Many other factors affect trout behaviour, current certainly being among the more important. To explain this further, the following are various areas where trout are usually to be located:

1.   A hatch or bridge pool containing fast 'white water' current, with the resulting foldbacks of slack water (not so important during May).

2.   A carrier or small stream entering the main river. This is always interesting and often very productive during the early season.

3.   That typical semi-straight area on a chalk stream where great mats of water-weeds (*Ranunculus* and starwort) gyrate in the current and the bottom is studded with a mosaic of pebbles, sand and small rocks. It is here that both trout and fly life enjoy the high oxygen content and that the largest hatches will occur. This area is well worth very careful observation. Even in such clear water, trout are often mistaken for twigs or weed until they fully show themselves, so it is important for the fly fisher to acclimatize himself to 'seeing' to the bottom; a whole new world will open up to the patient onlooker.

4.   Where the water is slow, dark and deep, which is an ideal habitat for *Caenis*, midge (chironomids) and mayfly (*Danica*) later in the season. During May, it might appear lifeless, but it is always worth trying in the evening as that is when the surface film is at its most dense, capturing any hapless returning female fly, a fact that trout is aware of and reacts to accordingly.

Hatches

Of the early-season hatches in late April, the large dark olive will predominate, but with the warmer weather the Lilliputians of the river world will start to hatch, offering the dry fly fisher, day-long hatches and rises. Of these, the more important will be the medium olive (*Baetis vernus* or *tenax*), the spurwings (*Centroptilum penulatum* and *luteolum*) and nature's wild card, the cold-weather loving iron blue dun (*Baetis pumilus*).

Towards the end of May, another serious contender for the trout's attention is the ubiquitous hawthorn fly (*Bibio marci*). One word of warning, especially in area 3; it is not uncommon to encounter two or more species hatching simultaneously. The trout will choose only one. Therefore, careful observation on the part of the fly fisher is essential. Trout, generally speaking, will be fairly evenly distributed throughout the stretch, but always look closely behind, beside and between banks of weed. Both these and the riverside margins offer the necessary criteria of cover and food.

Selective trout are rarely encountered in May, especially in area 3. However, it does pay any fly fisher to look closely at trout rise forms. Some, similar to midge pupae, may be fractionally subsurface, or in the surface film. Both indicate emerging flies rather than hatched adults. In the evening, these rise forms may

(Overleaf) The anatomy of a rise. Stage 1: the trout from its lie sees the insect enter its feeding cone. Stage 2: the trout allows the river current to lift it toward the food form. Stage 3: the trout intercepts the food or fly, opens its mouth on acceptance, aiming to return to the original position. This is called the simple rise form and a strike (lift) should be made as the fish is suspicious, it may continue to a fourth stage. Stage 4: the compound rise. Generally, this happens on fairly slow/medium currents and where catch and release is a firm policy. If the trout continues to Stage 5: the Complex Rise, then you have encountered a trout that has either been hooked and lost before (perhaps repeatedly) or caught on a number of occasions or at least 'knows' of man and his ways with a fly rod. Often, this type of trout will be facing downstream when it finally makes up its mind to take the fly, drifting often some feet in doing so: this type of rise corresponds normally to slow moving currents, though it can occur in medium flow. Delay in the strike is essential.

simple rise

cone of vision

stage 3

stage 2

stage 1

re

compound rise

complex rise

stage 4

stage 5

ervation post

mean an impromptu and unusual fall of spinner (egg-laying/returning female upwings). Never, at this time of year, expect the water upheavals associated with caddis or mayfly rises; all will be subtle pin-pricks of disturbance, even to hatched duns, and so often missed.

This leaves only areas 1 and 2; of these 2 is possibly the best bet, as carriers are a mere extension of area 3 and worth as much attention, particularly where there are any small bridges (it has always amused me that wherever one goes there are always fish beneath them). Area 1 is of little interest during May, coming into its own later in the season when it is an ideal place for caddis hatches.

Therefore, with our stream neatly dissected, let us consider tackle and tactics. Chalk stream trout are wary of every unusual movement, their vision is aided not only by the water's clarity, but by minimal surface disturbance. Therefore, leaders have to be long and fine – 12ft is not too long from a maximum (even in May) of 3lb down to 12oz for the tiny *Baetis* imitations. Of course, these have to be matched to appropriate lines and rods if breakages are to be minimized.

I generally carry two outfits, a 9ft Sage #5 to #6 for the often infuriating breezes that mischievously spring up and, for quieter days and a delicate presentation, a 9ft Sage #3 to #4, which I find to be fast, accurate and delicate in the strike. However, these rods are costly and there are good and cheaper alternatives, but try before you buy! If necessary, put on a matched line and tippet of the lowest strength (i.e. 1lb) and get someone to hold the tippet. Strike into them and you will soon know if it will suffice.

It is useful to carry a quick floatant such as gink, Orvis Hy Flote or Masterline Gell (waiting for Permaflote to dry in a heavy hatch and rise can be mind-bogglingly frustrating). An absorbent agent is also a good idea. Orvis Powder is superb and will render the soggiest fly spritely and fishable again. Fly patterns, apart from local considerations, will revolve around Ephemeroptera, the up-winged day flies.

Now to tactics. Someone once related how simple they thought fishing the upstream dry fly was – I wish it were so. The actual execution of this method, when compared to other forms, such as nymphing or deep-lure fishing and imitative fishing on stillwaters, is comparatively easy, I suppose, as several criteria work in the stream angler's favour: the rise form indicates when and where the fish is feeding and the current and behaviour of the trout suggest it will not move from that particular feeding station. Therefore, all we, as fly fishers have to do, is delicately land our imitation of the natural fractionally above the rise form from a downstream position.

The chances are that we can also deduce accurately which insect the trout is intent upon taking. However, the problems arise in actually getting the dry fly where a trout expects to see it and, therefore, behaving naturally enough to fool the fish into accepting it. Trout, especially on chalk streams, are ever vigilant of imposters and a floating fly dragging (creating a 'V' wake in the current) or a splashy touchdown will alert these instincts. This is where casting and presentation take over from fly choice. Indeed, control of fly line and its delivery are prerequisites in any chalk stream situation. Distance is seldom necessary, but being able to pitch a fly with precise accuracy is, and very often this may have to be done under overhanging bushes or tight into pockets surrounded by reeds. Two suggestions for obtaining accuracy: firstly, a practice session on open ground, using plates (or similar) as targets at various intervals, say 5, 10 and 15yd, and learning to hit them consistently with the 'fly' (preferably a piece of wool without a hook attached, for safety); secondly, seek out a good, qualified casting instructor who, for a few pounds, will show you exactly what you need to know.

The next problem is that of angles between you and the trout. Again this is a casting-and-delivery associated problem, and here the angler would be well advised to look closely at the water flow between rising fish and the casting area on the bank. It may contain two or three, possibly more, speeds of current, necessitating a slack line cast if the imitation fly's path is to match that of a natural's route. Too tight a line here and the fly will skate away from the rise in an alarming manner. Take each trout as a separate entity; it may be that one fish requires you to cast from an opposite position, another from further downstream, so angles are important.

Another consideration may be the trout itself. Watch it, as it may be seeing a natural from a considerable way off and *then* rising (these fish tend to sit lower in the water), or occasionally it may be accepting every second, third or fourth fly coming over its head. Vigilance is the key, followed by a good, accurate and delicately landed fly where the trout expects to see it. Even with a less than accurate pattern, this will deceive far better than a meticulously tied creation that is badly or splashily presented. Striking a fish should be as fast as you can make it, even with a dry fly. There is always present, a cushion of surface film that will momentarily delay reactions. This delay can often result in lost fish.

In addressing the basic principles of dry fly fishing in May, I am also mindful of the need first to locate the quarry. Always, especially on new water, do a little reconnaissance first; this is best done without a fly rod and accoutrements. All one actually needs to do is to work stealthily from the bottom boundary upstream, at a respectful distance from river and trout and, using twigs or broken reed stems, mark down any feeding fish, either rising or nymphing, by placing a twig opposite the feeding position at a spot approximately 10ft from the bankside. This allows for a roundabout return *without the trout spotting you* – that way the upper hand has, momentarily, been won.

10

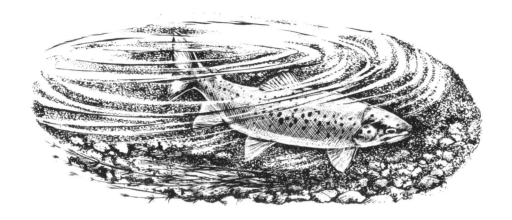

Green Meadows and Gentle Breezes

JUNE: the Month of the Mayfly

One of the most important hatches in the river fly fishers' calendar is that of the mayfly. It is rather a short-lived affair, lasting but a few weeks, but what a productive and glorious one it is. There can be few fly fishers who have not at least heard of this insect, and yet many have never had a chance to encounter their legendary hatches. This could be for a number of reasons, location, perhaps, being the greatest obstacle.

This fly, the largest of the upwinged (Ephermeridae) dayflies found in this country, is a dedicated lover of rich conditions and only areas of limestone or chalk are likely to produce anything like fish-interesting numbers.

Another reason and, regrettably, a reflection on our modern lifestyle, is the combined menace of various forms of pollution, be it abstraction, run-off or any similar potential destroyer of river systems. Yet the mayfly still hatches and it is a tribute to our progressiveness in creating stillwater fisheries that many more anglers now have the opportunity of 'matching' this, our most interesting of hatches.

The mayfly.

The mayfly's life is probably the best documented of any anglers' insect and yet (perhaps thankfully), we still do not know all there is to know even about the two most common of the species – *E. danica* and *E. vulgata*. However, rather than become too waterlogged in entomological minutiae, it is probably sufficient merely to outline their hatching behaviour. This is important for two reasons: firstly, because it typifies this whole group of river flies (the antics of the nymph being the only variable) and the stages at which they interest the trout; secondly, to pin-point various factors that have become apparent to me, which directly affect both the fishing of the artificial and its construction.

168

A typical area for the downstream dry fly.

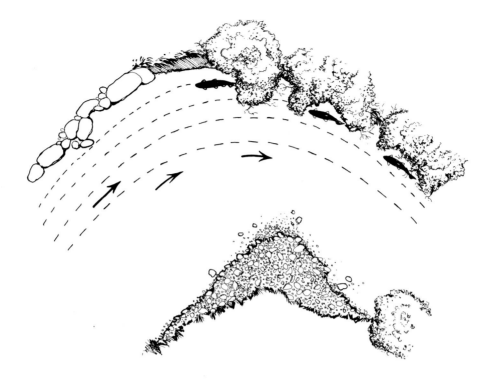

First it might be prudent to give some indication of where, geographically, you might encounter the mayfly. Generally speaking, the most important hatches occur in the southern area: the Rivers Test, Lower Itchen, Avon, Kennet, Lambourne and Frome, all play host to this insect. Also, the River Stour, near my home (in Kent) is, after this fly's absence for many years, slowly re-establishing a good emergence, so perhaps all is not lost. Sadly, it is scarce in northerly areas, but is present, the most significant of the mayfly rivers being the Derwent and Wye in Derbyshire. Locations aside (and by no means is the list above comprehensive), let us now look at the insect, its artificial counterpart and both our own fly fishing reactions and those of the trout.

The mayfly is a curious barometer of spring temperatures. Its often watch-like accuracy can suffer malfunctions especially in cold weather. A stretch of the Test I knew well would always produce mayfly in varying degrees of number on 14 May at 10.30 a.m. and from that point, for two to three weeks, they would grow in intensity. That was a few years ago and, latterly, with colder spring temperatures, their emergence timetable has fluctuated dramatically. On some rivers, 'the June fly' would be a more appropriate title. Therefore, if you hope to fish a hatch, and you are travelling some distance, a telephone call is very advisable.

Another interesting feature concerning the initial first wave of insects is how trout appear almost intimidated by the sheer size of the mayfly. I suppose the sight of something three to four times larger than normal insect proportions looks, not only incongruous, but decidedly dangerous. Trout appear to have to condition themselves to this natural orgy of foodstuffs, and this may take a week or so of constant daily hatches. Even then, for no apparent reason, fish may switch their attention to an entirely different fly form. In many ways this closely parallels

169

human nature, for, given a staple diet, day in and day out, of say fillet steak, I feel certain we would crave for variety and our enthusiasm would wane for steak! So, during even the heaviest hatch of mayfly, watch for those idiosyncrasies. A small black gnat or the ever-present pale wateries and spurwings offer an exciting variation and hors-d'oeuvre, and an imitation of such may well prove the undoing of a seemingly preoccupied mayfly trout.

As with other species of river trout food forms, the different stages of the mayfly's life require different approaches and aspects of imitation:

Stage one sees the nymphs emerging from tunnels sunk in river-bed silt. The duration of their incarceration in such places is a matter of some conjecture; for many years the accepted opinion was that the nymph cycle, when hatched from the egg, took two years until maturity and adult emergence, but, with evidence of an identical but smaller mayfly hatching simultaneously, it appears that some nymphs may miss one year and operate on a yearly cycle. This is important, for if nymph fishing is allowed (very often on mayfly waters it is openly discouraged), a smaller pattern may well prove more successful, as might a dry fly of more diminutive proportions.

The lively mayfly.

Stage two is the nymph's ascent to the surface film to ultimately hatch. It is at this point that the fly becomes serious prey for the trout, as are the similar species of day flies, caddis and other waterborn insects, and should be imitated with upstream nymph tactics.

So to stage three, the ecloding or hatching nymph. This aspect, above all, I find the most fascinating and one of the most rewarding to fish. It is, of course, at this stage that the unfortunate insect is at its most vulnerable, caught between adolescence and adulthood. Its struggles against the surface film undoubtedly fire the trouts' enthusiasm and, given that during a long hatch a proportion of insects will die in the process of emergence, the trout are rewarded with easy pickings of stillborns.

Stage four is the freshly hatched dun or sub imago. This is the penultimate stage of the insect's life, and recognizable by the ivory, mahogany-brown-flecked, body, and yacht-like olive wing, with heavy veining and three brown tails. This provides fly fishers with the first real opportunity of imitation with a dry fly, although, even at stage three, the question is posed as to whether one is imitating the nymph or the adult fly. This is a matter of conjecture and opinion, but certainly I feel that if one was fishing a dry-fly-only water, the emerging fly or stillborn would be tolerated.

However, back to the surface. It is this stage, the hatched adult, which provokes the totally uncharacteristic acrobatics and general idiocy in trout behaviour. You will witness a fish display every conceivable kind of contortion, cartwheel and odd antic, just to capture an airborne fly. Nature presumably tells trout that its efforts will be repaid nutritionally, and it is worth the trouble. However, it must be added that even with flies, both natural and artificial, of up to 1in or so long, rise forms are generally very delicate and not lavish upheavals of water. I believe trout operate on a similar system of feeding as can be found on stillwater with adult caddis or fry and that is the 'stun first – eat later' policy, requiring the angler to delay on the strike, and also with mayfly (as with daddy-long-legs), the size of fly dictates striking at lower speeds.

This leaves only stage five, the egg-laying female or returning spinner or, colloquially, spent gnat. A tragic creature, as death occurs after she has laid all her

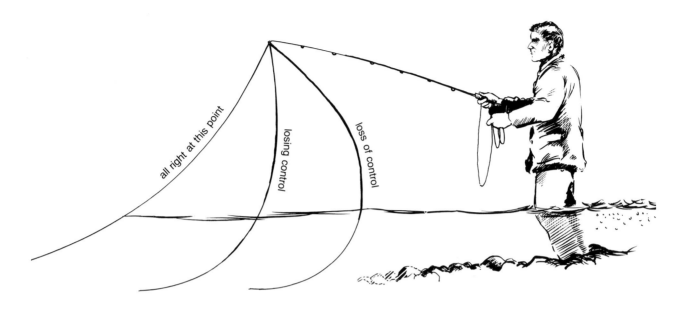

Keeping control of slack line by your feet is essential when dry fly and nymph fishing if a speedy strike is suddenly required.

eggs. Indeed, it is not uncommon during heavy falls of this fly, to see in an evening after, say, a week or two of persistent daily hatches, a veritable carpet of dead or dying flies stretching across the entire river. The trout, in customary fashion, revel in this natural carnage, and fly fishing becomes a question of whether the trout sees your artificial amidst so many naturals.

Traditionally, the spinner imago, or perfect fly, is the most spritely. All spinners, irrespective of species, wear a distinctly brighter coat than the newly hatched dun. In the mayfly's case, this is cream, verging to a white body and almost black-looking wings (due to their heavy veining) and ending with three long tails of very dark brown. Whenever I have witnessed large falls of spent gnat, I have found the late Dick Walker's 'Chinaman' policy of suggesting and emphasizing to be at least halfway successful, if not wholly.

Now to tactics and, although these conform very closely to those used in May, subtle variations do exist. In order to clarify one or two points, I shall deal with these in sequence as with the natural. Stage one is of no great interest with respect to angling, the first real opportunity at imitation existing at stage two, the ascending nymph. I must confess to adopting the late 'Master of the nymph', Oliver Kite's, approach who believed that, at mayfly time, the nymph is not normally necessary and, if it is, 'I give them best' since 'in such circumstances it would be spiritual prostitution'. However, I do realize that if an angler is perhaps fishing on one day only, every opportunity must be made to count, be it good, bad or indifferent. Here a nymph, if allowed, can make the difference. You actually only need one, but in two types: the Richard Walker Mayfly Nymph pattern in both leaded and unweighted, in sizes longshank 8 and 10. You will find none better; when fished upstream to trout visually seen in mid-water, it is deadly.

Trout that are feeding on the nymph can be quite easily recognized by their deft feints and flicks to left and right to intercept passing naturals, or by their tilting in mid-water like a cannon rising to a high trajectory, then gently returning to their original position. Both situations, and indeed other permutations, merely require

171

the upstream approach, the key to it being accuracy and drifting the nymph at the same level as the feeding trout. At any odd movement of the leader, the fly line on the surface or the fish – strike!

Moving higher in the water, stage three holds all manner of exciting possibilities, and fishing the stillborn has given me some of my best days during the mayfly hatch. In actual execution, it is really dry-fly fishing, but a partially sunk fly. Indeed, any fish actively feeding in, on or near the surface can be covered by this method. Again, fish upstream to fish seen, and watch for any underwater movement or subsurface whirl, as both mean that the artificial has been accepted.

Stage four, the dry fly at the dun stage, is perhaps the most visually exciting of all. Methods will vary little from those of May, except that you will require – whether fishing wet or dry – stronger tippets of say 5 or 6lb in order to turn over the bulky fly patterns. Therefore, stronger leaders are also advisable because of the very real chance of encountering the river heavyweights. Mayfly time has a happy knack of goading the larger trout to feed at the surface, which is perhaps the only time in the whole season that they will do so. Even salmon (in water where they run) have been known to succumb to the charms of the 'may'. Therefore, couple your stouter leaders with a size 6 rod, reel, and line system, rather than the lighter 4 or 5. Other than that, both tackle and tactics need vary little.

Fly choice for the dun stage could run into volumes. It is an area where, quite honestly, imagination can run wild. I have, over the years, cropped my amount of dun patterns to two perennials on which I lavish the utmost faith, they are Peter Deane's Shadow Mayfly and my own Lively Mayfly. One tip: do anoint your dry flies heavily in Permaflote prior to fishing.

Finally, stage five, and here the angler is largely placed in the lap of the gods, as success depends, especially in a heavy fall of spinner, on whether the trout even sees your artificial. If he does, the chances are he will take it, not as ferociously or splashily perhaps as the dun, but serenely, as with the smaller flies. A word on patterns: at this point of imitation, whatever you do, make certain that the artificial spinner floats flush and in the surface film and not *on* it.

Strangely, even after the last spinner has gone for another year, mayfly patterns can be successful, a form of conditioning in reverse. Therefore, even two weeks after the last hatch of the season, the odd flick with a dun pattern might prove worth while. The mayfly evokes curious feelings in me and I think all fly fishers owe it to themselves to fish this most spectacular of river hatches at least once. They may find it easy, difficult, impossible, frustrating, euphoric, perhaps even sad, but never dull.

But beware of two endemic problems: firstly, the 'masked hatch' – trout feeding on a totally different type of insect, more often smaller, such as a small spurwing or black gnat, which requires lighter tippets and close observation – and, secondly, 'sequence feeding' to mayfly, dun or spinners whereby a trout feeds on every other insect, allowing a number to pass overhead. Other types of fly, especially blue-winged olive, also evoke this feeding pattern in trout. The angler, in order to stand any chance at all, must make certain that the artificial conforms to the specific order and floats toward or over the trout at the right time, in the right place. Both instances require acute observation, but, then again, that is the byword of chalkstream anglers.

172

11

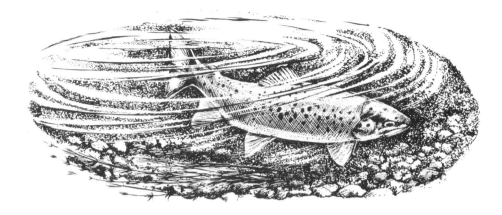

The Mid-Season and
The Impossible Trout

This period, covering July and August, presents the most difficult challenge to the fly fisher. These are months of interest, intrigue and tactical awareness, when subtle changes to approach, tackle and fly choice can lead to the downfall of ultra-shy, selective trout. It is a time of long summer days, warm breezes, heatwaves, and desperation and sullen nights; periods when sleeping anglers are missing the magic and mist-laden coolness of dawn and the feeding browns. A time, too, of often tiny flies, low-diameter leaders and the need for confidence in one's judgement and accuracy of presentation, calling for every vestige of the angler's skill.

JULY

There has, for many years, been a long established belief that trout in rivers are 'civilized', not necessarily in their general demeanour (they can be as uncouth as any stillwater fish when hooked or aggrieved) but in the hours which they keep. Traditionally, fly fishers have confined their efforts on streams from latish morning to that most evocative of all periods, the evening, but are they perhaps missing some of the best fishing midsummer has to offer on trout rivers?

   Surprisingly little, it seems, has been written on the distinctly uncivilized hours of darkness and, indeed, dawn (except about nocturnal sea trout) and yet exciting possibilities await the insomniac angler in the hatches and trout reaction he may find. Therefore, I would like to move away from the specifics of previous months and explore these twilight possibilities, and perhaps offer some alternative minor tactics for the traditionally oppressive weather systems and shimmering 'dog days' that July very often produces.

'Whoops!' The perfect cast foiled by an alder.

It is, I believe, fairly true to say that during such breathless and searing, heat-filled days, the river angler is offered distinct advantages over his stillwater counterpart and, although the rivers of early season may have shrunk, exposing their skeletal foundations, and are perhaps now trickling where, earlier, white waters rampaged, there is always somewhere an area of tree-shrouded coolness and depth, as well as oxygenated pools and shallows, offering both food and seclusion for trout, and thus possibilities for the angler.

Another critical element is water temperature. Even during some of the hottest summers, rivers often flow with cool water (be they spring-fed or rain-fed), seldom suffering the escalating tepidity of lakes. All this is good news for the fly fisher.

The one common denominator between still and moving water is the brightness of light and its angle to the water. Far greater proportions of water are subject to intense light over long periods. This is not such good news. Trout will be at their shyest and most wary during such harshly lit periods, resulting in some exceedingly demanding fishing. Therefore, it logically pays to confine efforts to either areas of shade or times of less intensive light. This is traditionally evening, but what about dawn? The late maestro of river keepers, Frank Sawyer, saw the advantages of this period on chalk streams and these I will discuss later – but, firstly, tackle.

Perhaps for the first time during a season on rivers, one really does have to pay

(Overleaf) Wild brown trout.

attention to lightness of tackle. Having enjoyed the cavalier attitudes of the past three months, both of the trout and of our own vague insect imitation, it is now necessary that more specialized approaches are adopted and, although I would still recommend a long rod (of between 8 and 9ft), AFTM line sizes need to be low. If you have unlimited funds, I recommend investing in either a Sage or Orvis 2, 3 or 4 weight rod. If not, look to lengthening your leader, should situations allow, to a minimum of 12ft, better still, 14 or 16ft, making certain that tippets do not exceed 3lb or, more realistically, 2 or even 1.1–1.4lb.

This brings us a full circle to rods. Light, softish-action rods are essential when using such light leader strengths, although one may minimize breakages by using 'high power gum' or a braided leader, which both nullify shocks to the tackle system. Better still is a suitable rod with the ability to present another essential criterion – delicacy – even when nymph fishing.

Let us move on to daybreak and the 'angler's curse' hatch – *Caenis*. Just why this should be so described, I have always wondered, as it can be among the most productive of any emergence on both still and running water during the whole season. Arguably, the main requirement for success is a change of mental attitudes on behalf of the angler. In fact, I would go further and say that in a majority of cases, fly fishers in this country have a straight mental block to any fly patterns tied below size 18. *Caenis*, like many other Ephemeroptera species, necessitate a hook size of between 20 and 26 if their size is to be imitated accurately. Indeed, other food forms that are equally important to river and lake trout encompass sizes as low as 28 and, given modern tackle technology, these tiny flies can only be fished with confidence if a slight readjustment of fly fishing values, or prejudice, are made. Landing a 3lb brown on 8x and a 28, can be – shall we say – exciting?

Dawn, above all other periods, offers these opportunities. I have witnessed some colossal hatches of *Caenis* as the mists roll off the river in approaching daylight. It is also a period of fairly intense activity for the remnants of spinners, enmeshed in various obstacles from the previous evening. Often the first sight or

Trout feeding on spinner or duns at dawn, taking advantage of a little back eddy which traps spinners like bees in a honey pot. The arrow shows the water movement's variation: the reverse current circulating the trapped spinners, whilst the main slipstream current on the outer edge brings down a trickle of duns. Difficult to fish, although a slack line cast will give a few vital extra inches of drifting time.

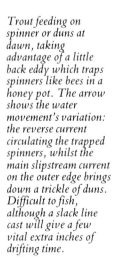

sound to greet the early-rising angler is a trout nebbing through these fallen harvests of insects with greedy, but casual gulping sounds, usually in slack water behind rocks, fallen brush or trees, the back eddies in pools, or slack water at bridges or similar obstructions.

Throughout this low-light period, the careful observer might notice some peculiar and uncharacteristic mannerisms in the trout, which suit the nymph fisher admirably. Trout generally fin in the water in the higher layers, perhaps not rising as such, but seldom so deep that they are unnoticeable. All are prey to the deadly upstream Sawyer Nymph method: a lightly leaded imitation is cast ahead of a moving trout, allowing for current variation to drift the artificial back towards the angler, until the fly is judged to be in the range of the fish, and then the rod is agitated, thus imparting a certain movement and attraction to the fly.

This can be done at very much closer quarters than during the midday period. Of course, care is required in the stalk, and a low profile is an essential ingredient, but trout do appear very much more tolerant of outside intrusions at this time of day. Just why, I do not know. Possibly it is because of the weakness of the light transmission from the sky. Given that a trout's eye is very similar to our own, it may just take time to re-adjust after a lengthy period of operating in near darkness and seeing only rod vision, which determines everything only in outline, not in colour. Whereas, during the day, the cone vision takes over, and so they can decipher colour. Whatever the reason, it merely emphasizes that dawn is possibly the most underrated time on rivers and, during periods such as high summer, should not be disregarded even at the expense of a warm bed and a little sleep.

With regard to the various insects one might encounter on chalk streams during this period, you should carry imitations for blue-winged olive, small spurwing (pale watery), *Caenis* and medium olive. One fly that ought to make a large impact this month is the caddis or sedge. However, although an essential part of mid-season stillwater fishing, it is, from my own observation, far less important on rivers. Certainly the opportunity exists for both searching the water with a dry representation and casting a dry fly to fish heard and not seen in semi-darkness but, as regards using the adult fly in its own right, I feel the opportunities are rare. This may be due to the timing of various hatches, that the point when a caddis might be deemed suitable for imitating coincides with a 'compound hatch', i.e. a variety of species all hatching at once. Experience has led me to question the caddis and rely on the upwing in such circumstances.

An adult caddis.

Having said that, in broken water or under trees and ridges, an Elk Hair Caddis, or a Tent Wing, can be exactly the right medicine and mark a slight departure in tactical terms. Normally, when discussing dry-fly tactics, the upstream method is immediately adopted, a dragging fly being the anglers' bitter enemy and a potential fish frightener. However, trout appear to like dragging caddis, indeed the more 'wake', the better it is. A word of warning: this minor tactic only seems to work during late evening or in very shadowed areas and not usually during either dawn or midday in open water. In such circumstances, a static float is far more desirable.

July also offers the first real opportunity for another form of fly fishing on rivers – which reaches its zenith in August – buzzers and terrestrials. My last word on July is to reiterate that old axiom, 'The early bird catches the . . . trout', but in doing so tread lightly, wear very sombre clothing and fish as fine and small as you dare.

AUGUST

If one stops to analyse river trout fishing, very little has actually changed throughout the centuries. Our knowledge of aquatic life has improved enormously, as indeed have our tactics and the tackle now employed to deceive trout, yet we still conform to an almost myopic viewpoint about which fly patterns are most appropriate for our re-creation of nature. Running parallel to this is the stillwater angler – a comparative newcomer in the fly fishing traditions – who has not been hide bound by former prejudices; his tactics, flies and theories know no barriers.

The river angler, be he a fly fisher on chalk, limestone, freestone or rain-fed water, tends to concentrate on the familiar: the upwinged species, caddis and stonefly, and their various stages of development.

Little, in this country, has been documented on their lesser streamside brethren, (but none the less important alternative food forms), apart from the odd shrimp or beetle, and yet, festooning every bank, tree, bush or silt build-up is a whole new vista of potential trout food forms and legitimate fly patterns – terrestrials. Perhaps the only author in recent times to see the significance of these less familiar insects has been Taff Price.

I would like to explore at least one or two possibilities that may prove successful during those often breathless, humid weeks of August, when traditionally angling on most waters is at a low ebb, especially on those rivers relying on rainfall which conceivably, given a normal summer, will have shrunk to boulder-edged trickles and rivulets, interspersed with dark, tree-shrouded, seemingly lack-lustre pools.

Amid these distinctly unfavourable conditions, the fly fisher must toil and make the most of what can best be described as a bad lot. However, help will be at hand as, wherever there is a tree or bush or, indeed, tall grasses by the bankside, you will find a natural larder: grasshoppers, spiders, moths, lacewings, ladybirds and many more. Of course, the ubiquitous ant will also be present to some degree. How often have we cursed our fly fishing deficiencies in not having an imitation to hand when these brown, red and black creatures induce a rise of seemingly limitless and ferocious magnitude? I always carry ant patterns!

Given the sheer diversity of terrestrials, it will make things simpler if I pin-point certain significant individual insects of importance and their imitations and tactical uses. For this purpose, it is necessary to mentally dissect a river into manageable proportions.

The first is areas margined by trees and bushes. Such conditions will always harbour trout, not by accident, but by design, and generally they will be the bigger fish of the river system. Trees have roots, and roots provide protection. They may also make fly fishing a challenge. There are, happily, one or two criteria which work in favour of the angler, the main one being the eagerness of fish to rise, even on the warmest day, due to the coolness afforded by the canopy of leaves. The other is an almost constant conveyor belt of foodstuffs and an eagerly awaiting trout's mouth.

Over the years, I have experimented a great deal with patterns for these circumstances, varying from latex painstaking accuracy, to absurd fly-tying liberties, and it appears that trout, in such circumstances, are simply not that fussy, possibly due to the variety of insects that the fish encounter. Therefore, patterns can be catholic, but buoyant, such as Deer Hair Beetles, Woolly Worms (in various sizes) and Bushy Palmers. These are traditional and effective. What *is* important is presentation, and here the angler may be at a slight disadvantage because, generally, such tree-fringed areas appear as an impenetrable jungle with few options to get a fly even tolerably close to the water, let alone near the trout. One method, if the tree allows it, is to actually (and very carefully), climb on to or into the tree and merely poke the rod through the branches and, on a very short leader, dap the fly over the water. However, catching trout this way can lead to a certain amount of amusement should there be any onlookers.

Another option, and perhaps the sensible choice, is to cast if possible from the opposite bank. This should again be done with stealth, with the fly fished upstream to the fish or from opposite the designated area. It may well require a 'flat' cast, i.e. a cast made parallel to the bank and water so as to get under any overhang. A good policy is to practise such casts at home. If possible, slightly open an up-and-over garage door and aim your cast into the aperture. Alternatively, place a box at about 12–15yd and, casting parallel to the ground, aim the fly into the box. Garage doors and boxes are far more forgiving on a fly box than an alder or oak branch.

The third and final option open to anglers covering this area is wading, which is probably the most practical. The methods described in April will serve you well, but nature may have contrived certain barriers. Despite my usual advocacy of long rods, on this one occasion I strongly recommend 6 or 7ft wands, rather than a 9ft rod. Nevertheless, the long rod can be employed.

Generally, tree-lined areas will not allow for a complete overhead cast due to overhang. Should you be stranded in such an area with a 9ft or longer rod, you can, as I explained earlier, merely separate the sections, put the butt end in the left wader top, strip sufficient line off the reel and use the 4½ft tip section for casting. The fun really begins when you hook the trout! I once tried to reconnect the two sections while playing the trout, a gymnastic feat which was not very successful. I now opt for 'playing out' fish with the top section only. Incidentally, wading should be generally conducted downstream of the trout but it may on rare occasions, be impossible to do so. In this instance, it can pay to very stealthily, using cover if possible, get upstream and float on imitation down to the fish on a slack line, the one big drawback being the poor hooking qualities of this presentation. However, it may be the only option, so take it if allowed. One final word about this style of fishing: do, I implore you, wear sober clothing, such as greens, browns and fawns.

I have said very little about patterns or indeed insects because no angler, no matter how exhaustive his fly box, can hope to carry all the patterns necessary. General representation, in this instance, is to be favoured over calculated accuracy. However, apart from the ant, two patterns are well worth carrying. Generally, there will be some areas which will be fringed with bankside grasses to a larger or lesser extent and, during August, these may well be the habitat of both grasshoppers and cranefly. Trout enjoy both! It has always surprised me that more river anglers do not carry these patterns as they can be absolutely deadly on their day.

Fishing either pattern can be a straightforward river tactic of upstream to a rising fish or likely holding spot, and both benefit from the odd twitch and animation when dead-drifting through the fishing areas. However, there is one tactic that I learnt when fishing the Letort in Pennsylvania, where 'hoppers' are treated as one of the important hatches, but this is, perhaps, not for purists.

Side strain (playing trout). The best way to turn a trout from an obstacle is to 'fold' the rod to either side of the body on a flat plain and apply constant pressure.

Choose a grassy bank and walk through it, brushing grass as you go in order to force insects out of their sanctuaries and into the water. Then retire for half an hour or so, letting the necessary commotion die down. Then return with a suitable imitation of the most frequently observed insect, hopper or daddy, this time using all available cover. On hands and knees (usually), very carefully lower the fly into either a rising fish's area or any undercut in the bank. One can also 'trot' the insect downstream. The important thing is not to cast, merely dap or offer slack line. It may seem a slightly odd way of fly fishing, but I assure you it can be very successful. Striking, by the way, should be conducted by hearing rather than obscured vision. This can also heighten the excitement. One can also afford, because of the imitation's size, to be a trifle slower than normal.

August, as you may have surmised, is an odd month, even wind can be an ally rather than an adversary, as it bears with it all manner of potential trout foodstuffs. Of these innumerable edible delicacies, perhaps the most important are the jassids (brown or black), soldier beetles and, although a little later, the famous coch-y-bondhu. Once again, it would be sensible to opt for generalization, as trout in such circumstances are seldom fastidious, and fall to good and sound tactics rather than minute imitation.

The various methods discussed have, by and large, revolved around the hours

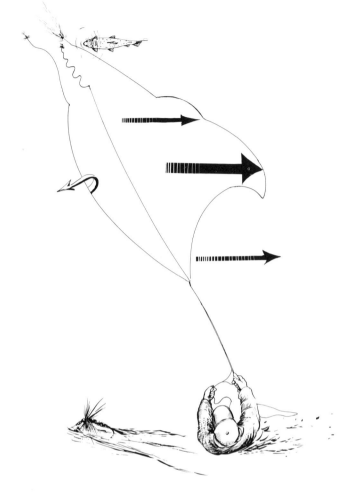

The effects of current on dry fly presentation.

of daylight; the evening may well see a more usual pattern, with hatches of caddis and upwing. However, as the sun slips behind the horizon and the streams fill with that purple oiliness of nightfall, it is the time when a moth pattern can be tried, especially the aptly named Ghost Swift. Like the ant, it is a pattern I would never be without.

I mentioned earlier areas of siltation. No water is without its population of the stillwater angler's friend, the midge (chironomid), which is not a terrestrial, but is nevertheless an important alternative hatch.

12

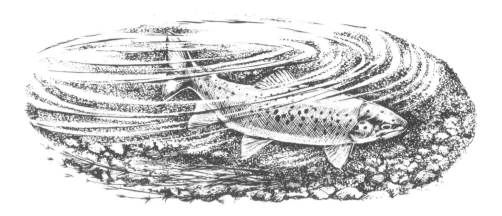

The Late Season of Mists and Sunsets

With cooling autumnal influence and the close proximity and harsh realities of approaching winter, the river once more becomes vibrant. There is an urgency about the insects and, equally, trout are alert, on the fin, and fuelling their bodies for leaner times and for spawning energy. September and October hatches can be exciting and surprising: the blue-winged olive will be in evidence, as will the *Baetis*. The trout are the survivors of a season, winners of countless battles, and practised in the ways of the fly fisher pursuing them. Fine leaders, careful imitation and approaches are the only guide-lines I can give, even these are often greeted by the heart-sinking underwater 'V' wake, as a fugitive trout bolts for cover. It is a time when the larger trout make their presence known. A sad time of golden days, red sunsets and oily river reflections.

SEPTEMBER

'Variety is the spice of life' is a highly appropriate saying for the river fly fisher during September. Throughout this month, rivers offer limitless permutations of style, tactics and fly choice, and provide a cornucopia of piscine delights. It matters little whether you fish freestone, rain-fed, chalk or limestone – all provide a wondrous array of hatches.

The water itself, after fluctuating temperatures throughout the season, will usually have levelled off, providing an ideal habitat in which nymphs and crustaceans can proliferate. More importantly, the light strength and angle of the sun will be indicating that the leaner times of winter are just around the corner, and nature, with instinctive urgency, will be encouraging these tiny forms to take to the air and propagate before time runs out.

Trout, with their uncanny instinct, will be on red alert. They too will be sensing the increased activity along with the climatic shifts, promoting feeding sprees reminiscent of May and early June. Be warned, though, they will not be the naive early-season fish, but the survivors, the trout that have seen it all.

It was in Colorado, USA, during a September some years ago, that I took my first tentative wadered steps into the internationally acclaimed Frying Pan River. It was a stream of infinite variations in a landscape of uncompromising grandeur, not dissimilar to examples found in more hilly and mountainous areas in this country. However, thereafter the parallels dissolved; the wake of fly hatches there would put any of our chalk stream to shame. Everywhere along its course was the flutter of tiny insect wings. At any one time, there were at least five different species of upwings (Ephemeroptera) at least three caddis types and two stonefly (Plecoptera). During a heavy hatch, the bankside vicinity was a blizzard of gauze-like, delicate creatures. The trout, needless to say, rose with apparently suicidal gusto. How could a fly fisher fail? After many fruitless casts, it appeared that one could fail. It soon became obvious that these trout (and subsequent observation in this country bears this out) would only feed on one particular species and at one particular stage only, under such heavy-hatch circumstances. This leads to some extremely demanding fly fishing. The following instance makes a perfect example.

Running parallel to a wide boulder-flanked pool, formed by the main river careering through rock-strewn rapids, ran a small stickle isolated from the main flow by a 'pebble dash' island. This flowed back into the pool at right angles, leaving a corridor of choppy water across the flanking slack water for about 20yd. Along this length fed some fifteen or so rainbows, so condensed that, in their eagerness to grab the constant conveyor belt of fly life, they writhed over one another, bumping noses. Their separate rise forms seemed to fuse into one undulating feeding mass.

It seems impossible, but for two hours I threw every conceivable type, style and variety of fly at the continuous chain of fins, tails and gulping mouths, from 16s to 28s, tippets up to 12oz! Nothing – I gave up. On turning my back on those uncatchable fish and musing on a Shakespearian tragedy in the making, I spotted a few of the *Baetis bicaudatus* (the American small blue-winged olive) at my feet. Some were wingless, some half in and half out of the nymphal shuck, some just plain dead on arrival. So large were the hatches, that the law of averages had thrown up non-survivors. 'Surely not', I thought 'The trout couldn't be . . .', but indeed they were. After wincing, as a wing was unceremoniously ripped from a painstakingly tied spent wing spinner pattern, giving a passable match of this hitherto hidden hatch, I actually deceived one of those trout.

I cannot report unqualified success, for only two more graced my tattered fly, but it did work, and taught me many valuable lessons. It gave me an understanding of both masked hatches, i.e. when the obvious fly is not even being taken and a smaller or different stage is being accepted, and compound hatches, i.e. when more than one species of fly is hatching at any one time, with only one variety being greeted with any acceptance at all.

I also learnt never to accept the obvious or trust first impressions, and always to look before you leap and, lastly, that persistence pays its own rewards! I might have written the whole episode off as a rarity in a foreign land if it were not for similar experiences I have had since in this country, and almost all have fallen in the same period, September.

mayfly

yellow may dun

large black olive

large spurwing

blue-winged olive

olive upright

medium olive

iron-blue dun

pale watery

small spurwing

broadwing

small dark olive

The upstream nymph. A simple dead-drift tactic is being used, requiring a leader slightly over depth which is cast, together with the chosen pattern, sufficiently ahead of the trout to allow the fly time to sink to the desired depth.

To return to British chalk streams in September, the day, as a whole, will be more or less predictable, given the longevity of the feeding period. The dawn may be hit or miss, but certainly from 10 a.m. onwards, the Lilliputian flies of the river scene will start to emerge: the spurwings, pale wateries and medium olives, indeed the whole *Baetid* tribe may be present, either singularly or hatching together.

Logically, it would appear that a dry fly would be the right tonic, but not necessarily. A tiny G.E. Nymph in 18 or 20, fished exactly as one would the dry, is often more successful. Why this should be the case, I can only wonder, but certainly autopsies and stomach pumpings have revealed equal quantities of nymph and adult naturals. This suggests that the rise forms of trout to these early morning flies, be they nymph or dun, are similar, possibly owing to the thin air of morning, as opposed to the heavy evening pressure, flies are galvanized into a faster ecloding/hatching rate. The trout, seeing little point in pursuing just the nymph, opt for the best of both worlds. However, do not ignore the dry fly and, once again, far, fine and small should be your bywords where tackle, tactics and fly choice are concerned.

This morning cavalcade of hatches will probably run through until midday or possibly threeish, leaving the afternoon for a siesta or a bit of experimentation. The one thing I would urge is that you save yourself for the evening period, as it will tax every sense you have and no angler – no matter how adept – fishes well with sore eyes, aching arms and a tired brain. Always remember, a less than accurate fly pattern, delicately presented and thoughtfully fished, will outfish every time a painstakingly accurate facsimile of nature, hastily or clumsily cast.

The afternoons are dominated by midges, which are present in enormous numbers. Trout, especially during very hot days and afternoon periods, can become entirely preoccupied with them in their pupae form. For some ten years, my nymph box has always carried a selection of 12s to 24s in brown, olive, golden olive, black, claret and emerald green, and also a few polythene ties to represent the phantom pupae. The style of dressing seems to matter very little, but certainly the most successful have been Bob Carnill's unique and superbly designed poly-rib 'close-copy' pattern and Gordon Fraser's version, which is a mere whisper of a thing. Both varieties are deadly when fished to trout observed displaying the tell-tale movements. Generally, these will be different to ordinary nymphers,

(Opposite) Common chalkstream/limestone upwinged duns.

185

Wading the river, and stretching for a good fish.

when the trout remain on station either tilting up or down, darting forwards or feinting sideways to intercept unsuspicious nymphs. Fish that are midging on rivers seem to throw all caution to the wind and do the most bizarre things, often travelling 2yd or more, gulping as they go, then abruptly falling back, swinging decisively from side to side, taking in pupae as they go. Indeed, there is no end to the permutations that trout will adopt. Therefore, if a feeding fish is doing very odd things under the water, try a pupa.

This brings me on to the *pièce de résistance*, the celebrated evening rise. To miss this during September would be to ignore the cream filling of the cake. One insect on chalk streams will predominate, the sublime blue-winged olive. It is, of course, encountered during many other months, but I always think of it and September as synonymous. It appears that most people have mixed emotions about both the insect and time of day; Skues, that late doyen of the Itchen, was rumoured to have had infinite problems with fly fishing at this period, and often declined invitations for the evening.

One of the problems may be that, traditionally, we think of evening as a time for the spinners, the egg-laying females, and so often miss the obvious – a hatch of duns. Trout will change, and do so extraordinarily quickly, the enmeshed, flattened spinner pattern being unceremoniously ignored in favour of the spritely upwing variety. Another consideration will be light. Sunsets infuse both river and insect forms with a golden reddish glow, making red a key colour for the trout's attention. Another factor, and one I was made painfully aware of recently, when fishing on the River Stour, is how, even in near darkness, size is of vital importance. At 9.30 p.m., with light fading, a flurry of blue-winged olive started to hatch. I had been imitating a fall of small spurwing spinner (*Centroptilium luteolium*) and using a 22. Rise after rise, I cast to – nothing – it was not until I changed to a 16 Adams that I was once again 'in the fish'.

There is throughout September as a whole, one key factor and route to success: observation – look before you cast.

OCTOBER

If there is one period that makes my fly fishing pulse beat just that little bit faster, then it has to be the somewhat unlikely month of October. This might appear slightly curious. Certainly the monumental hatches of May and June are a memory, and the twilight cavalcade of caddis during July and August a mere twinkle of the streamside year. Indeed, in many areas, trout fishing will have ceased. However, where it is allowed, and for those fly fishers who can actively fish the stream throughout this month, possibly some of the most intriguing fishing awaits.

I ought to explain that October fishing is vastly dependent upon the climate of early autumn but, given our now almost traditional Indian summers, then one can reasonably expect some superb late imitative fishing. Yet, it is not this that provides the irresistible temptation to cast a fly, nor is it the heady and bewitching atmosphere of hazy, gold-laden river landscapes. It is instead the rare opportunity to ensnare one of the stream heavyweights. For October, more than any other month, belongs to the 'glass case' brown trout.

There is a natural answer to this phenomenon which revolves around two key elements. Firstly, the onset of winter austerity with its lean, insect-sparse months which lie ahead and, secondly, the trout's unquenchable desire to spawn. Both present the angler with exciting possibilities, though for vastly differing reasons.

Let me explain the importance of the first: brown trout (indeed rainbows, when naturally reproductive) will, with the shortening days and crisper air streams, assemble generally in pairs and make what can be best termed as migratory journeys to areas of the river which afford them the correct criteria for their spawning. This, in many instances, necessitates an upstream movement that may cover many miles of river until the right location is sensed, and is, of course, of far greater interest to the fishing biologist. However, the fly fisher should watch carefully, for it is these primeval instincts which coax the larger browns from their areas of season-long solitary seclusion into both visible and extremely fishable portions of the stream.

The second element concerns winter's harsh notes of arrival, when the trout's instinct to harvest and store up essential food protein for the rigorous time that may lie only weeks away; this period affords the stealthy late-season angler a very real opportunity to success with a fly for larger trout.

I should quantify at this juncture, precisely what I mean by large trout. This covers any fish that is bigger than the average for the particular water. As an example, the fish of the west of England or northerly stream may attain an average of only 6–10oz, and there the 1 or 2lb trout is, therefore, a giant and certainly as noteworthy and estimable as a chalk or limestone fish of 4 or 5lb. It is all a question of relative values!

However, back to the stream and the tactics and location which will form the launch pad of our October activities. Never fall into the trap of imagining that these fish, for reasons discussed, will be easy prey. The migrating or 'upstreamly mobile' trout is, and will be, at its most wary and alert. Gone are their familiar locations and solitary hide-outs of gnarled roots, boulders and fish-hiding densities of weed. Instead, their world is an alien one which will demand all the caution that nature has imbued in them to ensure survival. Stealth must be the angler's by-word. However, many features will assist their pursuit, and certain stream areas will literally shriek trout.

*Getting fish out of
awkward, weeded areas
by holding the rod
above the head. This
will force the trout on
to the surface.*

Normally, fish-holding areas will conform to an overall pattern and be denoted by an area of shallow, pebbly water, either up or downstream of a feature that offers cover and depth. These, of course, will vary drastically from river to river and area to area. However, and merely as a guide-line, three possibilities emerge as candidates for daylight fishing and one for evening or low-light periods. Because, as we have found throughout the season, river fishing can be divided into two distinct categories and fish will operate differently in both.

First, the areas frequented in daylight hours, and how to tackle them tactically. Shallows are almost a prerequisite and will be obvious, but the deeps above and below may not be so well defined. However, one of the most familiar features will be a deep channel below a riffly shallow stretch and, although such deep runs can occur anywhere across the stream, far more likely will be the gorges scoured by the current into either bankside. These, indeed, may undercut the actual solid bank, and are a perennial favourite. Another area is where there are large obstacles, such as large boulders or bridge columns and buttresses, that break the river's flow and disperse current, scouring out undulations and crevices in the river bed. These, again, occur downstream of shallows and, occasionally, above. Weir pools, hatch pools and tributary entrances are perhaps the main areas for concern, and generally occur upstream of the shallow areas.

There is one common denominator between all three areas, namely a high oxygen content, which seems to be essential at this time of year. Therefore, any areas where you feel this occurs offer the possibility of the larger trout to the fly.

Now to tactics, and I am tempted to say that the method is far more important than fly choice; and it is very largely dependent on the rules of your particular fishery. If the nymph is not allowed then, sadly, the previously mentioned areas will be largely unfishable, save for a heavy hatch of fly. However, should the wet fly be permissable, three methods immediately spring to mind, two upstream methods and one downstream.

The upstream 'dead drift' is merely the upstream wet fly technique, but it may require, especially in cloudy water, a few adjustments. The sight of line or leader is of paramount importance, as is gauging accurately the speed and deviations of your chosen fishing area. The river current's path can often be read by throwing in a small twig or visible natural object (not cans, etc.!) that is approximately the same weight as the fly, and watching closely how it travels down your intended stretch. The twists and contortions of its passage will pretty much reflect how your nymph will travel.

Thereafter, actual fishing is conducted from a downstream position, casting a fly up to the required area, calculating the drift time as the path of the fly will need to reach the trout's seen or imagined area. The angle of the cast should be at either a right or left angle to your position, and control of line coming towards you done by stripping-in with the left hand so that as little slack line as possible travels towards you. Takes are lightning quick and necessitate instant reaction from angler and tackle. One very useful device for this dead-drifting method is the fluorescent Sight Bob of wool/propylene or cork, which acts as a mini float and enables maximum visibility at all times, the fluorescent yellow or orange blob being placed just over depth of your run.

The Sawyer or 'induced' tactic is a variation on the previous theme. The angler simply follows the exact same strategy to a point of approximately 2–5ft off either the seen or imagined 'station' of the trout. The fly, when it reaches this area, is agitated either upward or sideways by a movement of the rod tip alone or in conjunction with a quick tweak on the line with the left hand, thus mimicking the fleeing, darting, panicky flight of any aquatic insect in mortal danger. If done at the right time and within the trout's line of vision, takes are swift and positive.

The third tactic that can be tried is American, and best termed the 'downstream twitch' is, in essence, the 'Sawyer induced' method downstream. (This strategy is outlawed in some waters, so do check your rules before trying.) The angler will, for this tactic, need to be upstream of the quarry and chosen area and cast short of the target, allowing line, leader and fly to slacken and drift into the 'hit zone'. Thereafter, the line is immediately trapped by the forefinger on the rod butt and the downstream line allowed to bow and swing across the fishing area, accelerating the fly through the underwater, past the trout's line of vision. To achieve an effective swing of the fly, the angler might have to ensure a more acute angle between himself and the fished area than in either of the aforementioned tactics.

Another consideration in both the downstream and Sawyer methods is the shape of pattern in employment. Whereas, on the 'dead-drift' method, by and large flies should have a hunched and crumpled appearance, masquerading as aquatic forms caught up in the current's contortion and grip, the downstream swing and Sawyer methods require flies which look spritely and exude vitality and athleticism. Even the traditional humped appearance of a shrimp, when swimming, will straighten, and fly patterns must echo this feature. Trout, especially the larger brethren, can detect imposters with quicksilver ease.

This fact is of even more importance when applied to the evening period. This will be a decidedly spasmodic event, controlled largely by the temperature and sunlight. Indeed, there may be little use in staying for the period at all. However, if there is a mild period, then some very odd things can happen. Some years ago, while fishing the Upper Avon one late afternoon, I encountered a unique and uncharacteristically heavy emergence of mayfly – yes, *danica* in October – closely followed by great red sedge, then a 'mega' fall of cranefly, ending in a profusion of blue-winged olive. The fishing was rather good!

If the elements are in your favour, then concentrate on the shallows with approaching nightfall. Trout will lose some of their caution and will forage in these insect-rich areas. Also, be aware of the often heavy, although late hatches of blue-winged olive and returning egg-bearing females.

Many other upwinged flies are also relevant, the pale watery, dark olive and late march brown, medium olive, spurwing and the appropriate autumn dun. However, most will emerge during the warmer period of midday and early afternoon, offering some often exceptional daytime dry fly fishing in the accepted traditional sense. Never pass up such opportunities, because even large trout, given a heavy hatch, will incline to surface feeding. Be ever watchful during the evening period. Tactics should merely follow the familiar upstream dry fly method for fish that are seen actively feeding on a particular insect. However, it might pay to 'chance your arm' at likely areas at the approach of darkness. It was during such an October period, in near total darkness, that I extracted a brown of 5lb 8oz on a size 20 Midge pupa. Nothing was seen, I just felt the form and hoped it was my fly, which it was, thankfully. Initially, I thought the fish weighed about a pound or so and I afforded her the playing privilege I felt her weight warranted. You cannot possibly imagine my reaction after towing it, unceremon-

iously, from yet another weed bank to my waiting net. It was a hen fish and, of course, was returned. I urge you, wherever possible, especially at this time of year, to return all female fish. They represent, after all, our future seasons with a fly rod, both themselves and the thousands of potential giants they may spawn.

I have a memory that has haunted me for many years and one which might encourage even the most fair-weather angler. While fishing a hatch pool in Hampshire during early October, patiently seeking out deeper areas with shrimp, two fish gently glided into view. The male brown I estimated to weigh approximately 8lb, the female was much bigger. They cruised past my vantage point mid-stream and slid noiselessly into the depths, to provide a constant reminder of spoils, secrets and mysteries that are the very essence of October fly fishing.

13

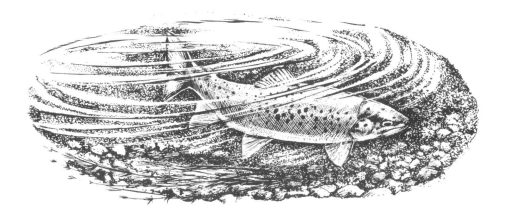

The Lady of the Stream

Gone is the evening rise, the gently swaying greenery is a memory, the air is thick with the musky tang of fallen discarded leaves and the landscape a fusion of blue greys, soft indigos, purples and madder. The stream fisher, rods hung, reels shelved, is left to ponder a myriad river-born reminiscences. However, stirring amid river valleys awash with amber, russet and gold is another angler – still the familiar fly rod, and feasibly with similar fly patterns – and his season is only just beginning. His quarry, the 'Lady of the Stream', is a unique blend of lilac silvery effervescence and salmonoid caution; the grayling anglers' time has just arrived. I would encourage you to brave the elements and resist the temptation of easy options – fireside fly tying, book-bound study and other winter-orientated pisca-torial preoccupations – and, if you have not already done so, give grayling a go.

To understand the grayling's role in the crystalline streams of these rich south-ern downlands, one has to cast one's thoughts back to the infancy of dry fly doctrines at the turn of the century and the subsequent sixty or so years during which these rivers were the cherished domain of brown trout and Salmo Truttas' well-being was the only area of concern. This, of course, necessitated regular weed cutting, river husbandry, the careful balance 'twixt nature and man, insect preservation and pest control; in a sentence, the creation of a brown trout Utopia. Grayling, in the eyes of these 'creators', simply had no place in the streams' structure, nor indeed did pike or similar coarse fish, and their eradication was an annual and perennial duty. Man, in his quest for fly fishing, has wrought a drastic change and (save for a handful of rivers and stretches that offer truly wild trout fishing), the norm is now 'put and take'. Whereas the grayling once proved a threat by feeding on minute organisms, the essential foodstuff of infant brown trout, they prove less so to a 2½lb rainbow. Indeed, many associations and owners now have come to terms with the grayling, seeing them not only as a viable second crop, but as estimable quarry in their own right and perhaps not quite the villains they were once thought to be.

Grayling areas.

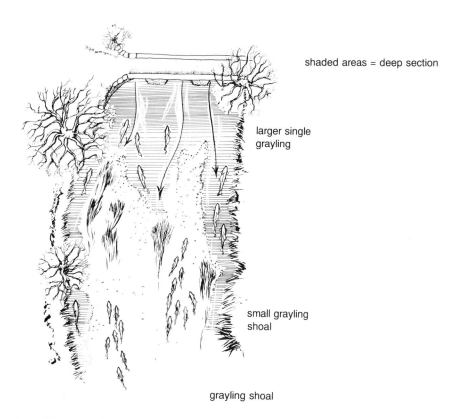

shaded areas = deep section

larger single grayling

small grayling shoal

grayling shoal

For this new thinking one has mainly to thank the various champions of the grayling's cause: the Grayling Society; John Roberts, whose book *The Grayling Angler* is essential reading for enthusiasts, and the late Reg Righyni whose passion for the fish remains legendary. The result of this is that many waters will now be available to the would-be grayling fisher that during the familiar trout season would have had their doors firmly shut. It has to be said that a few letters may have to be penned and detective work done to discover such areas, but most owners and clubs look kindly on genuine grayling addicts, offering the *crème de la crème* for remarkably little.

Certainly on southern streams grayling fishing follows an almost identical path to trout fishing. Obviously, personal preference will out, and mine leans towards the dry fly. But even on these temperature-stable rivers – seldom during the coldest weather will a chalk stream water temperature be lower than say 48°F (9°C) – opportunities will be rare. I strongly believe that barometric pressure, air temperature and the sun/light angle combine to promote hatches. Given the winter conditions, aerial fly life will be sparse save for the various mild days. This leaves us with the nymph as the corner-stone of our grayling angling activities, and it is rare that interest is not shown in these various subaqueous forms, even on days of extreme frost and cold. Rationally, then, we should look at this form of fly fishing and its relevance to grayling. Indeed – and this to a grayling *aficionado* may appear a heinous crime – I see it as a testing area for theories and patterns for future trout seasons. It is as good a honing device as I know of to keep reactions and instinct in shape, for if there was a byword in grayling fishing, it would be 'reaction'. I know of only one faster-biting fish to a fly, and that is dace.

193

It is in location that grayling differ quite markedly from trout. They are of a nervous disposition and seem at their happiest with good, all-round vision. Not for them the shady secluded spots and secret patches of gravel amid channels of weeds. Instead, long gravelly runs and pebble-dashed weed-free pools seem to suit them best. They are also a shoal fish, a factor worth considering when fishing: spook one and the others will fade and ghost away, so caution too is a prerequisite.

leaded shrimp

However, as always, fly fishing is full of contradictions and I have often found the larger fish (the magic two pounders and upwards) to lead a fairly separate existence from the rank and file. They are often encountered in unlikely grayling water, notably deep pools, fast-flowing hatches and weirs, while the smaller fish generally seek an even current and depths of between 4–6ft.

Another facet of this fish's lifestyle is its love of the bottom. The grayling appears to find comfort hugging the stones, and the rise to a surface fly is a polaris-like upward projection, unlike the trout's languid lift form a preordained station to intercept enmeshed fly life.

red tag

Grayling flies.

Having outlined a few areas which may offer grayling, the approach with a fly rod is next on the agenda, and here winter tactics combine with summer. If anything, more caution and stealth is necessary than during the trout season. Gone is the bankside cover of reeds and other vegetation. The sun's angle may also prove a problem, being much lower during the winter months, and so casting longer shadows. Also, grayling are even more susceptible to these fleeting patches of dark than trout. I have witnessed shoals scatter like panic-stricken hordes at the mere shadow of a bird in flight. Imagine what effect a human's attenuated form would have!

Having established that our quarry is nervous, flighty and a lover of clearer areas of the stream, it goes without saying that one must adopt tactics suited to these idiosyncrasies. Fishing upstream is not only desirable (and possibly essential to comply with chalk stream strictures) but is also tactically the best method. The feeding habits of grayling are catholic to say the least. Anything within vision that appears edible will be immediately pounced upon. Therefore, there is seldom any need for intricate trout-fishing nymphing ploys of accelerated or induced movement. I have generally found a dead drifted nymph to be all that is required.

The trick is gauging the taking and feeding depth accurately. To assess this, one has to act on streamside information. By merely watching passing leaves and twigs (and there will be no shortage of these on the river surface) one can gauge accurately the variations of current, speed and river distortions, and by employing a pair of polarized glasses (preferably with amber lenses) one can deduce depth. Combine the two and, allowing for a slight slowing down of river movement close to the bed, the angler can accurately assess how far he needs to cast and what weighting the nymph would need to achieve a fish-taking depth.

The real problems start when and after the fly has been pitched; it is now that tackle is of paramount importance. The fact that fly rods glimmer and sparkle is a shopkeeper's dream and a grayling (not to mention trout) angler's nightmare; causing rod flash is a sure-fire way of becoming a grayling conservationist. As I actually enjoy catching fish, my rods are matt, and also very light. Seldom, even in the strongest blow, will you need higher than size 5. Your rod should ideally be fast actioned or tip inclined, and loaded with a 4. A grayling missed is a shoal bothered. Leaders' needs vary little from those used for trout. A standard 14ft, including a braided butt, suffices in the majority of situations.

Because of the average size and tenacity of these fish, there is seldom any need to use heavier than 3lb/5x tippets. Indeed, such diameters will fish your fly more realistically, the artificial being allowed to convulate and tumble with current variation in a realistic manner – a simple fact that is often overlooked, especially in trout fishing. There is also another advantage in these diminutive leader strengths: they allow a quicker descent of fly pattern owing to less water resistance. Again, this is another factor worth consideration when trout fishing as well.

Let us now imagine that you have located your grayling shoal, deduced the river's depth and speed and are pondering on a nymph pattern. The choice will be almost limitless, the constant water temperature ensuring that all the usual up-winged nymphal forms will be present and, therefore, agile prospective food items. However, there is one creature that seems to hold enormous fascination for the grayling: the freshwater shrimp (*Gammarus pulex*). If in doubt, try one of these first, but err to small, 14s being more acceptable than 10s and 12s, unless a heavyweight is required to combat heavy, fast-water situations. Another similar insect, which is seldom considered on chalk stream, is *Corixa* (the lesser water boatman). It would, I think be an ideal candidate for the grayling's affection; certainly chalk stream trout like it. Sawyer's ubiquitous Pheasant Tail and Grey Goose and my own G.E. Nymph are all worth a wetting in either a leaded or unleaded form, as the stream dictates. Another consideration, also for bottom-tumbling tactics, is Gordon Fraser's Eyebrook Caddis; both grayling and trout love it.

As I have already mentioned, they are susceptible to an upstream dead-drift ploy and their outward caution belies their avarice in feeding. Getting them to accept the artificial may not be a problem; hooking them may well be. You will have little time to ponder 'has she or hasn't she?' – strike fast, ask questions later.

As with trout to the nymph, a flick of fish or fin right or left, or a concerted dart forward, or slight drift backwards, are all you may get as an indication that your fly has been accepted. However, unlike a normal trout (is there such a thing?) you may find a grayling will accelerate upward and intercept a fly passing through mid-water. On all these instances, lift instantly! It is the ultimate visual nymphing experience in cloudy or deep water. Alternatively, watch your greased leader butt like a hawk, if it slows up or zips downwards, act accordingly. On your first grayling adventure you will miss many, but learn from every instance. There is simply no substitute for winning one's spurs in the field of conflict.

This, of course, leaves the most loved of methods – the dry fly. Traditionally, this method has given us a wealth of permutations, yet, compared to trout dry flies, they can appear gaudy and lacking in any imitative quality: Bradshaw's Fancy, Rolt's Witch, Grayling Witch, Priest, Imp and Sturdy's Fancy are just a few to brighten a fly box. This lineage hails from the tumbling streams of the north and seems strangely incongruous on the somnambulant and, by comparison, doleful, rivers of the south. That is not to say a well-presented Treacle Parkin or Grayling Fiddler would not catch a fish or two – of course they would – but it is to pure imitation that one looks for the bulk of the sport.

Dry fly fishing, given hostile conditions, may prove to be a very sparse affair indeed. The bulk of grayling fishing revolves around the use of nymphs of one sort or another, primarily for the practical reason that they are active and much in evidence the whole year through, as are shrimp and hoglice. However, there is the charm of the unexpected about deceiving a grayling with a dry fly. Quite often a

(Overleaf) Lady and the shrimp.

195

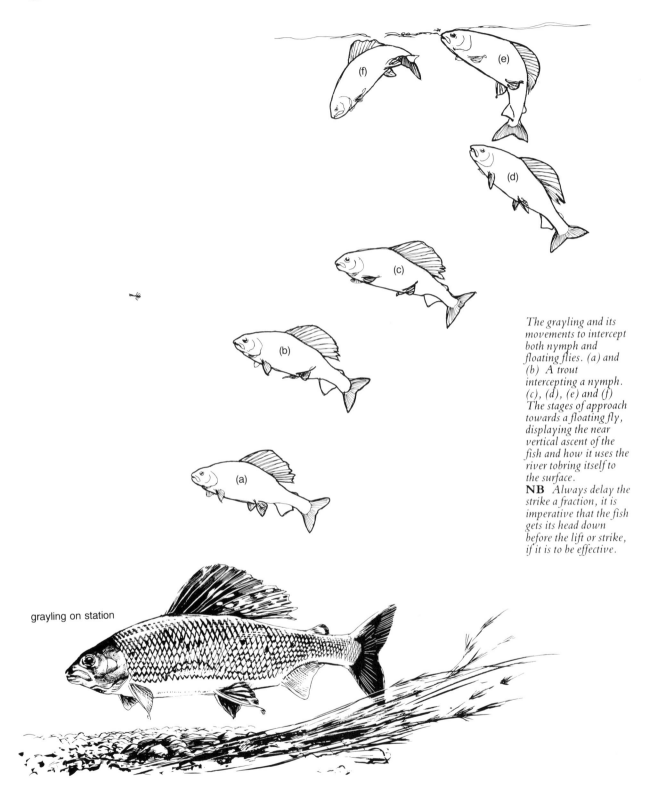

The grayling and its movements to intercept both nymph and floating flies. (a) and (b) A trout intercepting a nymph. (c), (d), (e) and (f) The stages of approach towards a floating fly, displaying the near vertical ascent of the fish and how it uses the river tobring itself to the surface.

NB Always delay the strike a fraction, it is imperative that the fish gets its head down before the lift or strike, if it is to be effective.

grayling on station

grayling will intercept a passing fly when lying in comparatively deep water. It is possibly because grayling tend to hold deep and rise abruptly. That slavish attention to detail concerning dry fly construction need not be paramount – a Beacon Beige or Adams are as good general 'olive' concoctions as one needs, as their vision must be extremely blurred, even more so considering the autumn or winter conditions and murkiness. There is also another factor: the grayling's speedy ascent. Its alacrity leaves little time for precise judgement. Yet there are other times when good hatches of fly will emerge to bring about those series of pin-prick rises in close proximity, which is a sure sign of a busy shoal of grayling. The most common hatches are large dark olive, the odd pale watery and small dark olive.

When employing or tying dry flies for grayling, bear in mind their mouths, as they are vastly different from the trout's and, I would perhaps venture, more sensitive. This, in turn, requires a fairly careful consideration of fly design. The removal of sharp edges and stiffness would seem an excellent idea. This necessarily demands a rethink about hackles. Whereas, for years, we have been desperate in our search for high riding, good-quality hackle, whether they be genetic or dyed, I am now suggesting a turnabout to the fully wound style. Given the modern fly floatants, almost anything can be made to float after a fashion. To listen to the claims that some manufacturers make, you would think this included concrete blocks!

Obviously a fly still needs a spread of hackle over an area about the body to both support and keep it from sinking and to create the illusion of legs. However, one does not need hackle immediately below or hackle that is one and a half times the gape. A small hackle, clipped into a 'V' underside, supports but offers delicate mouths little in the way of hardness, whereas clipping a Metz hackle is a painful experience. Wings also should be given some consideration: hackle points and feather fibre are admirable, but better still is *cul du canard* or polypropylene.

Tails should be afforded equal consideration, as it is these appendages which are engulfed first and thus felt on acceptance. Hen hackles or soft animal fibres, such as hare or rabbit, should be prime candidates. Stiff cock hackles, sprouting out like bristles on a yard broom, are far more of a deterrent than we probably actually realize.

The next heinous crime after denigrating the traditional dry fly is to urge the use, or at least the consideration, of downstream styles. In Austria you would be considered really quite odd if you were seen fishing upstream – and the Austrians catch a great many grayling. If you decide to try this style make sure it is legal on the water you intend to fish. I would hate to be the cause of black balling!

In conclusion, I would say that a nymph is the main line of attack when fishing for grayling. It is deadly at least nine times out of ten, at any period of the season, if correctly executed. The dry fly, as lovely as it is, is an 'interlude' during winter, as fleeting as the hatches it represents. However, it does have a charisma that will have you straining to find your tiny floating creation amongst the golden leaves on the oily, leaden winter stream's surface. We, all of us, live for the sight of that tiny dimple as a fly vanishes amidst a slight whorl, kindling an inner warmth as surely as sloe gin or cherry brandy by a log fire.

Appendix

Nymph Patterns

G.E. Nymph

Hook   Partridge E6A 16–18.
Silk   Olive, yellow or maroon Sparton micro.
Tail   Wood duck fibres (x3) or substitute (summer duck).
Rib   Fine gold or silver tinsel.
Body   Yellow olive feather fibre (either goose or swan).
Thorax   Olive dyed mole (Fraser).
Wing pads   Pheasant tail.
Hackle   Wood duck fibres in figure of eight either side of body.

Pheasant Tail

Hook   Partridge E1A or STO wet.
Silk   Maroon Sparton micro (though Sawyer used copper wire).
Weight   Copper wire.
Tail   Pheasant tail.
Body, thorax and wing pads Pheasant tail.
Rib   Copper wire.
Thorax   Olive hare's ear.

Killer Bug

Hook   Partridge E1A or STO wet.
Silk   Sparton grey/fawn.
Weight   Copper wire.
Body   Chadwicks 477 wool (fawny pink).

Grey Goose

As for pheasant tail, but tied with grey goose fibres.

Corixa

As for pheasant tail or standard wet fly 12–16.
Silk   Yellow.
Shellback   Oak turkey or speckled feather fibre (pos. hen pheasant) (I spray web of fibres with Letraset 102 Letracote which holds fibres together and adds a natural gloss).
Body   White fluorescent wool.
Rib   Sparton pearlescent tape.
Hackles/paddles   Hen pheasant tail fibres tied in bunches either side of the body (five fibres approximately to each side).
Head/eyes   I like to highlight the head with a pair of jungle cock sub eyes which highlight the natural's prominent feature.

Shrimping Patterns

Hare's Ear Shrimp

Hook   Partridge yorkshire sedge 8–16.
Silk   Hot orange sparton, pre-waxed.
Body   Mixed natural hare's mask fibres.
Rib   No. 25 or No. 26 gold wire.
Egg sac   (Optional) Figure of eight sparton fluoro, wool, orange or red.
Weighing   Lead wire wrapped the whole length of body and if desired bulked in the middle of the hook.
Legs   Picked-out body material with dubbing needle.

Red Spot Shrimp

Hook   10–14 code A or K2B.
Thread   Waxed olive.
Underbody   Fine lead wire.
Body   Mixed olive seal's fur substitute and olive mohair, dubbed either side of and around a tuft of fluorescent red wool which is trimmed to leave a red blob on either side.
Rib   Gold wire.
Back   Double layer of clear plastic.
Legs   Body fibres picked out.

Emerger Patterns

Jardine's Emerger

Hook   14–16 fine wire L3A, L4A or E6A.
Silk   Crimson.
Tail   Lemon wood duck or light blue dun fibres.
Rib   Stripped quill.
Emerging wing   Two grey mallard slips tied short and rear-facing either side of the body at the rear of the thorax.
Hackle   Lemon wood duck tied either side of the thorax only.

Jardine's Floating Nymph

Hook   Sizes 14–20 Cpt. Hamilton medium weight L2A.
Silk   Sparton micro to match natural (yellow, brown etc.).
Body   Blended rabbit or mole to match natural (e.g. 50 per cent yellow, 40 per cent white, 10 per cent blue).

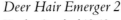

APPENDIX

Thorax Ball – polypropylene – pale grey, dubbed in a tight ball shape then placed on top of thorax.
Tail and whisks Blue dun hackles or wood duck.
(A pair of wing slips can be added for total accuracy but are not essential.)

Jardine's Floating Nymph Mk. II

Hook 14 code L3A or E1A.
Tail Wood duck fibres.
Body Dark olive Orvis Antron/hair mix tapering from the rear.
Rib Fibres of white synthetic parcel string or a translucent substitute.
Thorax A dubbed ball of grey Poly II (polypropylene) with parachute hackle.

Cripple 1 (Swisher & Richards' style)

Hook Partridge E6A 16–18.
Silk Olive, yellow or maroon sparton micro.
Tail An olive hackle stroked opposite way then varnished and tie extended.
Body Olive mole.
Wing Mallard primary (x2) tied in as 'stubs' either side of body.
Hackle Olive – clipped both top and bottom (essential!).

Cripple 2 (Jardine)

Hook As above.
Silk As above.
Tail Olive cock hackle divided into two by tiny ball of dubbing at bend.
Body As above or Orvis Antron mix in olive.
Wing Hen hackles in blue dun tied sloping back.
Hackle Golden olive, trimmed top and bottom.

Deer Hair Emerger 1

Hook Any light wire 12–16.
Silk Any. Hot orange is ideal.
Tail Jungle cock spade hackle fibres (black and white sub: grizzle hen or soft).
Body Mixed *soft* deer hair, colour to suit, mixed with Antron, approximately 60/40.
Hackle Cul du cannard – one turn only at head.
Wing Polypropylene/Antron either mixed or singly – sloping back to bend and clipped short, that is one eighth of an inch.

Deer Hair Emerger 2

Hook Standard 12–18 or l.s. 10–12 for Mayfly.
Silk Any – primrose or cream are ideal.
Body Dubbed fine deer hair and Antron mix in fawns, creams or greys.
Wing A small stub of white or grey polypropylene.
Hackle (Optional) One turn of cul-du-cannard.

Hare's Ear Emerger

Hook Jardine living nymph, partridge 18–20.
Silk Any. Danville or sparton micro: olive – brown – hot orange – claret.
Tail None.
Body Well mixed hare's mask (various colours), a shellback of Lureflash pearl tinsel, ribbed by 2lb b.s. mono.
Hackle None.
Thorax Hare fur over Polycelon, either white, grey or black, which should be tied in first, projecting $\frac{1}{8}$in of eye of hook. Dub over Polycelon base, then reverse material back toward the bend and tie down at jucntion between abdomen/body and thorax.

General Dun Patterns

Adams

Hook Partridge L2A in 14 to 22.
Silk Sparton micro black or yellow.
Body Grey mole or rabbit.
Wing Grizzle hackle points.
Hackle Grizzle and natural red cock hackle wound together.
Tail Mixed natural red grizzly fibres.

Beacon Beige

Hook As above.
Silk As above.
Body Stripped peacock 'eye' feather.
Hackle Grizzly and natural red cock hackle.
Tail Grizzly and natural red fibres.

Greenwell's Glory

Hook 12–16 E6A or L3A.
Silk Waxed yellow.
Tail Greenwell or furnace cock fibres.
Body Waxed tying thread.

Common, scientific and parochial names	Period and time of day of emergence	Nymph	Dun Appearance	Spinner Appearance
Large dark olive *Baetis rhodani* Winter, large Spring, olive	October–early May Peaking April–early May Daylight and dusk	Agile darter	*Large* Tail: 2 Wing: mid- to light-grey (pale brown veins) Body: olive brown or green body	*Female* Tail: olive grey Wing: transparent with brown veining Body: reddish brown with pale olive wings Eyes: dull red/underwater laying (called red spinner)
Medium olive *Baetis tennax, vernus* and *buceratus* Olive Blue dun Red spinner	April–November Peaking May–June Daylight and dusk	Agile darter	*Medium* Tail: 2 Wing: grey/golden olive in veins Body: dark grey to medium olive	*Female* Tail: 2, off-white Wing: transparent, light brown veins Body: red brown with light bands Egg laying: underwater
Iron blue *Baetis niger* and *muticus* Jenny spinner (male) Little claret	Throughout summer Peaking in May and in September Daylight	Agile darter	*Small* Tail: blue grey Wing: blue black/grey Body: dark brown olive though some may appear 'claret'	*Female* Tail: pale grey Wing: transparent Body: claret brown with light segments Egg laying: underwater during day
Small spurwing *Centroptilum luteolum* Pale watery Little amber Little skyblue	May–November Peaking June–August Daylight and dusk	Agile darter	*Small* Tail: grey Wing: pale blue/grey Body: brown, yellowy olive	*Female* Tail: pale olive Wing: transparent Body: pale amber ringed with cream Egg laying: dipping on water
Mayfly *Ephemera danica* and *vulgata* Green drake Spent gnat	May–June (also August and September) Peaking late May–early June Dawn, day and dusk	Bottom burrower	*Large to very large* Tail: 3, dark brown–grey Wing: yellowish green, heavy veining Body: creamy yellow with distinctive brown markings	*Female* Tail: very large, 3, near black Wing: transparent with heavy veining Body: creamy white with dull segments to the rear Egg laying: dipping/on surface (spent)
Black gnat *Bibio johannis* No see um's Smuts	Spring/early summer (also August) Peaking late May–June Day		*Small to very small* Tail: none Wing: brown tinged, transparent Body: blackish brown	
Small dark olive *Baetis scambus* Olive or July dun	June–November Peaking July/August Midday–late evening	Agile darter	*Very Small* Tail: 2, pale grey Wing: medium–dark grey Body: grey olive, last segment yellowish	*Female* Tail: 2, greyish white Wing: transparent with claret veining Body: dark brown – reddish chestnut Egg laying: underwater
Angler's curse *Caenis* spp/*Brachycerus* Broadwing	May–September Peaking June–July Dawn, evening and dusk	Silt/moss crawler	*Very small* This dun is of little fishing consequence as metamorphosis is so fast yet looks similar to the spinner	*Both male and female* Tail: 3, cream Wing: transparent Body: cream/white body, brownish thorax Egg laying: on water/spent
Blue-winged olive *Ephemerella ignita* Shiny spinner	Late May–November Peaking late June, July and August Late afternoon–nightfall	Moss creeper	*Medium* Tail: 3, ginger, ringed brown Wing: dark blue grey, very tall Body: brown olive–orangey brown	*Female* Tail: 3, olive grey, ringed brown Wing: transparent Body: apricot – chestnut Egg laying: aerially via an eggball
Pale watery *Baetis fuscatus/bioculatas* Golden spinner	May–October Peaking June–early July and September–early October Day long	Agile darter	*Small* Tail: grey-olive Wings: pale grey Body: washed-out olive hinting yellow (rear segment)	*Female* Tail: greyish white Wing: transparent Body: golden dun Egg laying: under and dipping

Importance and Peculiarities	Suggested Artificials and Sizes	Naturals' Size	Actual Size
A vital early season fly (the dun), it can hatch and tolerate awful weather. The spinner is of little use.	Nymph: Pheasant tail, GE (14) Emerger: Hares Ear (14) Dun: Greenwell, Pieckke dk olive, D.D. (14–16).	2b–3b	
A frequent, large hatch in late spring and an important spinner fall. Fish a smaller rather than a bigger fly.	Nymph: Grey Goose, Pheasant Tail, GE (16–18) Dun: D.D., Kite's Imperial (16–18). Spinner: Jardine Sink, Lunn's Particular, Chestnut Sunset Spinner (16–18).	4b	
Can bring about selective feeding and preoccupation. They enjoy both pleasant and ghastly weather. There is a need for accurate representation when trout are taking the fly.	Nymph: Grey Goose, Scandinavian (16–18) Dun: Iron Blue (pt. russet), Dark D.D. (16–18). Spinner: Pheasant tail, Houghton Ruby, Dark fallen spinner (18).	5b	
Very common but easily confused with pale watery. I suspect trout cannot tell the difference readily either. Important: the spinner fall, especially as night closes.	Nymph: Grey Goose, G.E. Grey (18) Dun: Little Maryatt, pale thorax, DD Light (18–20). Spinner: Amber fallen, Lunn's Yellow Boy, Tups Indispensible (18–20).	5b	
The mayfly is *the* hatch, yet trout can get fussy taking every other or every third fly (sequence feeding). Also, towards the end fish can get fed up with it and feed on something else (masked hatch).	Nymph: Mayfly Nymph (Walker) Emerger: Deer Body Sparkler Dun: Lively May, Shadow May, Grey Wulff Spinner: Poly May, Deerstalker (Goddard) (Patterson).	1b–2a	
Trout probably feed far more on this diptera than we think. It is always worth a try, especially if fish refuse during mayfly time. It is exceptionally hardy during very hot weather.	Goddard Smut, Halford Black Gnat, although any small (18–22) black fly will do. NB Useful anytime, anywhere.		
Trout often feed on this fly (dun) during the evening rise. Very often a switch to a tiny dun will work better than a spinner. Size is critical – err to 'tinyness'.	Nymph: Pheasant tail (18–20), GE (18–22) Dun: D.D. Light Olive, Thorax, Kite's Imperial (18–22) Spinner: Sunk, Jardine or Patterson's, Pheasant tail, Sunset (18–22).	5b	
Because of their size and the density of the hatch, this insect poses problems, yet small flies and light tippets and accurate casts work well enough.	Nymph: Caenis (Carnhill) Dun/Spinner: Cream Fallen, Caenis (Can), Last Hope (Goddard), Magic Wing. (All 20 or preferably 22–24).	5a (and smaller)	
Hatches of this fly can be heavy and late in the day, often as night falls. Duns will emerge. Trout feed on them avidly and selectively. Pattern match is essential.	Nymph: Pheasant tail (flattened to shape) (16) Dun: Duck's Dun/Thorax; (16–18). Spinner: Lunn's Particular, Egg Laying spinner (16–18).	3a	
Very easily confused with the small dark olive and small upwing, the trout probably is equally stupified. Light patterns are the order of the day.	The same as for small dark olive and spurwing.	5b	

APPENDIX

Rib Fine gold wire.
Wing Pale starling wing or moorhen.
Hackle Greenwell or furnace cock.

Hare's Ear

Hook 14–20 dry fly – light wire – down eyed.
Silk Any, that is hot orange or claret.
Tail Three or four soft blue dun hackles or hare body fibres (guard hairs).
Body Well mixed hare's mask (light and dark fibres).
Rib Fine gold wire or flat gold Lurex or Mylar.
Wing None.
Hackle Body well picked out by dubbing needle to suggest hatching 'chaos'.

Kite's Imperial

Hook 14–16 L3A, E6A or A.
Tail Honey-dun hackle fibres.
Body Grey feather fibre (heron/grey goose).
Rib Fine oval gold teist or wire.
Hackle Honey-dun cock.

Specific Duns

Compara Dun

Hook 14–22 Cpt. Hamilton, medium weight L2A.
Silk Sparton micro to match natural.
Body Blended rabbit or mole (for example, for medium olive: ten parts yellow, two parts red, four parts blue, seventeen parts white) or Hairtron in appropriate olive shade.
Wing Short deer hair from mask and leg areas, 'tied in' as for normal wing procedure.
Tail Blue dun hackle divided into two (nylon paintbrush Rowney No. 8, are also excellent for all tails) or clear Antron fibres to make a sparkle Dun.

Thorax Dun

Hook As for Compara Dun.
Silk Sparton micro to match natural.
Body As for Compara Dun or Antron in appropriate olive shade.
Wing Turkey body feather (Orvis) rolled and tied in an upright bunch in middle of hook.
Hackle Either tied parachute round base of wing or conventionally but clipped underneath.
Tail As for Compara Dun.

Sunset Dun

Hook Partridge E6A or E1A 16–18.
Silk Maroon sparton micro.
Tail Nylon artist's paintbrush bristles (Daler Oil 8 or 10).
Body Brick red-dyed mole 60 per cent, red Burgess body gloss 10 per cent, Orvis olive Antron/hare blend 30 per cent, or entirely rabbit and red and clear Antron.
Wing Turkey body feather fibres dyed dark blue dun tied centrally and upright.
Hackle Light blue dun wound in parachute style around the base of the wing.

Blue Winged Olive

Hook Partridge E64A, L3A, 14 to 18.
Silk Sparton micro olive or yellow.
Tail Light blue dun hackles divided into two, contianing approximately threee fibres each.
Body Yellow and olive mole or rabbit mixed in equal portions (a few fibres of pink may be added to darken hue).
Wing Turkey body feather (Orvis) dyed pale blue dun tied in a clump in the middle of the shank.
Hackle Blue dun tied in parachute style around the base of wing.

Piechke Dark Olive

Hook Partridge E1A Hooper dry (1x) short, 14.
Body Yellow Hairtron.
Tail Blue dun and olive soft cock hackles mixed (five of each).
Rib Peacock eye quill would close with narrow yellow banding – this should give an overall light and dark banding.
Hackle Furnace cock.
Wing Blue dun hackles by two, tied upright. The wing style is known as a 'wonder wing' and requires the fly tyer to reverse the fibres along the hackle stem against their natural direction – this is best done by stroking backwards with thumb and forefinger coated with a smear of varnish. **NB** This preparation should be done before tying the pattern.

Funnel Dun

Hook 14–18, L3A or E6A.
Silk Olive.
Tail Cock fibres tied slightly round the bend.

Body Seal's fur substitute or poly dubbing with a darker thorax round the hackle roots.
Wing Optional. Bunched hackle or feather fibres.
Hackle Cock hackle 'funnelled' forwards over the eye with a 'V' cut out on the side that will become the underside.

Spinners

Caenis 1

Hook Partridge L3A and K1A 20–26.
Silk Sparton black micro.
Tail Two fibres divided and spread, from a nylon Rowney or Daler artists' paintbrush (oil). A No. 8 brush will give you a lifetime of the best spinner tails one could wish for – merely felt tip pen in the desired shade on the white nylon fibres.
Body White rabbit fur dubbed.
Wing Very small hen hackle tips (x2) tied fully spent.
Thorax Dark chestnut brown or black mole or rabbit fur – around wing butts dubbed.

Caenis 2

As for Caenis 1, except wing which is a pale blue dun or cream cock hackle (fibres should not exceed the gape), wound through the thorax in open turns (three to four) then clipped in a 'V' top and bottom.

Sunset Spinner

Hook 14–18, L3A, L4A or E1A.
Silk Maroon.
Tail Two white nyulon paintbrush bristles (artists Daler Oil No. 8 or 10) widely spaced.
Body Well mixed and blended rust/orange Poly II, red-brown Poly II and red Burgess body gloss or Antron in the proportions: 5:4:1.
Rib (Optional) Lurez, Lureflash or Flashabou.
Wings Two good quality blue dun cock hackles wound together through the thorax and clipped to a 'V' top and bottom, with the option of two strands of Pearl Twinkle, tied spent.

Egg-Bearing Blue-Winged Olive

Hook E1A size 14.
Silk Maroon micro Sparton.
Tail Rowney No. 8 Oil paintbrush fibres (x2).

Body Russet brown/brick red polypropylene dubbing.
Egg sac Bright green (fluorescent) Antron or polypropylene dubbing in a ball shape at the bend of the hook.
Wing Grizzly hackle poionts (x2).
Hackle Dark blue dun (natural if possible).

Dry Fly Patterns

Duck's Dun

Hook E6A 12–20 or similar.
Silk Hot orange for medium olive; primrose for light olive; claret for dark olive.
Body Hairtran? to match insect, various olives.
Tail Fibres from the 'spade' hackle of a jungle cock (black and white) or a hen hackle. (4/5 fibres only.)
Wing 2 x *cul du cannard* back-to-back projecting upright and slightly sloping toward hook bend.
Hackle Very short blue dun or grizzle clipped under and over.

Lively Mayfly

Hook 10 or 12 Cptn. Hamilton L2A.
Silk Orange.
Tail Three pheasant tail fibres.
Body (1) Ten to twelve deer hair fibres.
Body (2) Buff/yellow/fawn wool or blended rabbit.

Caddis Patterns

Balloon Caddis

Hook 10–12 Standard light wire.
Silk Primrose.
Body Antron/polypropylene dubbing in olive, tan or amber.
Wing Deer hair/elk hair dyed chestnut or natural.
Head Polycelan re-doubled and tied down over thorax region.

Sedge Pupae

Hooks 10–12 nymph (x2) l.s.
Silk Cream or primrose.
Body Abdomen – Amber Irise (dub: thorax cream or yellow Irise dub.
Collar/hackle Cree (x2) turns clipped top and bottom and positioned between thorax and abdomen.

Further Reading

Historically Important

Frederick M. Halford *Floating Flies and how to Dress them and Dry Fly Fishing*, first published, 1889 (Barry Sherlock, 1973)
John Waller Hills *River Keeper* (Geoffrey Bles, 1934 and 1947)
George Edward Mackenzie Skues *The Chalkstream Angler: Sidelines, Sidelights and Reflections* (Barry Sherlock, 1976, first published in 1932), *The Way of a Trout with a Fly* (1921), *Minor Tactics* (1910) and *Itchen Memories* (Andre Deutsch, 1984, first published by Herbert Jenkins, 1951)

Historically Entertaining

These are a good read, fun and have sound information

John Waller Hills *Summer on the Test* (Barry Sherlock edition, 1972, first published 1924)
H. Plunket-Green *Where the Bright Waters Meet* (Wetherby, 1969, first published in 1924)
T. Donald Overfield *G.E.M. Skues: The Way of a Man with a Trout* (Benn, 1977)
C.F. Walker (Editor) *Angling Letters of G.E.M. Skues* (A. & C. Black, 1956 and 1975)
Frank Sawyer *The Keeper of the Stream* (A. & C. Black, 1952, Geo. Allen & Unwin 1985)
Sidney Vines *Frank Sawyer, Man of the Riverside* (Geo. Allen & Unwin 1984)

Tactics

These are timeless masterpieces worth any fly fishers' closest scrutiny.

C.F. Walker *The Art of Chalkstream Flyfishing* (Herbert Jenkins 1968)
J.W. Dunne *Sunshine and the Dry Fly* (A. & C. Black, 1924)
Vincent C. Marinaro *A Modern Dry Fly Code* (Winchester Press, 1950 and 1970) and *In the Ring of the Rise* (Crown, 1976)
Dermot Wilson *Fishing the Dry Fly* (A. & C. Black, 1957 and 1970)
Doug Swisher and Carl Richards *Selective Trout* (Nick Lyons Books, 1971)
Brian Clarke and John Goddard *The Trout and the Fly* (Benn, 1980)
Oliver Kite *Nymph Fishing in Practice* (Herbert Jenkins, 1963)
Frank Sawyer *Nymphs and the Trout* (A. & C. Black, 1958)

From the Other Side of the Atlantic

Migel and Wright (Editors) *The Masters of the Dry Fly* (Winchester Press) and *The Masters of the Nymph* (Winchester Press, 1979)
Datus Proper *What the Trout Said* (Knopf, 1982, Nick Lyons Books, 1989)
Solomon and Leiser *The Caddis and the Angler* (Stackpole, 1977)
Art Lee *Fishing Dry Flies for Trout on Rivers and Streams* (Atheneum, 1982)

Entomological and Tactical

S.D. 'Taff' Price *The Anglers' Sedge* (Blandford, 1989)

Entomological

John Goddard *Trout Fly Recognition* (A. & C. Black, 1966) Waterside Guide. Unwin, Hyman 1988

Fly Tying and Patterns

Caucci & Nastasi *Fly Tyers' Colour Guide* (Comparahatch, 1978)
Darrel Martin *Fly Tying Methods* (David and Charles, 1987)
Peter Gathercole *The Handbook of Fly Tying* (The Crowood Press, 1989)
Eric Leiser *The Book of Fly Patterns* (Knopf, 1987)
Randall Kaufman *The Fly Tyers' Nymph Manual* (Western Fisherman's Press, 1986)
John Roberts *River Trout Flies* (The Crowood Press, 1989) and *New Illustrated Dictionary of Trout Flies* (Unwin, Hyman, 1988)
Courtney-Williams *A Dictionary of Trout Flies* (A. & C. Black, 1949)

The Lady of the Stream

John Roberts *The Grayling Angler* (Witherby, 1982)
Ron Broughton *The Fourth Game Fish* (The Crowood Press, 1989)

Pictorial Documents

Dr E.A. Barton *An Album of Chalkstreams* (A. & C. Black, 1946), *Chalkstreams and Water Meadows*, *Running Waters* and *A Doctor Remembers*
Rod Sutterby and Malcolm Greehalgh *The Wild Trout* (Geo. Phillip, 1989)